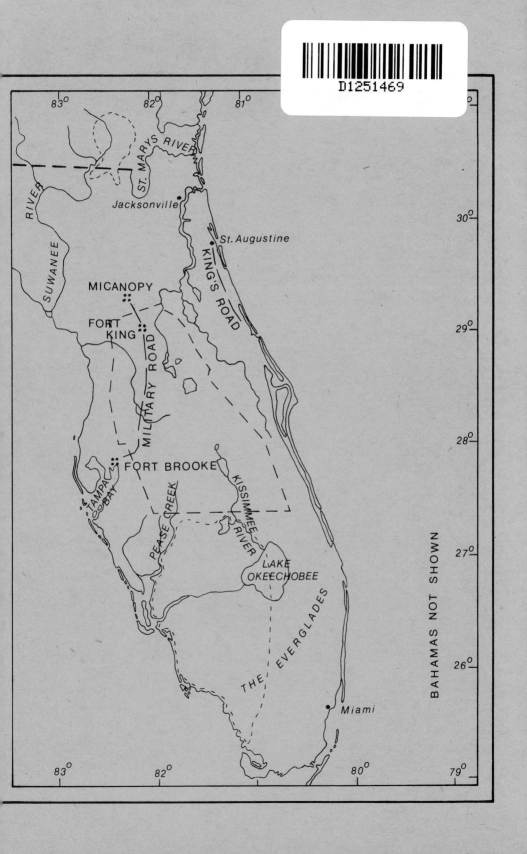

83°    82°    81°

ST. MARYS RIVER

SUWANEE RIVER

•Jacksonville

St. Augustine

MICANOPY

FORT KING

KING'S ROAD

MILITARY ROAD

FORT BROOKE

TAMPA BAY

PEASE CREEK

KISSIMMEE RIVER

LAKE OKEECHOBEE

THE EVERGLADES

•Miami

30°

29°

28°

27°

26°

83°    82°    80°    79°

BAHAMAS NOT SHOWN

D1251469

*The Florida Wars*

OSCEOLA. Painted by George Catlin. (*National Portrait Gallery, Smithsonian Institution*)

# The
# *Florida*
# *Wars*

VIRGINIA  BERGMAN  PETERS

1979
ARCHON BOOKS

Library of Congress Cataloging in Publication Data
Peters, Virginia Bergman, 1918–
The Florida wars.

Bibliography: p.
Includes index.
1. Seminole Indians—Wars.  2. Florida—
History—1821–1965.  3. Florida—History—
Spanish colony, 1763–1821.  I.  Title.
E83.817.P46          973.5          78-14739
ISBN 0-208-01719-4

First published 1979 as an Archon Book,

an imprint of The Shoe String Press, Inc.

Hamden, Connecticut 06514

Filmset in Bembo by Asco Trade Typesetting Ltd, Hong Kong   /
Lithoprinted in the United States of America by Cushing-Malloy Inc,
Ann Arbor, Michigan   /   Bound by The Short Run Bindery Inc of Medford,
New Jersey

*To Pete, Emory and Jeff*

This was one of the most troublesome, expensive and unmanageable wars in which the United States had been engaged; and from the length of time it continued, the amount of money it cost, and the difficulty of obtaining results, it became a convenient handle of attack upon the administration; and in which party spirit in pursuit of its object, went the length of injuring both individual and national character. It continued about seven years—as long as the Revolutionary War—cost some thirty millions of money—and baffled the exertions of several generals; recommenced when supposed to be finished; and was finally terminated by changing military campaigns into an armed occupation. . . . All the opposition presses and orators took hold of it, and made its misfortunes the common theme of invective.

Its origin was charged to the oppressive conduct of the administration, its protracted length to their imbecility, its cost to their extravagance, its defeat to want of foresight and care. The [enemy] stood for an innocent and persecuted people. Heroes and patriots were made of their chiefs. Our generals and troops were decried; applause was lavished upon a handful of savages who could thus defend their country; and corresponding censure upon successive armies which could not conquer them. All this going incessantly into the Congress debates and the party newspapers, was injuring the administration at home, and the country abroad; and, by dint of iteration and reiteration, stood a good chance to become history, and to be handed down to posterity.

SENATOR THOMAS H. BENTON
in *Thirty Years' View*

# Contents

## Part Three  The Second Florida War, 1835–1842

## Part Four  The Third Florida War, 1848–1858

# Illustrations

9

# MAPS

Map of Florida. By E. Glendon Moore, based on maps from the National Archives Collection. See the bibliography.

*Pages 20–21 and endpapers*

Site of the attack on Fernandina, 1812. By E. Glendon Moore, adapted from USGS Topographic Series (1 : 250,000) of Jacksonville, Florida-Georgia, 1957, Limited Revision, 1966, and Military Topographic Map of Georgia-Florida, (Bu Top Eng) Published 1862, NA, RG 77a. *Page 28*

Location of Seminole-Black Villages, showing movement south between the first and second wars. By E. Glendon Moore, after Michael Paul Duffner. *Page 46*

Seat of the Florida Wars, Upper Florida. By E. Glendon Moore, based on maps in the National Archives Collection.

*Page 112*

Seat of the Florida Wars, the Peninsula. By E. Glendon Moore, based on maps in the National Archives collection. *Page 222*

# Preface

A SERIES OF SMALL WARS fought in Florida during the first half of the nineteenth century appear, in the twentieth, to assume new significance for American history.

The first (1810–1818) consisted of three highly irregular military intrusions into Spanish territory which resulted in Florida becoming part of the United States. The second (1835–1842) occurred when the federal government sought to move the Florida Indians to reservations west of the Mississippi River. The third (1849–1858) followed because the second never accomplished its purpose.

All three were actually Seminole wars because Indians by that name made up the bulk of the aborigines involved. But I prefer to call them the Florida wars because the term Seminole was used to refer not only to that large group of dissidents who had seceded from the Creeks in Georgia and moved to Florida but also to remnants of many other decimated tribes living in the territory.

Furthermore, the Seminoles were joined in the first two wars by a contingent of blacks living in close harmony with them. In Florida these two minorities united in an effective alliance against a common enemy. Some Negroes had fled slavery in the United States to live under the protection of the Spanish government; they had children born to freedom. A number had been emancipated by the British for fighting against Americans while others had been acquired by the Indians through purchase or as trophies of war. But whatever their status, they lived in comfort as free people or in a state of benign feudalism whereby they paid an annual tribute to the Indians but possessed their own fields, livestock, and other property. Since there was frequent intermarriage between the two groups, there were close kinship ties as well.

In the first war, while the weak Spanish forces remained barricaded in their forts, the Seminole allies thrice faced American troops in defense of their existence. Although they lost their homes and much of their property, they did not suffer too many casualties and soon established themselves in other villages where they continued to welcome refugees from slavery.

When war broke out again in 1835, the blacks proved invaluable as interpreters and advisors to the Indians because, during their service under them, they had come to understand the language, customs, and even thought processes of the Americans. Thus Negro leaders played an active role in all the negotiations but their warriors were equally important on the field. If the Indian chiefs seemed more brilliant in the execution of hit and run attacks, the blacks—with more to lose if defeated—fought with greater resolution. When they found themselves unable to compete with the might of an industrial nation and a modern army, the allies simply retreated to the swamps where they let the climate and terrain undo their opponents.

Eventually the Americans learned to cope with that environment and the Seminole allies finally bowed to superior force but they were never completely vanquished. A number of black Seminole families accompanied the Indians to a freedom of sorts in the Arkansas Territory though many were killed or returned to slavery. By the same token, a few Seminole Indian families absolutely refused to leave Florida and their descendants live in the Everglades to this day. Whatever their fate, all members of this unique coalition benefited by combining their resources.

In addition, the Florida wars are interesting because they show how a government, having committed itself to solving a human and political problem with military force, was trapped in a policy as ineffective as it was costly. Unable to win the wars and unwilling to stop without total victory, several administrations continued to expend men and materials in pursuit of a goal they never reached. The records they kept are preserved in the National Archives where they continue to testify to this tragedy.

Finally, the experience of watching combat live on television almost daily has made us more aware of the impact of a major catastrophe on the lives of individuals caught up in it. No longer satisfied with an interpretation of war that deals only with military maneuvers and political implications, we look for a more human interpretation. The diaries, journals, and reminiscences of several articulate young Americans who fought for their country in these Florida engagements are replete with incidents which illustrate the personal misfortunes of all victims of war and make the Florida wars very contemporary and real for Americans today.

The modern historian is a fortunate heir of these Americans who left their eyewitness accounts to posterity. Since the Seminole allies did not share this literary tradition, their experiences and feelings must be deduced from a reexamination of the American records.

For doing just that, I thank Dr. Kenneth Wiggins Porter who, over a period of several decades, has gathered a mass of material to document the role of blacks in the Florida wars and Michael Paul Duffner for his unpublished thesis which provides anthropological evidence of the underlying structure of the coalition between the blacks and the Indians. I am also deeply indebted to Dr. John K. Mahon for his comprehensive annotated bibliography on the second Seminole war.

For providing every kind of help in seeking out sources, I thank the knowledgeable and dedicated professionals in the following institutions: the National Archives (NNS, NNFN, NNMO, the search room and library); the Library of Congress; the Smithsonian Institution Office of Anthropology Library; the Bureau of Indian Affairs Library; the Moorland-Spingarn Research Center at Howard University, Washington, D. C.; the Martin Luther King branch of the District of Columbia Public Library; all branches of the Fairfax County, Virginia, Public Library (especially the reference and interlibrary loan departments of the central branch); the interlibrary loan system of the Florida Public Library; the Navy Department Library, Washington Navy Yard, Washington, D. C.; and the Army Department Library, the Pentagon, Arlington, Virginia.

I wish to express special appreciation to Dr. Herman J. Viola, Director Smithsonian Institution National Anthropological Archives, for reading part of this manuscript and making many valuable, constructive criticisms and to Elsie Flemming and Nan Netherton for assisting with the indexing and proofreading. Very special mention is due my late husband who assisted with the manuscript proofing and who provided the "grant" which made this work possible.

All errors and weaknesses of the book are my own responsibility.

*Falls Church, Virginia*                    VIRGINIA BERGMAN PETERS

*Part One*

# THE FIRST FLORIDA WAR

*American Invasions of Spanish Florida*

*1810–1818*

# 1

# The Battle at Prospect Bluff

## A Threat is Removed

"The brave soldier was disarmed of his resentment and
checked his victorious career to drop a tear on the distressing
scene."
                                        MARCUS C. BUCK, *Soldier*

TODAY A TOURIST, following Route 98 along the coast from Pensacola
to Apalachee Bay, comes eventually to the mouth of the Apalachicola
River. This broad stream runs through incredibly lovely countryside
from the northern boundary of Florida where the Flint and Chattahoochee rivers merge with it, across the widest part of the state's
panhandle, down to the Gulf Coast. In 1816 its banks were bordered
with fertile land on which well-tended fields flourished and cattle
and horses grazed.

On 10 July of that year a small fleet, consisting of two transports
convoyed by a pair of gunboats, lay at anchor in the mouth of the
river. On the fifteenth, Lieutenant Jairus Loomis, the sailing master
in charge, sent out a crew in a small boat to obtain information about
conditions for proceeding up the river. The boat was fired upon.

On 17 July another group from one of the gunboats, searching
for fresh water, saw a Negro on the river bank. The midshipman
in charge put into shore and shouted to the man. Suddenly a blast
of musket fire hit the boat, killing three sailors and the officer. One
survivor fell overboard and swam to safety on the opposite bank;

the other was taken captive. The dead were stripped and scalped.[1]
The gunboat had fallen victim to an ambush of blacks who were
living in freedom in the Spanish territory of Florida.

How did a group of fugitives from American slavery and a
company of United States naval personnel meet in mortal combat
on a river in a foreign country? The answer to that question is found
in a fragment of American history seldom mentioned in text books
except by a passing reference or an unobtrusive footnote. Yet the
events that took place in Florida between 1810 and 1858 might well
be called another "Thirty Years War" with a "cold war" or two
interspersed.

What happened in Florida during that period has startling re-
semblances to more recent troubles which our nation has endured
in Vietnam and Cambodia. The places in which American soldiers
found themselves fighting had names as unprounceable; the conditions of battle were as baffling; the arguments for and against the
actions taken were as confusing and the moral questions raised as
embarrassing; the costs were as comparatively great in national treasure, human lives and property; and the results, in some ways, as
inconclusive. If a nation ever learns anything from its past, a look
at the Florida wars from today's perspective may be instructive.

The blacks who ambushed Lieutenant Loomis' party were maroons who had fled from their masters in the United States. They
had heard that American forces were coming to destroy them and
their homes and hoped to forestall disaster by attacking and frightening away the naval force.

As many as fifty communities of runaway slaves had existed in
various times and places in North America from 1672 until 1864,
but only those in Florida had lasted any length of time.[2] The communities in Florida had managed to survive because of three factors:
first, the Spanish had allowed the Indians driven from their homes
in the southern states and the fugitive Negroes to settle on the border
and had encouraged them to harass the settlers who were rapidly
taking up the Indians' lands; second, the English, operating from
Florida, had actively recruited slaves and displaced Indians as allies
in the Revolution and the War of 1812; and third, aborigines in the
south, seeing the prestige which accrued to slave owners, had bought
and stolen slaves or captured them in war.

But this was a different kind of slavery. In the Florida Territory
Negroes and Indians lived together in a rather relaxed relationship.
The Negroes built their own villages, laid out and farmed their own

fields (more efficiently and effectively than the Indians), and paid an annual tribute of corn, vegetables, beef, and hides to their Indian protectors. In return the Indian would insist that all blacks who paid this tax to him were his property and could not be claimed by slave catchers from the North. It was an ideal arrangement for both races.

The Spanish settlers had called the runaway blacks maroons, a West Indian word meaning "free Negroes," and had allowed them to settle among the Seminole Indians without paying much attention to them. The Negroes had even intermarried with the Indians so that often they were regarded as kinfolk and allies by their nominal masters. It is obvious why these free blacks meant to hold on to their freedom for even their present slavery formed a striking contrast to the hard life of unrequited toil under white overseers.

But now the maroons were in possession of a fort that threatened the peace of mind of Americans along the north boundary of Florida. The chain of events by which they had acquired the fort began in May of 1814 when an Englishman, Major Edward Nicholls, anchored at the mouth of the Apalachicola River in the British war vessel, *Orpheus*. He had sent Captain George Woodbine to recruit fugitive Red Stick Creeks by offering them a chance to gain revenge upon the American army. Only a month before, General Andrew Jackson, commander of the entire Southern Division of the United States Army, had literally destroyed that element of the Creek nation at the Battle of Horse Shoe Bend and forced on them a humiliating treaty in which they had ceded most of their good lands to the United States. Many who lost their homes had fled to Florida and would be happy to join anyone who meant to fight their recent conquerors. Woodbine was also authorized to offer the Negroes free lands in the British West Indies when the War of 1812 was over as well as providing a guarantee that they would never be returned to their former masters.

General Jackson, hearing that the British were on the Apalachicola distributing arms to the Indians, warned the American government of imminent attack. Then, on his own responsibility and without waiting for a reply from Washington, he took a group of volunteers from Tennessee, Louisiana, and Mississippi against the British in Florida. He found them at Pensacola and attacked. Nicholls fled back to the Apalachicola. There, on a spot known as Prospect Bluff, fifteen miles from the mouth of the river, he built a fort which he called British Post and which he used as his headquarters for negotiations with the Red Sticks, Seminoles, and Negroes. Americans

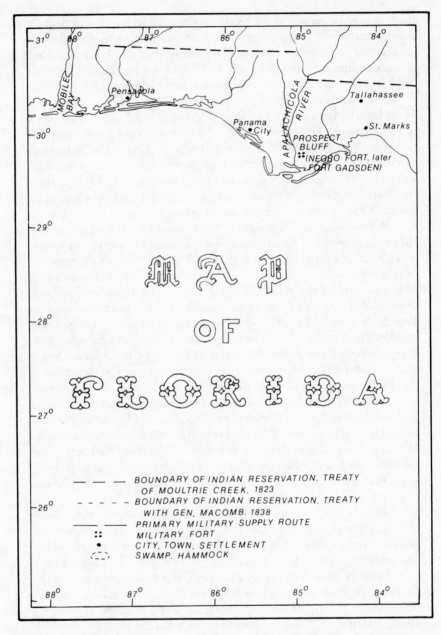

1. *Map of Florida. By E. Glendon Moore, based on maps from the National Archives Collection. See the bibliography.*

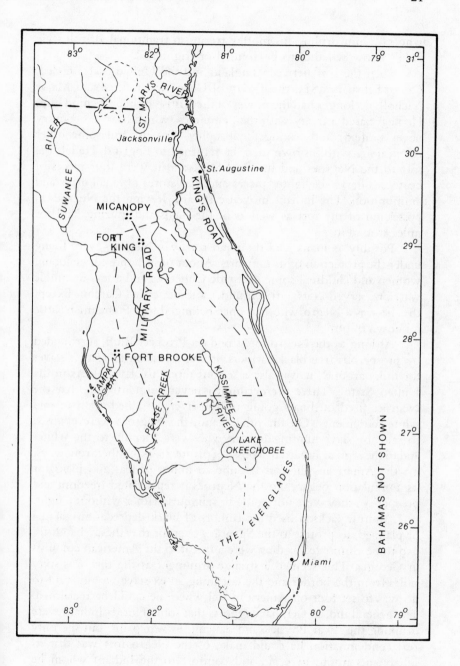

who saw him drilling his motley troops in traditional British style
didn't know whether to be amused or frightened.

Then the war between England and the United States ended.
On 17 February 1815, the Treaty of Ghent was ratified and Major
Nicholls no longer had the power of the British military behind him.
He negotiated a treaty with the Seminoles (which his own country
never ratified) and, taking the Prophet, Francis, and some other
chiefs along with his own men, he returned to England. He left the
fort to the Negroes and the Red Sticks; in it were four pieces of
heavy artillery, six lighter pieces and vast stores of small arms and
ammunition. The Indians moved eastward, leaving the Negroes in
possession of the fort as well as of the fields and grazing land for
miles around it.

Possibly as many as a thousand runaway Negroes were living
under the protection of its ramparts. About three hundred, including
women and children, some renegade Choctaw, and a few Seminole
warriors, served as its garrison under a leader called Garcon. Except
that he was a Negro who had once belonged to a Frenchman, little
is known of him.[3]

As long as the Negro fort stood on Prospect Bluff, surrounded
by prosperous free black farmers, it was a beacon to restless slaves
for miles around; it was also a serious threat to slaveholders in the
United States. There were rumors, never substantiated, that the
Negroes fired on boats going up the river or sallied forth to raid
white settlements. On the other hand, the Negroes were exposed
to raids by slave-hunting Indians who were friendly to the whites
and to the regular hazard of a posse of planters seeking their runaways.
To the Americans the fort became an object of fear and plans for
its annihilation began. To the Negroes it represented freedom and
prosperity; they were not going to relinquish either without a fight.

Andrew Jackson used the rumors of black depredations, actual
or planned, to protest to the Spanish governor that these "banditti"
had to be eliminated as they were a threat to the American colonists
in Georgia. This seemed a strange argument as the fort was sixty
miles from the border and the last thing an ex-slave would want to
do was to set foot on American soil where he could be reclaimed.
The general did, in fact, have reports that some Florida Indians were
drinking the "war Physic" and dancing in war paint, but the only
real condemnation he could make of the Negro fort was that its
inhabitants might give aid and comfort to the Indians whom he
planned to attack.

Jackson laid out his justification for a raid into Spanish territory and urged destruction of the Negro fort in a letter to Edmund P. Gaines who was then commander of the Division of the South with headquarters in New Orleans.

> The growing hostile dispositions of the Indians must be checked by prompt and energetic movements; half peace, half war, is a state of things which must not exist. . . . Any town or village affording them protection . . . must be destroyed.
>
> If the conduct of these people is such as to encourage the Indian war; if the fort harbors the negroes of our citizens or friendly Indians living within our territory, or holds out inducements to the slaves of our citizens to desert from their owner's service, this fort must be destroyed.[4]

Jackson had sent a messenger with a letter to the governor of Florida demanding to know under what flag the black fort operated and had insisted that if Spain wished to remain friends with the United States, it should destroy the fort and return the inhabitants to their rightful owners. When his emissary, Captain F. L. Amelung, returned to report that Pensacola had no troops with which to control either blacks or Indians and that the Americans themselves had little to fear from the Spanish, Jackson decided to take the initiative.

Without waiting for authority from Washington, he ordered General Gaines to move against the Indians in Florida. Gaines decided that supplies could be moved up the Apalachicola from the south much more effectively than overland from the north. He thus arranged with Daniel T. Patterson, United States Navy, commanding, at the New Orleans station, to assist in this effort. The plan was to destroy the Negro fort which would surely attack either the supply convoy or the army as they moved past; all captured inhabitants were to be returned to their proper owners. Since many Negroes, as well as their former owners, had died since their separations occurred and since many descendants of original runaways had been born free, this order would pose some interesting legal problems!

The little fleet under Lieutenant Loomis, whose scouting crew met such a gruesome end on that hot July day in 1816, was part of the force which General Gaines had assembled to follow out Jackson's orders to punish the Indians and to destroy the fort. The two transports carrying ordnance and provisions from New Orleans were to steam up the river to meet Colonel Duncan L. Clinch who was coming down the river from Fort Scott, a base of operations at the intersection of the Flint and Chattahoochee rivers.

Under Colonel Clinch were two companies of American troops, one led by Major Peter Muhlenberg and the other by Captain Zachary Taylor, comprising altogether 116 men. There were also 250 friendly Creeks under Major McIntosh. Along the way this army met, by chance, and enlisted the aid of two detachments of Lower Creeks who were hunting slaves.

As this formidable force moved slowly down the Apalachicola River toward the Negro fort, scouts for Colonel Clinch intercepted one of Garcon's messengers with a white scalp in his belt. The man, who was on his way to seek aid from the Seminoles, admitted being on the raid against Loomis. With this evidence of danger to white settlers, the Americans moved resolutely towards their objective.

The convoy arrived first and the garrison at the fort, fearing the worst, fired; however, Lieutenant Loomis remained out of reach of their big guns and demanded that the fort surrender to him.

When the army arrived a few days later, the garrison fired on it too. On 26 July, Colonel Clinch sent a delegation to the fort to demand that its inhabitants surrender forthwith. The Negro commander's reply was abusive; in addition, he hoisted the English Union Jack along with the red flag of death and followed this with a burst of cannon fire designed to frighten the Indians who were in the forefront of the expedition.

There was no more action that day but Loomis and Clinch conferred on their strategy. Then under cover of night, the Americans set up a battery on the opposite bank of the river and positioned the gunboats to attack the fort. The next morning the battle began with a great deal of activity on both sides. Cannon and artillery fire from the fort was fierce but inaccurate while the range of light arms was too short to hit anyone. Eight balls from the gunboats crashed harmlessly into the walls of the fort. Then Loomis ordered the ninth to be heated red-hot in the cook's galley while he elevated the gun enough so that this shot went over the wall.

When the fiery ball hit, everything went up in flames. The explosion of hundreds of barrels of gunpowder sent logs, cannon, human bodies, and other debris hurtling through the air. Of the 334 persons in the fort, most were killed. After the fire died down, Colonel Clinch and his Creeks found 270 dead and took 64 prisoners, most of whom died of their wounds later. Two of the prisoners were Garcon and a Choctaw chief who were turned over to the Creeks;

the warriors scalped the latter alive before stabbing him to death and they shot Garcon.[5]

"The scene in the fort was horrible beyond description; the cries of the wounded and dying, mingled with the shouts and yells of the Indians, rendered the confusion horrible in the extreme,"[6] says the official report. But it adds that three thousand stand of arms and six hundred barrels of powder were blown up and that the whole amount of property destroyed and captured amounted to $200,000. More important, the free Negro fort on Prospect Bluff no longer beckoned slaves from the United States nor promised them a haven.

The next day "a formidable body of hostile Seminoles" arrived, prepared to help their allies, but finding such a large force, prudently declined to attack. Clinch let them leave and he took his army back to Georgia without completing his punitive mission. It seemed that once the fort was destroyed, the Americans lost all interest in punishing Indians.

When the engagement was over, the dead buried, the wounded cared for, and the Negro survivors taken into custody to be returned to slavery, the battle for the spoils began. Loomis felt his men deserved to keep all captured goods as they had destroyed the fort single-handed. This was, in effect, true since the army batteries were never fired and there was no one left of the garrison to engage the troops after the explosion. But Clinch prevailed upon the navy commander to give up enough items to reward the Indians. Their payment included spades, axes and other implements, 120 pairs of shoes, flints, cartridges, muskets, and one howitzer complete and mounted.

Then Benigno Garcia Calderón, Spanish ship captain, demanded the booty in the name of his government on whose soil it had been captured. The American lieutenant declined to give it up on the grounds that the fort had fought under an English flag. Commander Patterson wrote Secretary of the Navy B. W. Crowninshield asking that a generous government reward Lieutenant Loomis and his men by giving them the captured goods as a "just reward" for their gallant effort in behalf of their country. However, the Navy Department was uneasy about certain political, international, and legal aspects of the entire operation. It was thought best to inventory and store all captured goods at Fort Crawford, Georgia, until those issues could be clarified.[7]

While the administration privately approved the action, fear of giving offense to Spanish authorities and of incurring attacks from the opposition party caused the government to keep the campaign a secret from the American public. When the *National Intelligencer* obtained a copy of Colonel Clinch's report to the War Department and published it, there was a congressional hearing on the matter.[8]

Marcus C. Buck, who participated in the battle, wrote his father from Fort Crawford. "You cannot conceive, nor I describe the horrors of the scene. In an instant, hundreds of lifeless bodies were stretched upon the plain, buried in sand and rubbish, or suspended from the tops of surrounding pines.... The brave soldier was disarmed of his resentment, and checked his victorious career, to drop a tear on the distressing scene." After completing a detailed description of the entire battle, Buck added a postscript to his letter. "First rate land can be purchased in Florida for fifty cents per acre. What speculations! if it should ever be ours, which, I think, will be the case."[9]

The Negroes who had lived along the river on this fertile land (which would some day be available to settlers for pennies an acre) had looked to the fort for their protection. Now they left their fields of corn, sweet potatoes, melons, and vegetables, and their herds of swine, cattle, and horses to hide in the forest. The fact that their Indian friends showed up indicates that another messenger must have got through Colonel Clinch's lines, but the help came too late. The displaced blacks took refuge near the Seminoles who lived on the Suwanee River. They reorganized themselves and built villages all the way to Tampa Bay. Within six months they were established in their new homes, ready to resist future aggressions.[10] However, the people of Georgia, with the help of the federal government, began immediate plans for the protection of their frontier.

"Such was the commencement of the Florida War," wrote Monette.[11] But the Indians and their Negro allies believed that it had begun somewhat earlier.

## 2

# The East Florida Annexation Plot

*An "Unauthorized Intrusion" by Americans Destroys*
*East Florida*

"The Seminole Nation is completely in waste...."
LIEUTENANT COLONEL THOMAS A. SMITH
AND COLONEL JOHN WILLIAMS

AS THE NINETEENTH CENTURY dawned, an age of expansion was developing in the United States. The desire for more land and resources had become a fever spreading among frontiersmen like an epidemic. Those in the Ohio Valley wanted the federal government to take over Canada for its rich fur trade but England was too strong for such an attempt to succeed. Others in the southwest urged the annexation of Florida as settlers pushed relentlessly over the Spanish border into the desirable lands there.[1]

In 1810 about sixty young men from the South and the West were elected to Congress. Eastern and northern states wanted to avoid war with England at all costs but these young southern and western "hawks" were angry over England's impressment of seamen and over her tendency to foster border troubles between the Americans and the Indians. They had the votes to urge war. Encouraged by this development, a group of delegates from four districts in Florida west of the Pearl River met in July of that year on Saint

27

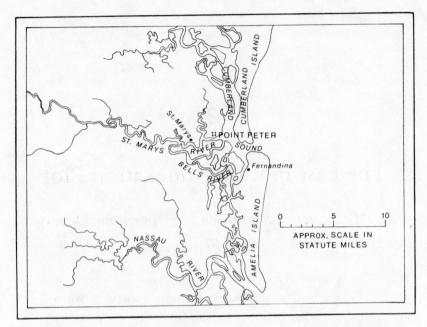

*2. Site of the attack on Fernandina, 1812. By E. Glendon Moore, adapted from USGS Topographic Series (1:250,000) of Jacksonville, Florida-Georgia, 1957, Limited Revision, 1966, and Military Topographic Map of Georgia-Florida, (Bu Top Eng). Published 1862, NA, RG 77a.*

John's Plains near Baton Rouge. They formed a government under the chairmanship of John Rhea. Collecting about eighty mounted men, they attacked and captured Baton Rouge on 23 September. To the Spanish government they sent a list of their grievances and to the United States a request for annexation.[2]

President Madison ignored the rebels but he ordered W. L. Claiborne of the Orleans Territory to take possession of West Florida from the Perdido River on the Alabama border to the Mississippi in the Louisiana Territory until a settlement with Spain could be worked out. This was done by a presidential proclamation on 21 October 1810 and confirmed by Congress on 15 January 1811.[3]

As General Claiborne was quietly working to add part of West Florida to the United States' Louisiana Territory, other forces were urging annexation of East Florida. Descendants of British colonists who had settled on the St. Marys River on the Atlantic coast were spreading westward all the way to the Flint and Chattahoochee rivers, bringing with them an inherited hostility toward the Seminole Indians. The territories of Alabama and Mississippi were filling up with settlers and those of Kentucky and Tennessee had acquired statehood.[4] The surge of white settlement was a tide that would not be stemmed. In the minds of the Americans of these areas, it seemed both inevitable and right that the Indians must be moved west of the Mississippi to make room for civilization and that Florida must not remain under the control of the weak but mischief-making Spanish government.

Rumors of Spanish plots and Indian uprisings always bred alarm among those who lived on the border and who would be the first to suffer if fears turned into reality. Often those on the fringes of the frontier were unscrupulous ruffians, eager to trade bad whisky for good furs, or farmers who had settled beyond areas open to whites and who quickly claimed protection when their intrusion was resented. Americans living north of Florida tended to exaggerate Indian depredations and to minimize the theft and violence of their own citizens.

But in spite of their distrust and even hatred of each other, both races on the frontier discovered that their well-being, if not actual prosperity, often depended upon mutual exchange of goods. Thus in 1811, the village of St. Marys in Georgia (population 585), at the mouth of the river, was a center of trade between Americans and Seminoles in which the latter gave beef, pork, venison, and furs in return for guns, ammunition, shirts, cloth, pots, and beaver traps.[5]

The Seminoles were a collection of decimated local tribes absorbed by dissident Creeks who had acquired their name, which means "Runaways,"[6] by leaving their own people to seek refuge in Florida. The first group, under Chief Secoffee,[7] had once lived along the Oconee River in Georgia, had been pushed to the Chattahoochee by the Creek-Yamassee War, and had finally settled on the Alachua prairie just west of St. Augustine about 1750.[8] When the Oconees reached these fertile plains, the Indians who had enjoyed possession of the entire territory when the Spanish first set foot upon it were virtually extinct. The Calusa-speakers on the lower peninsula, the Timucuans of central Florida and the Muskogean-speakers of the northern panhandle no longer existed as viable tribes. The Yamassees who had not been exterminated by earlier English and Creek wars were absorbed into the villages of the new settlers.[10]

As one community of Seminoles evolved in the east, others were springing up in the west. Conflict in the parent tribe was deep and strong among those Creeks who resented white intrusion on their lands and white demands for the Negroes in their midst,[11] and those who preferred to deal with the Americans through conciliation and cooperation. Those who clung to Indian traditions and feared that contact with whites could destroy the old way of life began to migrate into the "old fields" left vacant by defunct Florida tribes.

Early arrivals were the Chiaha who established their town, Mikasuki, in West Florida, absorbed some small groups, and soon became known as the militant Mikasukis who were to fight longer and harder than any other band in Florida. Like Secoffee's people, they were Hitchiti-speakers. They were followed in 1767 by a group of Upper Creeks from Efaula on the Chattahoochee River who settled northeast of Tampa Bay at a town known as Chocochatti. They spoke a Creek tongue, Muskogean, so different from Hitchiti as to be mutually unintelligible. However, the Creek emigrants all shared a core of cultural patterns strong enough to overcome language barriers.

In 1778 another large migration into West Florida brought both linguistic groups to settlements along the Apalachicola, Flint, and Chattahoochee rivers. Prominent among Creek emigrants were the Tallahassees on whose land the capitol of Florida stands today.[12]

By 1800, the Florida Indians, including remnants of early tribes such as the Yamassees, Uchees, Apalachicolas, Apalachees and such new arrivals as the Mikasukis, Tallahassees, Oconees, and others, were all referred to by Americans as the Seminole Indians. It is not clear whether this practice grew out of ignorance of differences too slight for whites to discern or whether, more likely, out of convenience, for it was easier to make treaties with and to control one tribe than to deal with many small ones.

Much more evident is the fact that the Seminole nation was not a tribe in the traditional sense. It is more accurate to call it an alliance. It was, in fact, a confederation born of dissidence and conflict. It held together for several years because all elements faced a common threat to which they refused to submit. Within its loose bonds were not only various Indian bands but also fierce rebels of another race.

For also living within the shadow of St. Augustine were several towns of free Negroes. There had always been an affinity between the runaway Seminoles and the runaway blacks. Just as they had settled near each other along the Apalachicola, Chattahoochee and Suwanee in the west, they had built adjacent villages in the vicinity of the St. Johns River in East Florida.[13]

As early as 1739 a colony of fugitive Negroes had grown up near St. Augustine and a fort had been constructed for their protection. It was known as Gracia Real de Santa Teresa de Mosé by the Spanish but the name was quickly shortened to Fort Mosé or Moussa by the inhabitants. Spanish records going back to 1688 show that Negro slaves who fled from English masters to Florida were given haven even if the Spanish had to pay the English for them. Although the Spanish government had decreed that the fugitives should be free in Florida, it was not until 1730 that a group of them brought a petition to the governor asking to be freed from the Florida citizens who now held them in bondage. Against the protest of the citizens, Governor Montiano passed the petition on to the Spanish crown which acted favorably toward the slaves. During the next twenty years various edicts confirmed this policy, which was ordered not out of compassion for the Negroes but as an effective method of disturbing the English. This procedure did all that was expected of it, for both the English and later the American planters found it a source of constant worry.[14]

Dispatches of Spanish officials bearing on this free Negro settlement indicate that a black sergeant actually operated from a post in Carolina to encourage desertions and even insurrection. His work apparently resulted in a slow stream of individual escapes and one uprising in which participants killed twenty whites but were caught and destroyed as they marched toward Florida crying, "freedom!"[15]

By 1756 the Negroes were self-sufficient economically on their farms. They had a regular priest, a Franciscan, to instruct them in the "true faith" and they boasted an army officered by their own men in a fort protected by four cannon.

Spain lost Florida to England in the 1763 Treaty of Paris, forcing the Spanish inhabitants, including the garrison at Fort Mosé, to move to Cuba. The French and Indian War (called the Seven Years' War in Europe) which this treaty ended, had profound influence on the Florida Territory. France was eliminated as a contender for the area and Britain took it from Spain. For administrative purposes, England divided it into two parts. East Florida included all land on the peninsula and east of the Chattahoochee and Apalachicola rivers with the northern boundary the St. Marys River west to the Flint. West Florida extended from the lower Chattahoochee and Apalachicola rivers west to the Mississippi.[16]

The end of the American Revolution brought another Treaty of Paris in 1783 in which the British were forced to return the Florida

Territory to the Spanish.[17] By this time Spain was weaker than ever and her hold on her New World possessions more precarious. The Spaniards were slaveholders themselves but they saw the steady stream of refugees from the United States as a source of potential strength for themselves and knew that it would stop at once if those fleeing found they were exchanging one form of thralldom for another. Thus the Spaniards continued to give haven to escaping blacks.

By 1810, many of the slaves who had fled before and during the Revolution had died of old age; their descendants had been born free and a fair number had intermarried with their Indian allies. Whether newly escaped or born to freedom, they now enjoyed a prosperous life on land they considered their own. Representative Joshua R. Giddings of Ohio, who had made an intense study of them, wrote: "When Mr. Madison assumed the duties of president, the Exiles were quietly enjoying their freedom; each sitting under his own vine and fig tree, without molestation or fear. . . . Discarding all connection with the Creeks, and living under the protection of Spain, and feeling their right to liberty was "self-evident," they believed the United States to have tacitly admitted their claims to freedom."[18]

All who observed them noted how both the free blacks and those who were slaves of the Indians had flourished in their new surroundings. One contemporary described the Seminole Negroes as stout, fine-looking people, more intelligent than their masters and longer-limbed and more symmetrical than their brothers on American plantations. They lived in separate villages in well-built houses fashioned Indian-style of "palmetto planks lashed to upright posts and thatched with palmetto leaves, . . . in the midst of well-cultivated fields of corn, rice, sweet potatoes, melons, beans, peppers and cotton."

The Negro male dressed like the Indian for special occasions in a turban of colorful bandanas or a brilliant shawl twisted about his head and topped with plumes. He wore a gaudy, long, full smock, belted at the waist and covered with polished crescents which hung about his neck and down his chest. His leggings were red cotton and his mocassins gaily decorated deerskin. For everyday a more somber, less elaborate variation of this custom sufficed. The young boys ran about nude until they reached adolescence whereupon they donned a long homespun shirt.[19] Both black and Indian Seminole women usually wore a calico or gingham tunic. They preferred leather stockings or leggings on which they hung strings of deer hooves which made a rhythmic sound when they walked or danced.[20] John Lee Williams, an on-the-scene observer, wrote: "The Seminole Negroes, for the most part, live separately from their masters, and manage their stocks and crops as they please, giving such share of the produce to their masters as they like. Being thus supplied, the Indians become idle and absolutely dependent upon their slaves. No one will suppose that negroes, thus situated, would be transferred to the sugar and cotton fields of the white planters, without exerting their influence with their nominal masters to oppose it."[21]

Actually the black slave was required to work his master's fields, tend his garden, keep his house, and prepare his meals. Thus, he also freed wealthy Seminole women to do more embroidery, weaving, or other crafts. On the other hand, the slave who policed his master's estate and handled his produce not only received a garden, stock, and house of his own but also gained prestige and power in the band. With such industry and knowledge of farming as he had gained in slavery under whites, he soon became an indispensable asset to his Indian master.[22]

Later, an Indian agent would report to the secretary of war that because of their idyllic conditions in Florida the Negroes abhorred change and would fight to stay where they were. He explained that the dependence of the Indian upon the blacks and their affection for them assured that "... an Indian would almost as soon sell his child as his slave, except when under the influence of intoxicating liquors."[23]

The Indians were dependent upon the Negroes in one other important respect. They were forced to use them as interpreters and advisors when dealing with the white man. Since former slaves often knew one or more European languages and had learned the customs and attitudes of their masters, they not only served as translators but could often suggest the best strategy for dealing with Americans. Thus such teams as Micanopy, ranking Seminole chief, and Abraham, Negro interpreter and negotiator, were to work together throughout the war with a skill that any diplomat might envy.

When the annexation movement in the United States began to gather momentum, the government of Spain had neither men nor materials with which to counter it. The local leaders could, however, turn to one group, the Seminole Indians who would lose their lands under American domination, and to another, the free Negroes who would lose not only their homes but also their freedom and dignity as human beings. There can be no doubt that it was the land of the Indians and the persons of the ex-slaves that were the real objective of the Americans who hoped to take over East Florida. It would be no minor tragedy for Americans that the two minorities chose to unite in order to protect themselves.

The coalition of Florida blacks and Indians against their oppressors would become unique in American history and would succeed, in the face of tremendous pressure, for several years. By 1812 the alliance was already firmly established. It had grown out of shared misery at the hands of whites and it was based on a complex of shared attitudes about the way life should be organized. Most of the blacks who resisted slavery and escaped to Florida were those who had come from West Africa. They seemed more aggressive and less willing to accept their fate than those from Angola or the Congo. A study of similarities between their West African cultures and that of the Seminoles provides a list of startling parallels between the two groups.

First, the West African tribes had developed a highly efficient system of agriculture based on corn as its staple. A sexual division of labor assigned to the women the drudgery of daily chores and tending the fields. The latter was not too difficult a task for they planted by poking a hole in soft soil with a stick that was pointed and fire-hardened. Into this depression, they placed a seed—sometimes adding a bit of fish for fertilizer—covered it with soil and tamped it down. The men would lend a hand in clearing a patch of land or any other heavy task; they also hunted and made war. In between these activities—while the women ground corn and carried water—they lolled about the village. They might pursue a craft or take part in religious ceremonies or political activity. As soon as they were among the Seminoles, the black males could slip back into this familiar pattern of life.

The Africans understood, as the Europeans never could, the communal sharing of land. Among them, as with the Seminoles, the entire clan or band worked the main fields of corn, beans, and rice while individual families cultivated their own small vegetable patches and fruit trees. Since the climate was very similar to that of Africa, the thatched roof houses—often raised a foot or two above the ground—were familiar and surely preferable to the slave quarters of American plantations.[24]

Second, the two groups shared basic religious beliefs. Both were animists who personified inanimate objects; the myths of both groups abounded in animal heroes. Both found power in certain fetishes concerning snakes and alligators both of which were plentiful in the area. In fact, one of the religious groups that allowed Negroes active participation was the Alligator Cult.[25]

Both groups observed the climax of their religious calendar by a ceremony of renewal when the major crop was harvested. Each year the Seminoles celebrated the Green Corn Dance. It began with three days of abstinence from all physical gratification; then all old or worn clothing, utensils, and possessions were placed on a huge pyre in the center of the village and burned. On the fourth day, the medicine man rekindled new fires for the village and for each household, symbolizing a new beginning. Debts were repaid or forgiven, village elders held court to settle differences or right wrongs; favorite myths were repeated, ritual dances danced to enforce clan values. When it was all over, everyone could begin the new year on a clean slate with new clothes and implements and a new fire on the family hearth.[26] With all ritual duties performed, the warriors took to the field to prove themselves in the chase or at war.[27] Seminole religious practices would be much closer to African black ones than those of Christianity.

If, among their creation myths, the Indians had several in which they placed themselves first among the races of mankind, the blacks could yield the point to gain obvious advantages. One Seminole favorite was the story of how the Great Spirit made a man, put him in the oven to bake but took him out too soon so that he was very pale. He made another which remained in the oven so long that he came out black. On the third try the deity was successful, creating a person whose color was just right right—a handsome brown![28]

There are several versions of how the Great Spirit offered the three races their choice of special gifts. What they chose determined their role in life. The white man selected a book, the Indian a bow and arrow, leaving nothing but a spade and other implements of labor for the Negroes.[29] No doubt, such a myth reinforced the role of blacks as those destined to perform the menial tasks of life. It also expressed the prevailing notion that the black race, having evolved last, was less well developed than the others.

A sense of hospitality (one of the Seminole's strongest characteristics) led the Indians to accept blacks in their midst. A feeling of superiority, based on the fact that many of the blacks came as slaves or refugees from slavery, soon gave way to one of respect as the Seminoles began to benefit from the knowledge of agriculture and the discipline to use it which the blacks brought to the union.

Third, the blacks found the Seminole government familiar. Their kings, like the Seminole chiefs, although hereditary, did not have absolute power. They were bound to follow the advise of a council of elders, made up of men who had proved themselves in war or at the conference table. Furthermore, a medicine man had great authority, for religious principles underlay all political behavior. Among the Seminoles, succession went most often to the son of the head-man's sister as was the custom in matrilineal societies.[30]

The Ashanti, one of the fiercest West African tribes, counted kinship by matrilineal descent.[31] This meant that the blacks were familiar with a system in which power and property passed through the mother's family to her children. The influence of the father was further diluted by the practice of polygamy which was basic to both cultures. Thus a child grew up secure in the undivided attention of his mother and her family while the father spread his time and influence among two or more homes. He might even have wives in different villages. One aspect of relationships between the two groups was that the Indian aristocracy seemed to seek out black wives, marrying those whom they captured in war or bought on occasion. There were even stories of Seminole raids to procure Negro wives.[32] Prominent blacks found it natural to revert to having more than one wife.

At ordinary times, blacks and Indians in Florida wore a minimum of clothing but for ceremonial occasions warriors of the two groups vied for the distinction of looking the gaudiest. Since the use of a turban had existed in Africa, the practice of wearing this exotic Seminole headgear became second nature to black males.[33]

Thus, under the benign attitude of the English and Spanish, the two groups fled from the United States, met and merged in Florida. Here they lived together in what Porter has called a form of "primitive democratic feudalism."[34] As the tide of white expansion spread like a blob of molasses toward the south, the Seminoles welcomed the addition to their numbers and wealth which assimilation of the blacks provided. As the two races had shared the good life in Florida for several decades, they would confront together the forces that now threatened that halcyon existence.

The Spanish coastal area which would be the battleground for the first Florida war was a fertile one in which Americans, Spanish, and English planters raised cattle, cotton, rice, and sugar cane in addition to other crops. Fernandina on Amelia Island was the focus of economic prosperity in Florida because it was a free port on the boundary between the United States and Spanish territory and largely unpoliced by either power.

In an effort to force England to respect American rights by any means short of war, Jefferson had put through Congress the Embargo Act of 1807 which prohibited all American trade with foreign ports. This hurt England by cutting off much of her food supply while she was at war with France but it also caused great suffering among the American commercial classes, "whose ships rotted at the docks." Fernandina profited by becoming the center of a vast smuggling trade. [35]

The population of Amelia Island was a polyglot of Negroes, squatters, merchants, and planters living in a hodgepodge of hastily constructed buildings. The island was also a natural funnel through which Americans entered Spanish Florida in search of land for settlement. [36]

During the twenty years that the British had occupied Florida, they had developed profitable indigo and sugar plantations and established settlements along the east coast. American planters had moved down with large numbers of slaves. [37] However, under Spanish rule and the American embargo, the thriving villages had dwindled to a few "dirty towns." These included St. Augustine, Fernandina and Picolata in the east, St. Marks and Pensacola in the west. Transportation throughout the area was accomplished mostly on the rivers as there were few roads worthy of the name.

The Spanish were, in fact, no threat in themselves but war between England and the United States over freedom of the seas seemed imminent. On 15 January 1811, a secret act of Congress had authorized the president to take possession of the Floridas "in case any arrangement has been or shall be made with the local authority of said territory for delivering up the possession of the same, or any part thereof, to the United States, or in the event of any attempt to occupy the said territory, or any part thereof, by any foreign government." [38]

On the twenty-sixth, Secretary of State James Monroe sent General George Mathews and Colonel John McKee of Georgia to negotiate with the Spanish authorities, to protect American interests and to carry out the intentions of the secret act. If, in the execution of their instructions, they should require military or navy assistance, they were to apply to the nearest forces available. [39]

General Mathews hurried to the Florida frontier where he soon discovered that the governor of East Florida had no intention of surrendering his province voluntarily. Nor were there any indications that England was planning to take over the area. These were the two conditions under which Congress had authorized the United States to take possession of the territory.

Mathews hoped to provoke a rebellion among the settlers but this proved very difficult since the farmers were prosperous and satisfied under Spanish rule. If the citizens of Florida were uncooperative, a group of Georgia volunteers calling themselves the "Patriots" were more amenable. They gathered on the banks of the St. Marys and organized an independent "Republic of Florida." Supplied with arms from the United States Arsenal at Point Peter, they raised their flag at Rose's Bluff on the Florida side of the river on 14 March 1812.

On the fifteenth, a flotilla of five gunboats descended the river. On the sixteenth, the commander-in-charge, Commodore Hugh G. Campbell, summoned all ship captains to his quarters and gave them written orders to go to the aid of the Patriots. They were to enter the harbor of Amelia and move as close to the battery at Fernandina as they could without going aground.

The boats were equipped with six mounted thirty-two pounders, one long eighteen pounder and six nine pounders. Leaving the commodore at the mouth of the St. Marys, the other gunboats moved toward Fernandina. The crews stood at quarters, guns pointed, tompions out and matches lighted. However, the orders were that the ships were not to fire unless the Patriots ran into trouble.

When the Spanish in the fort saw the gunboats approaching, ready for battle, they sent a messenger to ask for an explanation. The gunboat captains stood mute. Then the Spanish hauled down their flag and sent it to the ships; the flag was returned. The Spanish had just hoisted it again when two hundred and fifty Patriots approached in flatboats through Bell's River. After a brief consultation, the Spanish flag was lowered again and that of the Patriots' flown from the mast. At this signal the gunboats left the harbor and sailed for Point Peter.

When the ships returned, the captains were summoned to return their written orders to Commodore Campbell. These orders were never seen again.[40] There had been no need to fire a shot since the mere presence of the fleet with guns at the ready had convinced the unprotected Spanish garrison that the whole force of the United States government was behind the Patriots.

Meanwhile on the shore, the Georgians held Fernandina under the Patriots' flag until the next day when a detachment of United States troops from Point Peter arrived with General Mathews. The Patriots surrendered to him and the American flag was raised over the city.

A few days later, the Patriots, accompanied by part of Lieutenant Colonel Thomas A. Smith's regiment of regular troops, began to march toward St. Augustine while the rest of the American force went by gunboat down the St. Johns River to Picolata. The two groups met and joined just before they reached the city. As the conquering legion approached St. Augustine, the Patriots moved in advance of the American forces. They took possession of each area and then as the "local authority" they surrendered to the United States agent, Mathews, repeating this procedure until they reached the walls of the city.

Scouting parties were sent out to bring in influential and respectable inhabitants; planters were told that those who were co-operative would be suitably rewarded while those who were ob-structive would suffer under the new regime. Those who resisted were kept in the American camp until they agreed to support the cause. In the meantime, the Spanish authorities sent word for every-one in the countryside to come into the city where they could be protected. Thus all the plantations along the St. Johns River were left to the mercy of the invader.

In order to maintain their force, the Americans collected droves of cattle, barrels of corn, and other food supplies from the abandoned farms. As the seige of St. Augustine continued, the thriving planta-tions disintegrated from lack of care and the constant inroads of foraging soldiers.[41]

Back in Washington, under heavy pressure from Federalists and northerners, Secretary Monroe apologized to the Spanish govern-ment saying that General Mathews had exceeded his authority and would be dismissed. But in his letters to the general and other officials, the secretary expressed his great admiration for Mathews and at-tributed his errors entirely "to his zeal to promote the welfare of his country."[42]

To the Spanish he promised that all American troops would be removed from East Florida. But the secretary of state then appointed Governor D. B. Mitchell of Georgia to assume control and to arrange for the withdrawal of the troops. Furthermore, the governor was authorized to demand amnesty for the Patriots in return for a "res-

toration of the original situation." Since the Spanish governor
resisted such a stipulation, the United States forces remained. In
addition, as governor of Georgia, Mitchell could call upon the state
militia at a moment's notice. In fact, he proceeded to mobilize a
contingent of that organization at once. The commander of that
group was quoted as saying that he hoped the Indians would come
to the aid of the Spanish since this would afford the Georgians a
pretext to penetrate their country and attack a Negro town which
he considered an evil existing under their patronage.[43]

The Indians were not rising to the bait for General Mathews had
sent a messenger to warn them that if they took up arms, their
towns would be destroyed. Still, with Mathews removed and the
Patriots temporarily subdued, the Spanish had a chance to gather
their forces. The Georgia press estimated the St. Augustine garrison
at four hundred white and five hundred black troops. Mitchell
announced that "they have armed every able-bodied negro within
their power, and they have also received from the Havana a re-
inforcement of nearly two companies of black troops." He warned,
"It is my settled opinion that if they are suffered to remain in the
province, our southern country will be in a state of insurrection." He
then protested to the Spanish governor that his knowledge of "the
peculiar situation of the southern section of the Union," should have
compelled him in common decency not to arm blacks.

On 12 December, Governor Benigno Garcia wrote from St.
Augustine to the governor of Georgia that the colored population
served in the militia in all Spanish provinces on a parity with whites
and compared Mitchell's protest to that of a burglar insisting that a
householder lay aside his blunderbuss and meet him on an equal
footing with pistols.[44]

The Spanish garrison at St. Augustine, although reinforced from
Havana, could not obtain provisions from the land side and was in
danger of falling from starvation if not military conquest. Unable to
move the Indians, the Spanish appealed to the Negroes. In July 1812,
a black arrived at Payne's town of Alachua to warn the Seminoles
that the Americans intended to take the Indians' land and to re-enslave
the Negroes. He urged that the best defense was an offensive strike.

Aware of the American troops at Picolata where they had
settled down to maintain their seige of St. Augustine, the warriors
were convinced of the messenger's logic. On 25 July, a combined
force of Indian and black Seminole warriors fell upon the St. Johns
plantations of Americans cooperating with the Patriots; they killed

eight or nine settlers and captured a number of "probably not un-willing slaves."

Patriots began to desert the camp in order to save their families and property. On 21 August, Colonel Smith reported: "The blacks assisted by the Indians have become very daring & from want of a proper knowledge of the country the parties which I have sent out have always been unsuccessful." [45] Colonel Smith could not foresee how many military commanders in Florida would send that same unhappy message to their superiors in the decades to come.

On 15 August, Major Daniel Newnan of Georgia had arrived with 250 volunteers but he and his men had been met by the Spanish forces, strengthened by a contingent from Cuba and another group of Georgia volunteers—the ex-slaves and their descendants. Slaves, taking advantage of the confusion among the planters on the St. Johns River, began to desert and to join the Spanish, Indian, and Negro allies. On 9 September, Governor Mitchell declared that the Spanish governor "has proclaimed freedom to every negro who will join his standard, and has sent a party of them to unite with, and who are actually united with the Indians in their murderous excursions. Indeed the principal strength of the garrison of St. Augustine consists of negroes. . . . The most of our male negroes on the seaboard are restless and make many attempts to get off to Augustine, and many have succeeded."

While the Spanish garrison at St. Augustine wondered how long it could survive the siege, the American forces were having their own troubles. Their logistics problems required that supplies be hauled over great distances through hostile territory. On 12 September, a train of wagons under escort of twenty United States Marines and Georgia volunteers was proceeding from Davis Creek to the besieging camp. The detachment had just reached Twelve Mile Swamp—named for its distance from the St. Johns—when the men were ambushed by a group of Negroes and a few Indians under the leadership of a free black named Prince.

Captain John Williams, in charge of the marines, was mortally wounded and Captain Tomlinson Fort of the militia was badly hurt. The sergeant was killed and six privates wounded; several horses lay dead in their harness. As Negroes and Indians leapt out of their hiding place, knife and axe in hand, the dozen marines and militiamen still on their feet responded to the commands of their officers with a charge so fierce and unexpected that the enemy melted into the darkness. The American survivors managed to escape with their wounded but they had to leave their baggage behind. The Seminole allies, meanwhile, replenished their stock of provisions from the abandoned wagons. Although the brief engagement was not an unqualified success for the attackers, it caused Colonel Smith to summon enough Georgia militia to help him take his men from St. Augustine back to Davis Creek where he could rely on American gunboats for support.[46]

Major Daniel Newnan, adjutant-general of Georgia and commander of the Georgia volunteers in Florida, had received orders in August to move against the towns of the hostile Indians and thus remove the threat to the Americans' rear guard at St. Augustine. However, malaria among the troops and problems of procuring provisions had delayed the campaign. When the catastrophe at Twelve Mile Swamp occurred, his volunteers had less than a week left to serve but he asked for men who were willing to stay with him as long as they were needed and got eighty-four to agree. With some Patriots and militia from other detachments, he brought his force to over one hundred men. He set out on 24 September, with twelve horses and four days' provisions, to destroy the Alachua towns.

On the fourth day, when the expedition was only six or seven miles from its destination, it was met by a force of seventy-five to one hundred Indians under the aged Head-Chief Payne (eighty-year old grandson of Secoffee) and his brother and war leader Bowlegs. A fierce battle ensued in which old King Payne, mounted on a white horse, urged his men on until he was shot from his horse. After two and one-half hours of fighting the Indians retreated. They carried with them the body of their dead chief but had to leave some of their comrades on the field.

Newnan and his men erected a log barricade and dug some trenches from which they watched the Indians painting themselves and preparing for another attack. Meanwhile, word of King Payne's death had reached nearby Negro villages and black warriors joined the Indians in avenging their protector's death. The Seminole allies, who now numbered about two hundred men, crept up on the Americans and opened fire. When the United States troops again replied with fatal accuracy, the Seminoles retired. In his report, Major Newnan said that the Negroes were the best fighters, attacking more fiercely and consistently than the Indians.[47]

Now the Georgians were in trouble, for although they had beaten back two assaults, they knew that they were being constantly watched from the surrounding swamps. Having planned to take the beef and corn when they sacked the Alachua towns, they were out of provisions and reduced to eating their horses. The Seminole allies, in turn, had learned that they could not face the deadly accuracy of the Georgian rifles and resorted to sniping at the Americans from hiding places. After five or six days of this, Major Newnan's men were so incapacitated from hunger, wounds, and illness that he decided to retreat. His force set out in the dead of night, carrying the sick and wounded on stretchers. The enemy, who had suffered about fifty casualties themselves and wanted, in any event, only to save their homes, let them go.

It took Newnan and his troops several days to reach the St. Johns River. During this time, the men were forced to live on "gophers, alligators, and palmetto stocks." As they struggled back toward their base, they missed one unit sent to relieve them and were attacked once more by a party of Indians before they finally met a relief expedition that took them by gunboat to Colonel Smith's camp.[48]

Reports of large numbers of free Negroes in Florida, of their fighting ability as testified to by Major Newnan, and of defections from plantations along the border, spread general alarm. A group of two hundred mounted volunteers from Tennessee, under Colonel John Williams of Knoxville, arrived at Colerain on the St. Marys River on 7 January 1813 and put themselves under the command of Thomas Flournoy, adjutant general of the United States Army.

Thomas Pinckney of South Carolina had replaced Governor Mitchell as representative to Spain. He opposed President Madison's ambiguous policy toward Florida. He urged that the United States either occupy the Spanish territory with forces strong enough to hold it against any British attack or else withdraw completely. Benjamin Hawkins, United States agent for the Southern Indians, pleaded with Pinckney to use federal troops to prevent this new invasion of Florida. But Pinckney did not intervene and, in the end, Colonel Williams was actually supported by Colonel Smith with two hundred regulars when the troops moved out. The expedition was under orders from General Flournoy to punish the Indians, burn all property which could not be transported, execute without mercy Negroes captured under arms, and take all others prisoner.[49]

On 7 February the combined force moved upon the Alachua towns. The Seminole allies knew they could not muster more than two hundred warriors nor face an enemy with twice as many troops. They hurried their women and children deep into the swamps and contented themselves with harassing the army as it marched towards its destination. When the expedition reached Payne's deserted town on the ninth, Colonel Smith remained there while Colonel Williams took his men to raze Bowlegs' village. Taking advantage of the divided American forces, the Seminoles attacked the Tennessee volunteers but were repulsed with heavy losses. All they could do was to stave off the inevitable until the twelfth.

The expeditionary force burned 386 houses and thousands of bushels of corn; it appropriated great numbers of deerskins and took away three hundred horses and four hundred cattle. The Seminole allies, watching their homes and livelihood destroyed, attacked over and over but were beaten back each time. However, their resistance was strong enough to force the expedition to abandon plans to take one more town farther away. At any rate, the army had more spoils of war from the two villages than it could handle. The soldiers returned to their homes insisting that "the balance of the Seminole Nation [was] completely in waste." To be sure, they had destroyed the food supply of a large segment of the East Florida villages but the population was relatively intact although the *Niles Register* reported that fifty or sixty Indians had died as compared to one white man killed and seven wounded. More important, the Alachua region was now open to white settlers.

For the second time, the resistance of the Seminole allies created a situation which forced the national government to take note of illegal American military intervention in Spanish territory so that all troops were withdrawn by 15 May 1813. But while the Seminoles were described as "virtually starving" and driven from their homes, the Patriots were settling on the site of their ruined villages. The Americans built a fort there and again requested annexation. This was definitely and finally refused on 18 April 1814.[50] Thus ended the East Florida annexation plot.

When the Patriots took over the area from Fernandina to St. Augustine, "the province was in a state of high prosperity." White planters grew all their own staples and food for their livestock; they profited from the sale of such cash crops as cotton and timber; families of Spanish, English, and American descent lived and worked side by side in peace. Indian and Negro towns flourished too, providing a good life for all. There was no trouble among the races.

When the American troops withdrew a year later, Indians and blacks had been set against whites and their villages destroyed. With their sustenance taken from them, they were homeless and hungry. In fact, the whole province was in "a state of utter desolation and ruin." "Almost every building outside of the walls of St. Augustine was burned or destroyed; farms and plantations laid waste; cattle, horses, and hogs driven off or killed, and immovable property plundered or destroyed; and in many instances slaves dispersed or abducted."[51]

Citizens of Florida agreed that "but for the aid, countenance, and protection of the United States forces, those Patriots, so called, could have made no progress whatsoever; that not only would their efforts at overturning the provincial government have been entirely abortive in the outset, but they could not, at any time during the insurrection, have maintained themselves or their position in the country for a week, if unaided by the American troops."[52] By aiding and abetting the Patriots in their bid to take over East Florida, the United States government had, contrary to Governor Garcia's metaphor, been the burglar with the blunderbuss. Having subdued its victim by merely aiming the weapon, it held the territory hostage for a year while Secretary of State Monroe and President Madison made soothing speeches about Mathews having exceeded his authority. What did such a policy achieve—what loot did the burglar gain?

At the end of a year's occupation, the army was withdrawn without effecting the annexation of East Florida although the occupation had outraged Europeans. The British, who were the ostensible threat against which Americans were protecting themselves, never appeared on the scene. Even the Spanish military remained safely barricaded behind the walls of St. Augustine.[53]

The troublesome blacks and their Indian allies had been impoverished and driven from their towns but most of them were still alive and busy erecting new homes and villages. There was some personal advantage to the individual Patriots who remained on the land they had taken up; there might have been some peace of mind for Alabama and Georgia planters who could report to their slaves that their free brothers had been routed from their comfortable homes. But in every other respect, the whole incident had all the clumsiness of an attack with a blunderbuss and did as much harm with its indiscriminately scattered shot.

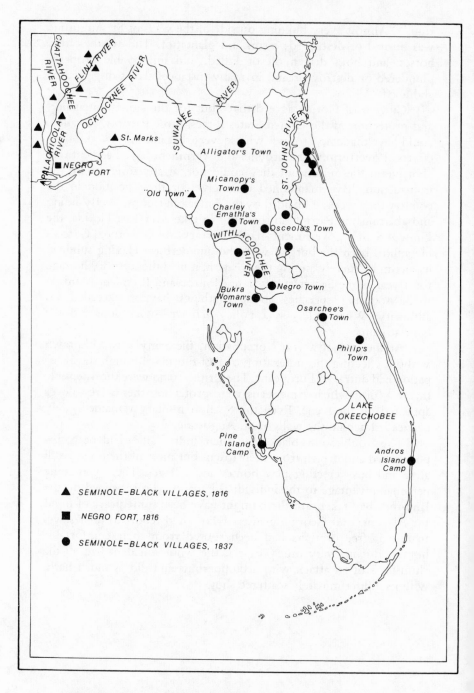

3. *Location of Seminole-Black Villages, showing movement south between the first and second wars. By E. Glendon Moore, after Michael Paul Duffner.*

# 3

# A Third Invasion of Florida

# for the "Great and Sacred Right

# of Self-Defence"

*The Spanish, Bowing to Superior Power, Give up*
*Florida to the United States*

"The Seminole War may now be considered at a close...."
MAJOR GENERAL ANDREW JACKSON

THE ANNEXATION PLOT OF 1810–1813 was the beginning of the
Florida War as far as the Seminole Indians and Negroes were concerned. It had shown the American determination to remove the
Seminole allies, even from foreign territory, by any means possible.
During 1814 and 1815 the machinations of the British had brought
the Seminole allies to the attention of General Andrew Jackson and
had resulted in the destruction of the fort at Prospect Bluff and all
of the Negro plantations along the Apalachicola, but the people
had survived. By 1817 there were large settlements of Seminole
allies along the Suwanee River. The two groups had again united
to save their persons and their property. After their protector, King
Payne, was killed, the Negroes had chosen Bowlegs as their chief
with his head slave and advisor, Nero, as their commander.

Nothing specific is known of Nero but some things may be inferred from his actions. We know that he was able to control and lead a band of angry, free Negroes and runaway slaves and that once he intervened to save two captives from torture and death. The men he rescued were Scottish traders at Prospect Bluff named Hambly and Doyle who were seized by Fowltown Indians and brought to the Mikasuki and then to the Suwanee towns. They were tried for complicity in the destruction of the fort and were about to be turned over to the Choctaw survivors when Nero sent them to a Spanish fort under "protective custody."[1] It must be assumed that the black leader understood diplomacy as well as war.

Besides Bowlegs and Nero, the Seminole allies along the Suwanee had another mentor—Alexander Arbuthnot, a Scottish trader from Nassau, who had befriended them and won their respect by his fair dealings. He, in turn, was indignant at the treatment they received at the hands of unscrupulous traders and land-hungry frontiersmen. He wrote often to United States officials asking for fairer treatment for the Seminoles. One of these letters protested against "the pressing solicitations of the chiefs of the Creek Nation, and the deplorable situation in which they are placed by the wanton aggression of the Americans."[2]

Arbuthnot apparently regarded arming Indians as a means of providing for their self-defense. In the spring of 1817, he arrived at the Suwanee in his schooner, *Chance*, carrying tomahawks, rifles, flints, lead, and gunpowder along with paints, beads, blankets, and rum for his trading house. Aboard his ship were two other Englishmen noted for their activities among the Seminole allies. Captain George Woodbine had been a recruiter of Negroes and Indians in the War of 1812. Robert C. Ambrister was a dashing young English marine of good family, doubtful intentions, and dubious behavior, whose adventures would come to an abrupt end at St. Marks in Spanish Florida.

The situation on the Georgia-Alabama southern border in 1817 was tense and confused. In August General Gaines reported to the secretary of war that he was receiving constant complaints that settlers now on the lands acquired from the Indians by the Articles of Agreement and Capitulation between General Jackson and the Creeks in 1814 were being robbed by the Indians of corn and livestock. He added that he had referred all such cases to civil authorities because he questioned the authenticity of the charges.

That fall the Indians killed a Mrs. Garrett and her two children at St. Marys. The citizens called on the army to avenge their deaths, but Indian Agent David B. Mitchell reported to the secretary of war that "the peace of the frontier of Georgia has always been exposed and disturbed, more or less, by acts of violence, committed as well by whites as the Indians; and a spirit of retaliation has mutually prevailed." He explained that the difficulty began when "a set of lawless and abandoned characters, who had taken refuge on both sides of the St. Mary's River," and who lived principally by plunder, had attacked a party of Seminoles on their way to Georgia to trade, killing one of them. Mitchell had questioned the Indians and been told that when a party of them came to the Garrett home and found a kettle belonging to their dead friend, they assumed that Mr. Garrett was the perpetrator of the murder and killed his wife and children.[3]

General Gaines, nevertheless, summoned the Seminole chiefs for a conference. In his talk to them he called them "bad people." He warned them against harboring Englishmen who wanted to cause trouble and ended his remarks on a personal note. He accused the Mikasuki Chief Hatchy (Ken ha gee) of having some of his slaves and promised him that if the chief would allow him to go into the village to retrieve his runaways, the army would not harm the Indians. According to the interpreter, King Hatchy replied in part: "You charge me with killing your people, stealing cattle and burning your houses; it is I who have just cause to complain of the Americans. . . . While one American has been justly killed for stealing cattle . . . more than four Indians . . . have been murdered. . . . I harbor no Negroes. When the Englishmen were at war with America, some took shelter with them; and it is for you white people to settle these things among yourselves, and not trouble us with what we know nothing about. I shall use force to stop any armed Americans from passing my towns or lands."[4]

Up to this point the conflict had consisted of isolated killings followed by charges and countercharges. But in November of that year, Chief Neamathla of Fowltown, a Seminole village in southern Georgia, warned Americans who had been cutting wood on his lands and some soldiers to keep away from his town. General Gaines, hearing of this, summoned the chief to Fort Scott for a talk. When the Indian refused on the grounds that he had already said everything he had to say, General Gaines sent 250 men to arrest him. When Neamathla resisted, the army attacked the town, killing four warriors and a woman who was dressed in a blanket and mistaken for a man.

The Indians fled the village, leaving behind a British officer's uniform and a letter referring to the friendship between E-me-he-maut-by (Neamathla?) and the British. On the strength of this evidence, General Gaines ordered the town burned.[5]

Mitchell wrote to the acting secretary of war that he thought Gaines had blundered in his destruction of Fowltown because these Indians had never been beligerent, had not joined the Red Sticks against the Americans and had expressed a desire to live in peace. Testifying before a United States Senate committee, which was looking into the matter, the Creek Indian agent said, "Truth compels me to say, that before the attack on Fowltown, aggressions ... were as frequent on the part of whites as on the part of Indians."[6]

Reprisals for the burning of Fowltown were not long in coming. The Indians displaced by the razing of their village fled to Florida and on 30 November a party of them and some Negro allies attacked a boat traveling up the Apalachicola River. The vessel was carrying forty United States troops as well as seven women and four children —dependents of the soldiers. Lieutenant R. W. Scott, the commanding officer, and most of his men were killed in the first volley. Six of the women and the four children were also slain. The seventh woman was taken prisoner. Six soldiers dove into the river but only two reached the fort to report the disaster. A few days later, Major Peter Muhlenberg, ascending the river with three boatloads of supplies for Fort Scott, was pinned down by Seminole fire for some time before he was rescued with great difficulty.[7]

Both incidents involved ships in foreign territory, bringing men and supplies to an American military installation. Yet, on 16 December, Secretary of War John C. Calhoun issued an order to General Gaines, in the name of President Monroe, to demand reparations from the Seminoles for these outrages and, in the event that these were not forthcoming, to cross the Florida line and attack them within Spanish limits. Ten days later he ordered General Gaines to Amelia Island and General Andrew Jackson to Fort Scott. At the time there were about eight hundred regular troops at Fort Scott and one thousand Georgia militia which had been mobilized for national service. Since Seminole strength was estimated at twenty-seven hundred warriors, Calhoun authorized Jackson to "call on Executives of adjacent states" for whatever militia forces he deemed necessary.[8]

Jackson wrote the president that he thought the United States ought to take possession of Florida and that he could do it in sixty days. The general, obviously confident that he had Monroe's support, set out from Tennessee with one thousand volunteers and traveled by forced marches to Fort Scott. He and his army covered the distance in forty-six days but heavy rains and impossible roads had forced him to leave his supplies behind. Since there were no extra provisions at the fort, the general had to choose between waiting for his wagons or starting off without supplies down the Apalachicola River, where, it was reported, provisions from two sloops in the bay were being brought up by keel boat. On 10 March 1818, Jackson ordered all available livestock slaughtered and issued each man three rations of meat and one of corn. Then he and his army of volunteers and regulars set off for Florida.[9]

Five days march from Prospect Bluff, his force of two thousand men met the heavily loaded keelboat and the men had their first proper meal in three weeks. Heartened by the nourishing food, they moved on to the site where the Negro fort once stood. Another had been erected in its place and christened Fort Gadsden after Lieutenant James Gadsden, the army engineer who had built it.

On 1 April, Jackson was deep in Seminole territory. Here he met General William McIntosh with his Coweta warriors and Colonel Edward Elliott, who commanded five hundred men.[10] With their combined forces they easily drove the Seminoles back through the Mikasuki towns, burning three hundred houses and capturing large stores of grain along with a herd of cattle. Hanging from a pole in the center of King Hatchy's village were the fresh scalps of Lieutenant Scott, his soldiers, and the civilians, who had been ambused in November.

Jackson heard that some of the retreating Seminoles had taken refuge at St. Marks. He was convinced that if the Spanish had not actually instigated Indian and Negro raids, they had armed and supplied the warriors and harbored agents "who [had] long been practicing their intrigues and villanies in this country." He attacked the fort. As he took possession of it, he made an inventory of its contents which he gave to the Spaniard in charge before sending him under armed escort to Pensacola. The general intended to return the Spanish property intact and the inventory was to be his proof of the legality of his actions! He then set out for the Suwanee River where he hoped that by destroying the Indian and Negro villages, he could "put a final close to this savage war." [11]

Arbuthnot wrote to his son at the mouth of the Suwanee that he felt the main purpose of the expedition was to destroy the blacks and that it was folly for Bowlegs to throw away his forces in their defense. At first the Negroes thought it was a ruse to sow dissension among the two groups of Seminoles but sober reflection revealed that both races could muster no more than a thousand warriors while Jackson had thirty-three hundred troops and fifteen hundred Creeks, whom the Seminoles feared even more. The Negroes abandoned their villages which were on the west bank of the river and sent their families to the east where the Indians towns were. For nearly a year Ambrister had been drilling the Negroes and training them to defend themselves but when word of the approach of Jackson's huge force reached him, the Englishman retreated to Arbuthnot's schooner and left Nero to assume command over the blacks.

As the invading legion plodded through the wilderness, Indian scouts spotted the force and galloped to warn the Negroes. Bowlegs took Arbuthnot's advice and disappeared into the swamps with his people and the Negro women and children. Blacks began ferrying their possessions across the river. They were barely out of the village when Jackson arrived just at sunset on 16 April.

The general had marched his men since very early in the morning, hoping to be in a position to attack shortly after noon but it was past 3:00 P.M. when he halted to rest, still six miles from his objective. He wanted to stop there to rest his men for the night but he didn't dare because he knew that six mounted Indians, who were supposed to be spies, were racing toward the Suwanee to spread the alarm. Since his supplies were depleted, it was imperative that he secure subsistence from the villages he meant to destroy. He decided to push on.[12]

He formed his lines of attack and put them into motion. His left flank consisted of Colonel John Williams in command of the Second Regiment of the Tennessee volunteers and some friendly Indians under Colonel Kenard. With his own Kentucky and Tennessee volunteer guards, some regular army, and Georgia militia, Jackson led the center column. The right flank consisted of the First Regiment of Tennessee volunteers under Colonel Dyer and the rest of the Creeks under General McIntosh. As usual the Indians were sent on ahead of the rest of the force. They were to cut off the retreat of the Seminole allies at the river.

About three hundred Negro warriors had remained with a few Indians on the west bank to cover the retreat of the others. Their eyes dazzled by the sunset, their British smoothbore muskets out-ranged by the American rifles, outnumbered three or four to one, they clung to their ground for a few desperate necessary minutes. Two Negroes, their retreat cut off, had to surrender; nine lay dead with two Indian comrades; the rest ran for the river and struck out for the eastern shore. The Creeks and Colonel Kenard's Tennesseeans kept firing at any sign of movement in the water or on the opposite bank. No one knows how many bullets hit their mark.

Jackson's official report mentions finding a small party of Negroes, "surprised busily securing their moveable property." He blamed the Creeks for allowing the enemy to escape by way of the river and reported eight or nine killed and some taken prisoner. A story in the *Louisiana Gazette* stated that Jackson had slain eighty Negroes and the *New Orleans Gazette*, sneering at the way Bowleg's warriors had disappeared, charged that the black Seminoles, defending themselves with great courage, showed greater resolution than the Indians.

Governor D. B. Mitchell of Georgia announced officially that Americans had engaged Negroes at Suwanee. It is certain that whether the military records or the newspapers were right about the number of casualties, it was the Seminole Negroes who fought at Suwanee in such a manner that they won the admiration of observers and prevented the army from taking Negro prisoners.[13]

Jackson destroyed the towns, burned three hundred well-built houses, captured twenty-seven hundred bushels of corn, ninety head of cattle, and many horses. He scoured the swamps for six miles beyond the river but picked up only five Negroes and nine Indian women and children; his troops killed three warriors but could not find the main body of the Suwanee residents. They had broken into small parties that could not be hunted down.[14]

In the meantime at St. Marks, an American naval officer, Captain Isaac McKeever, had lured Francis, the Prophet (Hillis Hadjo), the old Red Stick Chief Himollemico, and Arbuthnot aboard his ship by flying the British colors. Ambrister was also picked up near the Suwanee and, after a court-martial presided over by General Gaines and twelve officers selected from the Kentucky volunteers and the Georgia militia, the two Indians and the two British citizens were put to death. Arbuthnot was found guilty of "exciting and stirring up the Creek Indians to war against the United States;" Ambrister of "aiding, abetting, and comforting the enemy, supplying them with the means of war . . . and leading [them] . . . against the United States." The Prophet and Himollemico were pronounced "prime instigators of the war." Arbuthnot was hanged from the yardarm of his own trading ship; Ambrister had been sentenced to fifty stripes on his bare back and twelve months in prison but Jackson reversed the court's verdict and had him shot; both Indians were also put to death.[15]

After his strenuous activities at Suwanee and St. Marks, the general rested briefly at Fort Gadsden before moving on to Pensacola. Throughout all of his maneuvers the Spanish had stood helplessly by. When Jackson arrived at the city, the governor had fled but the garrison at the fort refused to surrender upon the general's demand. There was a brief exchange of fire before the Spanish gave up and Jackson was able to take command.

In a few months Jackson had done what he promised his president he could do in sixty days. He had virtually conquered Spanish Florida. He had also punished Spanish Indians for depredations on Americans passing through Spanish territory, had occupied Spanish forts and cities and ousted Spanish officials without a declaration of war, and he had executed British subjects.

President Monroe defended his general's behavior to the House of Representatives in March 1818 by referring to Jackson's actions as "the measures which it has been thought proper to adopt for the safety of our fellow-citizens on the frontier exposed to these ravages."[16]

What were the "ravages" to which the people on the Georgia frontier had been exposed? After an investigation of allegations against the Indians, General Gaines reported to the secretary of war that the Indians admitted to killing seven citizens but claimed that ten of their own people had been killed by whites. The incident which touched off this war began when an Indian chief complained that American citizens and soldiers were cutting wood on Indian land and demanded that whites remain on their own territory. Because General Gaines felt the chief had not treated him with respect, without investigating the evidence of British collusion, he razed the town and drove the Indians into Florida. He killed four warriors and a woman. The Indians retaliated by attacking two ships that were bringing military personnel and supplies through foreign territory. These attacks resulted in the death of ten civilians and the capture of one, but none of these victims was assaulted on American soil. The soldiers, one would assume, must accept the risk of being set upon by the enemy against whom they were preparing to go to war. When all was over, it was Fowltown and the Mikasuki and Suwanee villages that were ravaged.

Even if one ignores the fact that every major incident was the direct result of affronts to the Indians by whites, the response of the American government and military seems to have been a consistent overreaction. Monroe argued before Congress that in view of the serious threat which the Florida Indians posed to the United States in the future and to inflict on those savages "the punishment which they [had] provoked and justly merited," he had authorized the major general commanding the Southern Division of American troops to move into Florida. The president forbore to mention that the Indians which so threatened the United States and which the army had pursued into foreign territory had fled there after their homes had been demolished by the Americans for what can only be judged by any criteria as exceedingly petty reasons.

Monroe's legal justification for the invasion of Florida was that as almost all of the Seminoles inhabited land within the limits of Florida,[17] Spain was bound by the Treaty of 1795 to restrain them from committing hostilities against the United States.[18] Her inability to accomplish this by reason of her "very small and incompetent" force, the government felt, "should not expose the United States to other and greater injuries." The president promised Congress that the movement of American troops in Spanish territory would be confined strictly to "the high obligations and privileges of this great and sacred right of self-defence." He went on to reassure Congress that, "orders have been given to the General in command not to enter Florida unless it be in the pursuit of the enemy, and, in that case, to respect the Spanish authority wherever it is maintained; and he will be instructed to withdraw his forces from the province as soon as he shall have reduced that tribe to order, and secured our fellowcitizens in that quarter by satisfactory arrangements, against its unprovoked and savage hostilities in the future."[19]

Dissatisfied with the president's justification, Congress went on to inquire into Jackson's activities in Florida but not until after the campaign was over. After hearing all the evidence the select committee issued a report which disapproved of his execution of Arbuthnot and Ambrister. They did not go into his violations of Spanish territorial integrity nor into the damage done to the inhabitants of the Suwanee villages who had not been involved in the attacks on Americans. Even this condemnation of the execution of the two

British citizens was not wholehearted. A minority report concluded that "the committee can discover much which merits applause, and little that deserves censure," in the general's behavior and commented on the "incalculable benefits resulting to the nation from the distinguished services of General Jackson, and the officers and men who served under his command." The report offered these men the thanks of their grateful country.[20]

Just what had General Jackson and his army of nearly four thousand men accomplished? He had destroyed the Mikasuki towns and had probably hurt some of the Seminoles sheltered there because they had fired on American ships. But he had also driven deep into Spanish territory to raze several villages and destroy the homes of thousands of blacks and Indians who had made no move against the Americans. If he intended to capture the Negroes who had escaped in the devastation of the Alachua area around St. Augustine, he had failed again. Only a handful of blacks were taken, while the majority of the people slipped once more from the grasp of the Americans.

Jackson had achieved one major objective when he overran and conquered Spanish Florida. The following year, on 22 February 1819, a treaty was signed making the entire territory part of the United States. Article six of the treaty reads as follows:

> The inhabitants of the territories which his Catholic Majesty cedes to the United States, by this treaty, shall be incorporated in the union of the United States, as soon as may be consistent with the principles of the Federal Constitution, and admitted to the enjoyment of all privileges, rights, and immunities of the citizens of the United States.[21]

For one group of inhabitants in Florida—the Seminole Indians and blacks—there would never be any privileges, rights or immunities. For the white settlers there would not be real peace in which to enjoy these promises for a quarter of a century.

Florida became part of the United States for a price of $5,000,000. However, this $5,000,000 was to be paid not to Spain, but to American citizens who had claims against her! Secretary of State John Quincy Adams won his reputation as a wily diplomat on this occasion. The new American boundary included not only East and West Florida but all the territory from the Sabine River on the Gulf of Mexico to the Pacific Ocean at the 42nd parallel. Spain had also relinquished her claims to the Oregon Territory in return for clear title to Texas.[22] When Adams and Luis de Onis, the Spanish minister, finally signed the agreement after protracted negotiations, the secretary of state wrote in his diary that it was probably the most important day in his life. He had all but realized his goal of making the world understand that the proper dominion of the United States was the continent of North America!

The first Florida war was over. It began with the invasion of East Florida in support of the Patriots and the destruction of the Alachua towns in 1812 and 1813; it continued with the blowing up of the Negro fort sixty miles inside the Spanish border because it was "a threat to Georgia citizens" in 1816; and it concluded with the invasion of West Florida to punish the Seminoles who had fired on boats carrying military personnel and materials through foreign territory to Fort Scott. By 1818 many Mikasuki and Seminole villages had been sacked, homes and food supplies burned or captured, and untold suffering inflicted on the victims of American military operations. But the Indian and black population, although widely dispersed and suffering at the dislocation inflicted on them, remained virtually intact.

Colonels Smith and Williams had returned from the Alachua expedition to report that the Seminole nation was "completely in waste." General Jackson had overcome the Spanish almost without opposition and had reported in June to Secretary of War Calhoun that, "the Seminole war may now be considered at a close; tranquility again restored to the southern frontier of the United States; and as long as a cordon of military posts is maintained along the Gulf of Mexico, America has nothing to apprehend from either foreign or Indian hostilities."[23]

If Americans felt safer as a result of Jackson's latest campaign, they had widely varying views on the ethics of it. Some saw the general as a great national hero, others viewed him as a monster. He responded to the House committee by attacking its methods and vindicated himself by saying that he felt his discretionary orders authorized and justified every measure he had taken. He had been ordered to engage in offensive operations, to bring the war with the Seminoles to a speedy and successful termination, "with exemplary punishment for hostilities unprovoked," and to establish peace on conditions that could be termed "honorable and permanent." He had done all of these things and he had done them under orders which had charged him with the management of the war and vested him with powers necessary to accomplish this task.[24]

The beleaguered Seminole Indians and blacks must have had mixed feelings too. Although their homes and possessions were gone, most had escaped with their lives. Jackson reported that they had fled so precipitately that they had left a trail of belongings behind them as they scattered into small groups to avoid pursuit.

Porter says that the Indian and Negro population was in motion like a muddy pool stirred violently with a stick. According to him, the Fowltown Indians migrated to the west bank of the Apalachicola; and the Mikasuki moved thirty miles west of the Upper Suwanee to a place called New Mikasuki while others went back to part of the Alachua region. Upper Creek Red Sticks settled around Tampa Bay while the Alachua drifted to a place twenty miles south of their old homes; the Alachua Negroes moved to a town known as Pilakli-kaha near their Indians. Other Negro villages were set up farther west and those blacks at Suwanee were with Bowlegs in a town sixty or seventy miles southeast of their old Suwanee towns. Both Seminole Negroes and runaway slaves went down to Cape Florida and the reef, from where vast numbers were smuggled to the Bahamas. Some even put to sea in dugout canoes, carrying corn, peas, and pumpkin seeds, and approximately two hundred made a perilous passage to Andros where their descendants still live.[25]

The official reasons for the first Florida war had been that of protecting American interests against Spanish and English intrigue and of securing the rights of American settlers in Florida and along its borders to the north. Little official mention was made of the problem of the free Negroes living in the area. However, the purpose of Jackson's order to destroy the fort at Prospect Bluff had been to exterminate or take prisoner the blacks who lived there. Since it is hard to imagine the Negroes marching several days to attack Georgia citizens in territory where they would automatically be considered slaves, it is more plausible to believe that such slaveholders as President Monroe, Secretary of War Calhoun, and General Jackson himself all saw the Negro fort as a threat to an entire way of life for the planters along the Florida border. General Gaines revealed an interest shared by many when he promised Chief Hatchy immunity for himself and his people if he would turn over Negroes under his protection.[26] Having punished the Mikasuki villages and captured St. Marks, Jackson need not have traveled a week through the woods to destroy Bowlegs' towns if it were not for the hope of capturing Negroes. Arbuthnot was right when he warned Bowlegs that the main purpose of the Americans was to destroy the black population at Suwanee.

The success with which the blacks and their Seminole allies eluded capture and destruction in the first Florida war boded ill for the future attempts to subdue them but no one was reading the true significance of the results of that struggle in 1818. Everyone was too elated over the acquisition of Florida to notice that while the Seminole allies may have lost some battles, they had survived to fight another day.

From the comfortable vantage point of hindsight, it is interesting to ponder what would have happened if the Seminoles had not reacted to the sight of a familiar kettle in unfamiliar circumstances with suspicion and murder. What if General Gaines had not responded to the presence of a British uniform in a Seminole town with death and destruction? Could all the cost in national treasure and human suffering have been prevented if the United States had been content to rely more on diplomacy and less on military action? Young as our nation was, she had infinitely more power than either the Spanish or the Seminoles. A string of forts along the border might easily have protected the frontier at much less expense than the three invasions cost. Such a military policy could not, of course, have brought about the annexation of a valuable and strategic territory.

The order of events throughout the first Florida war followed a pattern that had prevailed early on in New England and in the northern Mid-Atlantic states. The mutual distrust and violence of the conflicting groups on the frontier became a way of life fed and fostered by every new incident. The tendency of the United States government as well as of the Indians (when they could) to demand and secure retribution for every affront and to attack first in the name of "the great and sacred right of self-defence," had in the past and would in the future embroil all concerned in perpetual armed conflict.

*Part Two*

# THE COLD WAR

*Negotiation for Emigration*

*1818–1835*

# 4

# The Troublesome Presence

### *Free Blacks and Indians Threaten*
### *the American Way of Life*

"Shall the lordly savage not only disdain the virtues and enjoyments of civilization himself, but shall he control the civilization of the world?"      JOHN QUINCY ADAMS

GENERAL ANDREW JACKSON had entered Florida himself or sent troops into the territory twice without official sanction when he felt it was in the best interest of the United States. Both times Congress investigated his activities and the president was forced to apologize to Spain for them. There was a great deal of feeling against Jackson, both in the Congress and among the public, for his unauthorized campaigns into alien territory but he had his defenders as well. Influential friends like Henry Clay prevented actual censure by investigating committees.

The general's behavior had been, to put it politely, highly unconventional. Embarrassed by the show of naked force and defiance of international law in Florida, President James Monroe had restored St. Marks and Pensacola to the Spanish as soon as he felt they had acquired effective garrisons. He had sent Secretary of State John Quincy Adams to negotiate for the American acquisition of Florida. The Spanish, too weak to maintain control of the situation, signed such a treaty. When it was ratified in 1821, the president asked Jackson to go to Florida—legitimately this time—to set up a territorial government.

Whatever his public statements, President Monroe revealed in his correspondence that he secretly sympathized with the behavior of both General Mathews and General Jackson. While he censured them publicly, he praised them both privately for their devotion to their country and excused their behavior as the result of excessive zeal in promoting its welfare.

Certainly Jackson's campaigns were another example of the philosophy that nothing succeeds like success. His actions had led to the acquisition of a territory long coveted by the United States. His methods would be quickly forgiven and soon forgotten.

The president no doubt sent him back to Florida as a civil administrator because the general knew the terrain well and because his capacity for ruthless action would be useful in stabilizing the situation there. In a letter dated 24 January 1821, Secretary of State Adams offered Jackson the position of leadership in the new territory and commissioned him to occupy and govern the two Floridas and to establish a territorial government. The secretary, in his letter, expressed the certainty that the general would be able to control smugglers, slave traders, and pirates and to make sure that the Seminoles would cease to give trouble.[1]

Jackson did not want the job for he felt that he was being shunted off the scene in Washington where many people were incensed over his high-handed methods. But there was no war on now and the army was being reduced. The general's command had been abolished, leaving him little choice but to accept the position offered. He was not happy in Pensacola for he did not get on well with the Spaniards and he was disappointed when the president did not even allow him the privilege of appointing his own friends to important official positions.

He began his administration by organizing East and West Florida into a single territory with two counties. St. Johns included all of the land east of the Suwanee River and Escambia encompassed everything west of it to the Perdido. Jackson then issued executive orders setting up a civil government which provided for administrative and judicial offices. He obviously did a competent and efficient job of creating a framework for governing the area but he continued to have serious problems with ex-Governor José Callava who remained in Pensacola. In October 1821 the general resigned.

On 30 March 1822, Congress passed a law creating a territorial government which provided for the orderly progression toward self-government and eventual statehood. William Pope Duval, a judge in East Florida, became the first territorial governor and Colonel Gad Humphreys was appointed agent to the Florida Indians. Duval, as governor, became ex-officio superintendent of Indian Affairs.

The number of Indians in Florida at the time was estimated at about 4,000, including 1,600 men; the blacks at 800, of which 150 were adult males. Their villages dotted the countryside from St. Augustine to the Apalachicola River. Most of them consisted of log and palmetto huts, surrounded by cleared fields of from two to twenty acres.[2]

That year M. Penieres, subagent for the Florida Indians, reported to Congress that the exiles (Seminole Negroes) were afraid of losing their liberty and that they influenced the Indians strongly. He suggested moving them from the United States and General Jackson, who had been too busy with administrative matters for a year to bother the Indians, now added his insistence that all the Seminoles be sent west. He continued to assert that they must not only be removed from Florida but that they must be reunited with their bitter enemies, the Creeks.[3]

The Creeks were having their own troubles. The previous year, Georgia had demanded a new treaty with them and Secretary of War Calhoun had appointed General Andrew Pickens and General Thomas Flournoy of Georgia to negotiate one "for the benefit of Georgia." The Georgians had two goals—to obtain the fertile lands between the Flint and Chatahoochee rivers, now in the hands of the Creeks, and to secure lost slaves or indemnity for them. As adjutant general of the United States, Flournoy had given the order to punish the Alachua Indians and to execute without mercy any Negroes under arms. But even he and Pickens could not satisfy the Georgians' demands for the return of lost slaves—an issue in treaties with the Creeks since 1783.[4] Pickens and Flournoy were replaced by Daniel M. Forney and David Meriweather who finally hammered out an agreement satisfactory to the citizens.

In 1790, as allies of the British in the American Revolution, the Creeks had been forced to sign a treaty of peace, as the vanquished party, with the new American government. Article three of that document stated:

The Creek Nation shall deliver as soon as practicable to the commanding officer of the troops of the United States, stationed at Rock-Landing on the Oconee River, all citizens of the United States, white inhabitants or negroes, who are now prisoners in any part of said nation.[5] And if any such prisoners or negroes should not be so delivered, on or before the first day of June ensuing, the governor of Georgia may empower three persons to repair to the said nation, in order to claim and receive such prisoners and negroes.[6]

Another treaty in 1796 also asked for any Negroes among the Creeks and stated that " ... the governor of Georgia may empower three persons to repair to the said nation, in order to claim and receive such prisoners, negroes and property, under the direction of the President of the United States."[7]

In the Treaty of Indian Springs in 1821, the Georgians had demanded compensation not only for their lost slaves but also for the labor the slaves would have performed if still in bondage! Although there was no way for any person or court to determine who had been captured or deliberately lured from their masters in war or who had escaped by themselves or with the help of the Spanish, the Creeks were now held responsible for them all.

The agreement, as worked out, allotted $200,000 in cash to the Creeks for the lands between the Flint and Chatahoochee rivers ceded to the United States; furthermore, the government agreed to pay an indemnity to Georgia, provided the sum was no more than $250,000, for property taken or destroyed by Indians between 1775 and 1802. Thus the citizens of Georgia would soon be in possession of the valuable farm land given up by the Creeks and much of the money paid for the land would go back to the Georgians in the form of indemnity. No reparation was ever considered for destruction of Indian homes and property.

The amount due to Georgia was to be ascertained by the president of the United States. After investigating the matter, a group of commissioners decided that claims for ninety-two slaves were valid and their value in person and labor lost was set at $109,000. Congress appropriated the money.

... A very important point was the assignment to the United States, for the benefit of the Creek Indians, of the interest vested

in the claimants to the property and persons claimed—the United
States to hold such interest in trust for the Creek Indians.

By this arrangement, our government became owners of the
Exiles referred to "in trust for the benefit of the Creeks," according
to the construction which the Indians, the authorities of the United
States and those of Georgia, placed upon the assignment, the agreement and the treaty.[8]

Thus after thirty-eight years of persistent effort, southern legislators had involved the United States government in slave dealing;
Georgians had obtained compensation for the loss of the fugitive
bondsmen and their northern colleagues had let them do it!

Naturally the Creeks became intent upon securing as many of
these slaves as possible for each one returned to the Georgians who
claimed them meant a payment to a Creek by the federal government. This policy had, in fact, begun long before 1821 and it was
for this reason that Arbuthnot had been impelled to protest to the
American government that the Seminole Indians were victims not
only of American settlers trying to take their lands but also of "the
pressing solicitations of the chiefs of the Creek nation . . . ," hoping
to obtain "their" Negroes.

The attitude of the Americans was best expressed in a speech
made to the Creek chiefs by the Georgia commissioners in 1820.
They said, in part, "Brothers: As to the Negroes now remaining
among the Seminoles, belonging to the white people, we consider
these people (the Seminoles) a part of the Creek Nation;[9] and we
look to the chiefs of the Creek Nation to cause the people there, as
well as the people of the Upper Towns to do justice."[10]

General Alexander McGillivray spoke for the Creek chiefs,
assuring the commissioners that his people had delivered all the
Negroes they could find after the Treaty of 1790; he reminded them
that the Creeks had helped destroy the Negro fort and had delivered
all survivors to Colonel Clinch, while other Negro captives had
been turned over to Colonel Hawkins. He offered to go and find
any others he could lay his hands on. In spite of all Creek efforts, the
Americans were not satisfied and the 1821 treaty would now legiti-
mize slave hunting by both Creeks and whites.

At this time the missionary, Jedidiah Morse, found the Seminole
communities a "resort of pirates, smugglers, etc." and added that
"Our refugee slaves aim for their settlements with a view of escaping
to the neighboring islands.[11] Penieres estimated their number at

five thousand, the Negro slaves at forty and the fugitive Negroes impossible to estimate. But even as the good Reverend called their camps a haven for pirates and smugglers, he reported that the Seminoles were making a serious effort to conform to white customs. The women wore dresses and the men a belted shirt that reached below the knee. They had given up their "Indian fondness for ornaments and finery." He added that they were honest and attached to the British and Americans. The Seminoles had always been farmers, but Americans did not want to share Florida with Indians— farmers or hunters—irresponsible or praiseworthy. They pressed to have them sent west of the Mississippi or, at the very least, moved out of their way and off the valuable lands they now occupied.

Although the Indians who inhabited North America before the sixteenth century were as varied in their social customs, language, and cultures as the nationalities of Europe, the native Americans shared one common trait—their attitude toward the land on which they lived. No American Indian had any concept of individual ownership of land for individual personal gain. Whether it was a garden plot, a berry patch, a fishing spot, or hunting range, the land belonged to a clan or tribe and was used by individuals only as long as they did not abuse it and took from it no more than they or their group needed. While a few chiefs came to acquire land or property in the European sense after years of contact with the settlers, the natives on the whole never understood the "legal deeds" which the white man was always placing before them and asking them to affix their marks upon. Nor did any European have any concept of what land meant to the Indian. To the whites, the Indian attitude toward land was incomprehensible; it was also wasteful and inefficient.

In the eighteenth and nineteenth centuries, even such enlightened men as Thomas Jefferson felt that one of the justifications for taking the Indian's land was that he simply did not know how to use it efficiently. In a speech made in 1802, John Quincy Adams expressed this opinion for all Americans. "Their cultivated fields; their constructed habitations; a space ... for their subsistence ... was undoubtedly by the laws of nature theirs. But what is the right of the huntsman to the forest of a thousand miles over which he has accidentally ranged in quest of prey? ... Shall the exuberant bosom of the common mother, amply adequate to the nourishment of millions, be claimed exclusively by a few hundreds of her offspring? Shall the lordly savage not only disdain the virtues and enjoyments of civilization himself, but shall he control the civilization of the world?"[12]

Later Adams argued before the Supreme Court that Indian occupancy was not like European tenure: "... they have no idea of a title to the soil itself. It is overrun by them, rather than inhabited. It is not a true and legal possession."[13] The court upheld the view of Adams and the American citizens agreed. This point of view was particularly interesting in view of the fact that time after time the Iroquois and the Five Civilized Tribes had shown that they could farm as effectively as their frontier neighbors. The Mandan in North Dakota had been able to supply enough corn and vegetables for themselves and great numbers of nomadic tribes around them.

By 1823 the Florida citizens could wait no longer to remove the natives in their path; they demanded a treaty with the Seminoles. Governor Duval, James Gadsden and Bernardo Segui acted for the Americans at a meeting at a camp on Moultrie Creek just south of St. Augustine. The Seminole chiefs came in reluctantly and most of the influential ones refused to sign the treaty for it ceded to the United States government all of the good land on which their villages now stood. The treaty contained the usual promises. The federal government would protect the Seminoles, and would give them $6,000 for farming implements and livestock and an annuity of $5,000 for twenty years. At the end of that time the Seminoles were to emigrate to land west of the Mississippi. The United States government would also supply $2,000 to move the Indians from their fertile fields to the acreage now given them; would supply rations of corn, meat, and salt until they could plant again and would support a school, a blacksmith, and a gunsmith. The Indians did not want to leave their villages and the graves of their loved ones; they hoped to live peacefully near the whites; they resisted all efforts to move them. Finally six chiefs were induced to sign the treaty after they were given plantations along the Apalachicola River. The rest had to move.[14]

Again, an important clause in the treaty was one that bound the chiefs and warriors to be "active and vigilant" in seeking out and returning fugitive slaves.[15] The commission wrote Secretary of War Calhoun that the majority of Indians in Florida were warriors and that most of them wandered about without permanent homes. In view of the number of fields and gardens which the American army had in the past and would continue in the future to destroy, this was an incredible statement. In a talk to the commissioners, Neamathla stated that the Seminoles meant to incorporate fugitive Red Sticks that came to Florida and refused to state the number of

Negroes among them.[16] It was clear that the Indians were angry and that the commissioners did not know anything about the natives in their midst or were deliberately deceiving the officials in Washington.

At one time George Walton, acting governor of Florida, suggested to T. L. McKenney, superintendent of Indian Affairs in Washington, that in negotiating a treaty with the natives, government representatives have "no private interests or feelings to consult" and be "acquainted with the Indian character, and known personally to the chiefs."[17] Gadsden was a slaveholding planter, Duval the governor of the territory, and it seems likely that Segui's residence there dated back to Spanish rule. They had all had long and close contact with the Florida Indians but it seems clear that it was their "private interests and feelings" rather than an understanding of Indian character that dominated their thoughts and actions at Moultrie Creek.

The reason the Indians were forced to sign the treaty in 1823 was that Americans were finding the distance between Pensacola in the west and St. Augustine in the east too great to travel on matters of business and wanted a capital that could serve the whole area more conveniently. Governor Duval asked John Lee Williams of East Florida and Dr. William H. Simmons of West Florida to find a suitable site for the capital of the new territory. They settled on Tallahassee, a village on the lake of the same name. It was then inhabited by two hundred Indians under Sub-Chief Chefixico Hadjo, but scattered throughout the surrounding peach orchards were three hundred more of the same group under Neamathla, the head chief. Williams and Simmons were entertained by Neamathla with a dance and games and allowed to look over the land but the chief would not consent to their taking the home of his people for their capital. However, Duval went ahead with plans to move the executive offices there and, by using threats and promises, to clear all the Indians out first. He then called a council to gain public permission from the natives for placing his capital on their land.

By this time American settlers were clearing land and raising log cabins near the Indian villages. Other white men were gathering around the new seat of government, hoping for political office or land grants. As they built their shacks or raised their tents, they dreamed of the large estates or political opportunities that would soon be theirs. The chiefs were "grave, dignified, courteous;" their warriors seemed concerned only with protecting their stock and harvesting their crops. Neamathla was grimly silent.

The council met at Pensacola on 8 November 1824. A large number of Indians watching impassively from the rear of the room and through the doors and windows seemed a sign that portended well for the future. "It was the meeting, as yet not hostile, of the forces of the civilized and the wild."[18] Americans believed they could handle the natives easily; Duval knew better.

As the council was meeting to establish the capital at Tallahassee, Duval set out alone for the camp of Neamathla. He found the chief urging his warriors to resist removal to reservations. Duval broke in on the chief's speech to warn that those who refused to move would suffer. Unable to muster a war party, Neamathla went back to Georgia.[19]

And so during 1824, the Florida Indians were shunted to their reservations on the peninsula and the good land in north central Florida became available to settlers. After making a tour of inspection, Duval reported that no part of the Seminole allotment was worth cultivating. He added that it was by far the poorest and most miserable region he had ever beheld. Many Indians simply stayed on their old lands. In 1825 Acting Governor Walton wrote to McKenney that the problem of fugitive Indians who refused to go to the reservations was so serious that only armed force would impel them to comply with the treaty.

> ... I have determined, as the only course left to save these Indians from starvation, and the settlements from exposure to depredations from them, caused only by their necessitous condition, to place Mr. Doyle at or near the Suwanee River, with the double objective of preventing the Indians from entering the settlements of the whites, and to furnish them with some supplies of corn for their wives and children.

> I am convinced they cannot be concentrated within their limits without the aid of military force, unless some means of subsistence be there provided for them; in which case, I believe they would comply with whatever might be required of them. ... The situation of these unfortunate human beings is miserable in the extreme, and requires prompt and effectual relief from the humanity, if not the justice, of the Government.[20]

Doyle did his best. In October 1825 Chefixico Hadjo, chief of
the Tallahassee, had his camp on the Suwanee where he had taken
his people when they were displaced by the state capital. Doyle
finally convinced the chief to take his people to Tampa Bay on the
first leg of their journey to their new land. When the party reached
Tampa, they were met by a messenger from Chief Hicks on the
reservation. Hicks had been appointed by Duval as head of all the
Florida Indians and the one with whom the Americans would deal
although he did not hold hereditary rank. His emissary had just
enough corn and beef to issue each person about two days' rations
before they set out for the swamps which were their destination. At
the sight of such meager supplies, half of the hundred men, women,
and children in Chefixico's party deserted him and went back to the
Suwanee. Since sixty others had recently returned from Tampa to
their old areas, Doyle wrote to warn Walton that over a hundred
hungry Indians were scattered around Tallahassee.

Doyle listed his reasons for the Indian reluctance to settle on the
land given them: it was too poor to make their bread on; there were
no running streams and the stagnant pond water caused disease;
there was not enough maintenance at the agency to support all of
those who presented themselves; neither the chiefs nor the white
men were distributing the funds fairly; the Indians who had lived
near the reserve and knew it well refused to move on it; the Indians
had been forced to leave their homes against their will. A kind and
honest man, Doyle was one of many who were to recommend
moving the Indians west of the Mississippi as an act of charity. He
wrote, "I found all those Indians humble, and I believe would be
willing to go to any place where they could find good land and
water. It would be a most favorable moment to press on them the
idea of crossing the Mississippi." Although a year had passed since
the signing of the Treaty of Camp Moultrie, implementation was
far from accomplished. Yet whites were already urging a revision
which would authorize immediate removal of all Indians to the West.
Miserable as the Seminoles were, they did not want to leave Florida.
However much they hated their new treaty, they clung to a clause
in it which implied a twenty-year reprieve before they must move
again.[21]

Slaves continued to escape and seek refuge among the Indians.
The secretary of war gave whites permission to go on the reservation
to look for them; whites sometimes took blacks who had been born
free or who belonged to Indians. Yet Indians were flogged or mur-

dered if they appeared in white settlements; their slaves were taken, their stock killed, and their houses burned. Finally, in desperation, the Indians turned on the whites, stealing cattle and committing cruel murders among them. They attacked one family in Alachua, drove them from their farm, took all their provisions and destroyed some buildings. Duval asked McKenney for a fort in the Alachua area to prevent depredations by both Indians and whites. There were attacks on the Tallahassee citizens as well.[22]

Through 1825 bloody conflicts grew up over the controversy of fugitive slaves; Negroes whose families had been free for generations were returned to slavery. Although the Indians were suffering severe want Duval withheld the promised annuities in order to force the Seminoles to give up more blacks. Duval, himself a slave owner, could not resist the importunities of his fellow citizens. He was courageous and able, but he had little regard for the deep-rooted customs of the Indians and no respect for the feelings of Negroes. The development of Florida into a state in the union was the governor's main goal; he underestimated the dignity of the Seminoles— of both races—and the love they bore for their land.

Angered by the withholding of their annuity because they allegedly harbored slaves claimed by whites, some Seminoles stole grain and meat from the settlers. Duval reported that because of drought and late planting the Indians were hungry; they hunted off the reservation—sometimes livestock of Americans when the deer were gone. Whites kept up an angry complaint about Negro slaves in the hands of Indians; however, the governor reported to Washington that many of the Indians' slaves were in the hands of whites.

Even as the governor was describing the wretched conditions on the reservations to the superintendent of Indian Affairs in Washington, he was upbraiding the chiefs because their people stole cattle and grain and he was ordering them to make fields in order to raise corn and vegetables. He ended his speech to the chiefs with a familiar refrain. "Chiefs and warriors: You hold negroes in your nation that belong to white people. By the treaty you are bound to deliver all the negroes that do not belong to the Indians to the agent; this you have not done, although you have promised in your talks to do so; you are now called upon to fulfill the treaty. You are not to mind what the negroes say; they care nothing for you, further than to make use of you to keep out of the hands of their masters."[23] It was true that Duval was under constant pressure from constituents in his territory to press for the return of slaves whenever he met with the Indians but it is also very likely that he, himself, could not believe that the alliance between the Negroes and the Indians was based on mutual respect, affection, and commitment to a common cause.

When Chief John Hicks replied to this talk, he reminded Duval that it was hardly his fault that his nation was destitute on the land to which they had been forced to move; he complained that whites had killed their cattle and hogs without ever having to pay reparations. He expressed a sense of deep injustice because bad Indians were always punished while bad white people seemed always to go free.[24]

What Hicks couldn't see and his adversaries couldn't admit— even to themselves—was that as long as the Seminoles were an unwanted minority in the area, they had little hope of social or legal justice. They were guilty of one basic crime. They were in the way. Wherever Indians existed, they stood in the path of American expansion and the settlement of frontiers. How to get them out of the way in some manner that we could justify to our collective conscience absorbed much of our energy and ingenuity for three centuries.

# 5

# Colonel Gad Humphrey's Campaign

## An Indian Agent Does His Best

"I am getting to be very old, and I wish my bones to be here."

CHIEF JOHN HICKS

TWO YEARS HAD PASSED since the signing of a pact between the Seminoles and the Americans but conditions had changed little. The Treaty of Camp Moultrie had forced all but a handful of chiefs from the good land of northern Florida.[1] After putting the Indians on land that, according to Governor Duval, was uninhabitable, the federal government withheld annuities promised the natives in order to coerce them into giving up blacks demanded by the citizens. With no crops and little game on which to subsist and with their annuity withheld, the Indians turned to raiding to survive. Each time there was a sortie, the Americans cried out that the Indians were treacherous and not to be trusted. Into this volatile situation came Colonel Gad Humphreys on 14 June 1825 to take up duties as agent to the Florida Indians.

Colonel Humphreys wrote Superintendent of Indian Affairs Thomas S. McKenney in Washington, asking for temporary help until the Indians could plant some crops and he asked for instructions on how to handle squatters who were settling illegally on public lands. The agent also wrote Acting Governor of Florida George Walton about the problem of settlers selling whisky to the Indians, reporting that the warriors would pay any price for a commodity which weakened and brutalized them and caused havoc in their camps. He noted that settlers shrewdly made all their bargains in secret so that they could not be caught and prosecuted for this illegal traffic. He begged that some effective remedy be applied at once.[2] There was constant trouble between the natives and the new settlers but Humphreys felt that if the sale of liquor could be controlled and illegal squatting on public lands prohibited, difficulties could be decreased.

Not long after Humphreys assumed his duties, an incident occurred which was typical of the friction which existed within his jurisdiction. A planter on the St. Johns River by the name of Salano arrived at St. Augustine to report that three Indians had come to his plantation swearing to have revenge for the death of three warriors who had been missing from their village so long they were presumed dead.

A Lieutenant Canfield was dispatched with twenty men to ascertain the facts. His party came upon the Indians' camp in a place called Cabbage Swamp. When they were within hailing distance, Salano ordered the interpreter to remain silent. Seeing the soldiers in the background, the Indians took a belligerent stance. Instead of explaining the reason for his party's presence, Salano fired his pistol. The Indians returned a volley. In the skirmish, two Indians were captured—one slightly wounded—and the others fled, leaving four rifles and a large quantity of skins.

Lieutenant Canfield finally took command of the expedition, sent one of the captured Indians after the others to explain that the whole thing was an accident. However, the Indians were incensed over the wounding of one of their men. Settlers near St. Augustine fled to the town lest they be victims of reprisals. The interpreter told Humphreys that Salano took the skins, the abandoned rifles, and other valuables which belonged to the Indians back to his own plantation.

In his investigation Humphreys, the Indian agent, was puzzled by many aspects of the story: first, Indians never boasted before they took revenge but always acted in secret; second, had the interpreter been allowed to assure the Indians that the party was merely looking for information, they would not have been alarmed; third, had Salano waited for the army officer in charge to take the initiative, no shots would have been exchanged; finally, Salano went home from the incident laden with booty.

As a result of this encounter, Humphreys was forced to send an infantry detachment to patrol the road between Fort Brooke and Camp King to deter any hostile acts; settlers had been frightened into leaving their homes temporarily and the government incurred the expense of making reparations for the injured Indians in order to prevent bloodshed. Yet Humphreys could not obtain censure for the man who had caused all the trouble. Ironically, when the whole thing was over, the missing warriors returned safely and a troubled peace descended temporarily upon the St. Johns area. In his report, Humphreys went on to say:

> The great disadvantage under which the almost proscribed children of the forest labor for want of credibility as witnesses in our courts of law, destroys everything like equality of rights; forbids the idea of their success in legal controversy, in opposition to their white neighbours, and thus virtually excludes them from our halls of justice. To this must be mainly attributed their proneness to take punishment into their own hands, despairing as they do of obtaining redress for injuries by recourse to the laws of the whites, which have in but few cases, when they have been appealed to by Indians, afforded any remedy for evils complained of. In the case before us, Mr. Salano, who is the author of it, being permitted to depose, has enjoyed and exercised the power to fix upon the Indians by imputation they could not merit, and which for lack of testimony, or want of hearing, they could not repel.[3]

At this time it was merely custom to deny Indians access to justice in American courts. It would soon be written into law in Georgia.[4] Negroes, of course, were not treated as human beings. A law was placed before the House of Burgesses in the colony of Virginia in 1723 authorizing owners to go before the court in defense of a slave because the Negro could not defend himself.[5]

A century later the greatest cause of friction between the Americans and the Seminole nation was over the Negroes in it. Humphreys reported that the Indians, possessing no rights in the court of justice and having paid in good faith but having no paper to prove it, found their slaves taken by force. When this happened, the Seminoles felt justified in taking them back the same way.

Governor Duval sent instructions that any slave properly identified by a white man must be turned over to St. Augustine at once; but if the white's claim was doubtful, Humphreys could wait until Federal Judge J. L. Smith had ruled on the validity of the claim.

He was to remove all free blacks from the Seminole nation at his own discretion and, where whites held a slave belonging to an Indian, justice was to be rendered the latter.[6] How the agent was to enforce these laudatory rules no one could imagine. The complaints from both sides grew apace. In March 1826, Duval wrote to McKenney.

> The persons who have been most clamorous about their claims on the Indians for property, are those who have cheated them, under false reports of their slaves, who have gone back to the Indians. I have been adjudicating these claims for some time almost daily, since my arrival here. The justice which the Indians are entitled to they cannot obtain, while they surrender to our citizens the slaves claimed by them, their own negroes that have been taken from them are held by white people who refuse to deliver them up. I have felt ashamed while urging the Indians to surrender their own rights, and property held by our citizens. The Government should have their property restored to them, or pay the Indians the value of it.
>
> To tell one of these people that he must go to law for his property, in our courts, with a white man, is only adding insult to injury.[7]

As governor of the state, Duval might conceivably have put the weight of his office behind his sympathy for the Indians, but this he was never able to do. Colonel Humphreys tried to adjust demands made by citizens while at the same time protecting the natives, but he stood alone. An outraged legislature at Tallahassee passed a law entitled, "An Act to Prevent the Indians from roaming at large, throughout the Territory." It stipulated that any Indian over the age of consent found beyond the boundary of the reservation without a pass could be apprehended by any citizen and brought before a justice of the peace who was authorized, empowered, and *required* to punish him by inflicting not more than thirty-nine stripes on the bare back and to take his gun from him. In a letter to the Office of Indian Affairs in Washington, the agent wrote that, although cruelly oppressed, the Indians were free men who would not submit to "the ignominy of stripes, and that for no other offence, than the mere exercise of a privilege common to all who are not slaves." He warned, "carry this law into effect and war in reality may be expected sooner or later to follow as a consequence." He quoted a Florida legislator as saying to him, "It is found impossible to bring them to negotiate for a removal from the territory, and the only course, therefore, which remains open for us to rid ourselves of them, is to adopt a mode of treatment towards them as will induce them to acts that will justify their expulsion by force." Humphreys blamed the outcries from settlers concerning disturbances on just such indignities which the Indians could not tolerate.

By 1827 the Florida Indians were starving on their unproductive reservation. In a letter to Duval, dated 6 March of that year, Humphreys wrote, "There is not at this moment, I will venture to say, in the whole nation a bushel of corn, or any adequate substitute for it." The people, he reported, had eaten all the coontie and briar root, their usual last resort, and were relying on the cabbage tree for a vegetable sustenance. Many of the warriors' guns had been confiscated during a recent alarm so that they could not hunt. Recently a group of "stragglers" had been rounded up and marched like cattle to the reservation. Old people, helpless children, and pregnant women had not been allowed to rest. One woman's child was born prematurely and she barely escaped death. Humphreys agreed that military force could be used to apprehend Indians who had been responsible for violence, but he decried the "parading of military detachments through the country in warlike fashion in time of peace." A practical military man, Colonel Humphreys ended his letter on the following note of despair: "... and any man who reads the history of this inglorious *war* and its effects, will learn and see much which, as an American, a member of a nation calling itself *Christian*, he must blush at." [8]

While Humphreys was in Washington on business, the local grand jury convened in St. Augustine and composed a list of complaints against him. Humphreys could only reply that he always had in the past and would in the future continue to act honestly and independently. The territorial legislature, in turn, wrote to Washington that the citizens resented, "probably not without cause," the additional land given to the Indians after the treaty of 1823. This was the only land fit for cultivation which the Indians received and it had been granted them at the recommendation of Governor Duval who had reported to McKenney on 22 February 1826 that, "I have therefore to advise, as my duty demands, and the honor and humanity of my country require, that the Big Swamp be also given to the Indians, and that the Northern side be fixed five miles north of the Big Swamp and extended to the Okelawaha River East and so far West as to include the Big Hammock: this line will take in no good land but the Big Swamp, of any consequence, but by extending it into the pine barren five miles, it will keep off settlers from the Indian boundary who would otherwise crowd near the line, and sell whisky to the Indians."[9]

A year later the Floridians' complaint was that this land lay in the pathway of their citizens and had already impeded the settlement of the fairest part of Florida. "The land in this vicinity," they cried, "is excellent, and but for the obstruction by this unfortunate though not less obnoxious tribe of beings, would, before this, have borne on the current of the St. John's all the rich and luxurious products of a tropical clime." They complained that Indians stripped their corn-fields, killed or stole their cattle, burnt their houses, and murdered their citizens. They begged for the speedy removal of "those people" from the territory. The citizens of Florida must have been decent people, yet they were incapable of recognizing that in 1810 the Indians and blacks had been producing all the "luxurious products of a tropical clime," that only since their own fields had been laid bare, their homes destroyed, and their people moved forcibly from the good land by a treaty,[10] had they resorted to obtaining food by raiding those who now possessed their territory.

The demand for Negroes, who were said to be among the Indians, continued to agitate the country and cause serious problems. Citizens wrote to the commissioner of Indian Affairs that the agent was not acting upon their requests that the Indians give up slaves. Duval supported Humphreys in a letter of 20 March 1827 in which he said, "I see no reason why Indians shall be compelled to surrender all slaves claimed by our citizens when this surrender is not mutual. . . . The negroes, claimed by the Indian woman, Nelly, may be given up to her; or if you believe it just and proper, the same can be retained under your orders until her case shall be determined."[11]

The claims for slaves were following a round-robin course: they were submitted to the federal court judge who turned the matter over to the agent; the agent, feeling the delicacy of the situation, referred the matter to the superintendent of Indian Affairs; the super-intendent avoided responsibility by saying that neither he nor the agent was vested with judicial powers and ordered the chiefs to decide. The chiefs were determined not to surrender their property to anyone for investigation. "Deprived as they were of a voice in the halls of justice, the surrender of the negro at once dispossessed them, without the least prospect of ever getting him returned. Discontent and the spirit of retaliation pervaded the entire country. The settler had no confidence in the Indian, which feeling was most heartily reciprocated."[12]

The Indian suffered every kind of personal abuse. He was made drunk and when he recovered, found he had been robbed of his ornaments and rifle or had sold his horse for a drink; he could never recover any of his property legally. In retaliation, he stole cattle and hogs, held up travellers on the road, and robbed empty houses. On 2 April 1827, a company of mounted militia moved out to hunt two Indians suspected of killing two white men. Neamathla, a respected chief, assembled his warriors and sent them to find and bring in the men. They were tried and acquitted; this incensed some citizens who felt sure the trial had been corrupted. (This was, in fact, the only case of an Indian acquitted in an American court in Florida during this time that ever came to the author's attention.)

In November 1827 an Indian was shot while accompanying a couple who had a pass to visit relatives. The acting superintendent of Indian Affairs wrote Humphreys to calm the chiefs while efforts were made to find the killer. Humphreys replied that the chiefs, while angry, were quietly awaiting the result of the investigation. There seems to be no record that the culprit was ever found.

In the midst of all these difficulties, a delegate of the territory, Colonel J. M. White, wrote the War Department, demanding immediate redress for the grievances of his constituents. Colonel Humphreys was ordered to deliver forthwith the Negroes claimed by one of them, Mrs. Margaret Cook. The agent replied to Colonel McKenney in Washington that he had sent four parties out after one of the slaves named Jack or John, but that no one could bring him in. In fact, one of the most valuable chiefs of the Seminole nation had been killed trying to arrest a runaway slave. Humphreys asked if he could have a military force to secure Mrs. Cook's slave.[13]

No one was prepared to send an army after one runaway slave, but Governor Duval again withheld the Seminole annuity, hoping to force the Indians to give up some Negroes. While one military authority after the other refused to lend his forces to hunt down missing slaves, the Seminoles were busy hiding blacks deep in the swamps and hummocks. "These proceedings naturally inflamed the passions of all," wrote Lieutenant Sprague. The young warriors, angered by repeated insults and demoralized by whisky smuggled to them across the border of their reservation, were fuming; but they dared not go to war against the wishes of the powerful chiefs.

Then an Indian killed a white man on the Oklawaha River and all had "reason to believe the deed was altogether wanton." The chiefs pursued the man, overtook and shot him. He fell but got up and ran to the river. It was believed he drowned trying to cross it. No one could be certain if he died in the water or managed to escape, but the Indians claimed to have exacted justice in their own way.

Claims for Negroes kept coming in all through 1828 and each one turned out to be more complicated than the next. In one instance, the Negroes demanded had been hidden deep in the swamp where Colonel Humphreys, who had only twenty-eight men, dared not venture. These fugitives had been among the Seminoles for twenty years and were not about to go back to slavery. In another case, that of Nelly Factor, her father gave her some slaves and then took them back and sold them to the Indians. Now she was trying to recover them.

Colonel G. M. Brooke, commanding officer at Fort King, wrote to Humphreys in May of 1828.

> ... I really pity those Indians, and although negroes are of little value to the Indians, being rather masters than slaves, still they view them as their property. So many claims are now made upon them, that they begin to believe that it is the determination of the United States to take them all. The idea is strengthened by the conversations of many whites ... which they have heard. I would assume the responsibility of not delivering the negroes, unless the claim was perfectly satisfactory, ... and in any or all events, I would be perfectly satisfied as to the perfect ability of the persons who have signed the bond. It is a delicate matter, after having received a positive order; but there is, and must always be discretion, unless the person giving the order is on the spot.[14]

That same month Judge Joseph L. Smith wrote Humphreys saying that no one could come and remove the Indians' property without their consent, that there was no legal reason for withholding the Indian annuity because they would not give up the white claimant's property which they alledged to own, and finally, the agent could not give up slaves to the citizen claimant on his ex-parte statement alone.[15]

Thus Humphreys received both military and legal support in his efforts to protect the Indians from the importunities of the slave owners. But since neither legal judgments nor government orders discouraged the whites, the agent kept trying to find those Negroes he felt should be returned. Often if a black were caught and brought in, he would escape again. In one case, a Negro born and raised among the Seminoles was "sold" by an Indian too drunk to know what he was doing. Chief Hicks, although feeling the Indian had been cheated, turned the Negro in—not just once but twice! Each time the man escaped. For this, the Seminoles' annuity was withheld again.

The governor was forced to listen to the settlers and adventurers that daily complained about their lost Negroes or the depredations of the Indians. He seemed powerless to stop their personal abuse of those Indians who came on business to the American community. When pressed to send the annuity, Duval wrote Humphreys that he would give no order nor take any step with regard to governing Indian affairs. Orders would have to come from Washington. Thus the ex-officio superintendent of Indian Affairs for Florida abandoned the Indian agent in the face of pressure from the legislature and citizens. The whites were recklessly looking for the time when they could go to war against the Indians to secure their property and remove the aborigines from the area. The Indians were ready to retaliate for any offense and to resist to the end any attempt to force them from their land. The governor was inclined to defend and vindicate the citizens.

Humphreys called the chiefs together and begged them to abstain from any form of hostility. He urged them to appoint a delegation to visit Arkansas. The chiefs had always refused to do this, but now they agreed to go if Humphreys would go with them. In October 1828, the agent sent notes informing Duval at Tallahassee and McKenney in Washington of the Indians' decision. For some unknown reason, now that the chiefs were willing to look at the western lands, the government took no action.[16]

In the meantime citizens complained that they were losing livestock and blamed it on the Indians. Chiefs had trouble controlling the braves, especially when they were made reckless by the whisky sold them by irresponsible whites. When meetings were called between the two races to work out problems, the young warriors were insolent and distinguished chiefs stayed away rather than be insulted by arrogant whites.

On 14 January 1829, Chief Hicks, recognized leader of the Seminoles at the time, made a speech which was to be forwarded to the president. He asked why the Indians must always pay for the death of a white man while whites rarely were held accountable for that of an Indian. He said that white men constantly took away Negroes which the Indians had captured in war or raised from children. He pointed out that although his people were destitute, their annuity was being withheld because they would not give up their property to citizens who claimed it. He said they were always being called upon to make reparations for lost cattle, hogs, or horses but had never been able to recover those taken from them. It was a long list of grievances. Chief Hicks ended on a poignant note:

> I am getting to be very old, and I wish my bones to be here. I do not wish to remove to any other land, according to what I told my great father. When great men say anything to each other, they should have good memories. Why does Col. White plague me so much about going over the Mississippi? We hurt nothing on his land. I have told him so before.
>
> John Hicks, his X mark<br>Coa hajo, his X mark<br>Tuskenaha, his X mark
>
> Taken in the presence of J.M. Glassell, Capt. 4th Infantry; Assistant Surgeon, Lt. L. D. Newcomb, 4th Regt., U. S. A.[17]

Citizens and Indians met in the woods, unable to decide whether to treat each other as friend or foe. The former knew their defenseless position if the Indians should act in concert, but felt the national government would come to their aid. The Indians, exasperated by repeated wrongs, cared only for revenge no matter what the consequences. The people applied again and again for troops to overawe and punish the Indians but commanders at St. Augustine, Fort King, and Fort Brooke declined to act. They were satisfied that those who were most alarmed had brought their troubles upon themselves and they were equally certain that as soon as a body of troops went in pursuit of Indians the country would be desolated. (It is interesting to note that civilians are more prone to urge shooting as a solution to problems than the soldiers who are going to have to do it!)

One justice of the peace, George Downs, sent to find Indians roaming off the reservation, swore in the presence of Surgeon H. S. Hawkins that he found only a man and his wife who happened to be staying with Colonel Piles. He added that whenever Indians strayed beyond their own lands, it was because they were lured there by the hope of buying liquor. On 4 April 1830, Humphreys asked for strict enforcement of the law forbidding the sale of liquor to Indians because they often complained about not being paid for skins and having other articles taken from them when they were intoxicated. Sprague summed up the situation.

> Through the years of 1829 and 1830 this critical state of affairs existed. No one knew at what moment open hostilities might commence, and the country be laid waste by fire and blood. In the face of this, demands for negroes were still authoritatively made, and most criminally persisted in; though the most unequivocal evidences had been given that a further prosecution of the subject would, ere long, involve the country in an Indian warfare. Enough had been done to place the matter upon equitable grounds, and, if necessary to urge it, the evils complained of by the Indians should have been removed, and their rights protected by some competent tribunal.[18]

Sprague may have felt that Florida citizens had been adequately recompensed, that they had been given "equitable" treatment, but few civilians would have agreed with him. Nor was there a tribunal willing to defend the rights of the Indians. On 16 February 1830 Humphreys had written to McKenney that certain Negroes sought by whites were within the Seminole nation but not within reach of the agent, since he had been denied "the means requisite"—that is, military force—to effect compliance with orders from Washington. It was the agent's last letter on behalf of the Seminoles; on 21 March, the secretary of war informed him that he would no longer be the agent for the Florida Indians. Colonel Humphreys had fought resolutely but he had won few victories; he had scarcely held the line for his charges. At the time, the citizens of Florida did not mourn the loss of this professional soldier whose integrity, determination, and sense of duty had been the only protection the Seminoles had enjoyed for five years. Eighteen years later, Lieutenant Sprague would defend him and, indeed, history has been kinder to the colonel than his peers were. Sprague wrote:

> It is not contended that, in the exercise of these functions, pressed on all sides by conflicting interests and motives, he was infallible. But his correspondence shows conclusively, a disposition to carry out fully the policy and designs of the government towards the natives, and which they had a right to demand. And though discouraged and ultimately defeated, he throughout was a sincere and

uncompromising friend of the red man. . . . In relative proportion
as his activity and intelligence protected and vindicated the savage,
so did the acrimony of the populace increase, until, by loud complaints to high authorities and constant murmurings among the
people, he was ejected from office.[19]

The man who replaced Gad Humphreys as the Seminole agent
was Major John Phagan. Many of the Indians seemed personally fond
of him, but it is hard to believe that the chiefs did not suspect early on
that he was mishandling their money. His successor, Wiley Thompson, was to find that Phagan had indicated in his books that he was
paying Cudjo, the Negro interpreter, about $500 a year when, in
fact, he had given him only $175 in three years and kept the rest
for himself. But that was a small amount compared with what he
appropriated for himself out of the Indian funds. This seems particularly despicable in view of the fact that another severe drought
occurred in 1831. Deprived of their cash benefits and suffering from
poor crops, the natives were again reduced to eating palmetto
cabbage and roots. Large numbers were naked and shivering in the
Florida winter.

With their staunch defender, Gad Humphreys, replaced by the
rank opportunist John Phagan, the Seminoles were vulnerable on
their home territory. To add to their difficulties, Andrew Jackson
was now in the White House. Under his policy of expansion, the
subject of Indian removal west of the Mississippi had become a
national issue. The president was always a controversial figure—
even among the Indians. He had enlisted the Creeks to help him in
the War of 1812 and had then turned around and taken for the United
States not only the land of the hostile Red Sticks but also that of the
Creeks who had been his allies and absolutely essential to his victories.
Even after this betrayal, many Creeks followed him into Florida to
fight against their Indian brothers there.

Now as chief executive of the country, Jackson urged Congress
to pass a bill authorizing the removal of all Indians to lands west of
the Mississippi in order that civilization might progress without
hindrance. Most congressmen were willing to pass the bill, especially
since missionaries approved it as the only way to save the Indians
from extermination in the east. But as the debate progressed, it became
clear that the citizens of the southern states were interested merely in
getting rid of the natives and not in helping them. The northern
legislators, whose constituents had already expelled the natives from

their states, could afford to be virtuous about southern Indians and began to oppose the bill. But after a bitter debate, it was finally passed on 28 May 1830.[20]

By the Removal Act, the legislature "abolished and took away all the rights, privileges, immunities, and franchises held, claimed or enjoyed by those persons called Indians within the chartered limits of that state by virtue of any form of policy, usages or customs existing among them."[21] The Indians had never been considered American citizens but now they were stripped by law of all prerogatives enjoyed by whites. As fast as treaties could be signed and arrangements made, all tribes would be deported west of the Mississippi and civilization in the east would march forward. It was time to make a new treaty with the Florida Indians.

# 6

# The Treaty of Payne's Landing

*Removal of All the Florida Indians Is Legalized*

"This is the only way I sign!"                                    OSCEOLA

CHIEF HICKS MIGHT WELL QUESTION the memory of his Great White Father who, in 1832, appeared to have forgotten the promise his agents had made at Camp Moultrie in 1823 that if the Seminoles relinquished their best lands in north-central Florida, they could remain on their reservation for twenty years. That spring Secretary of War Lewis Cass wrote to Colonel James Gadsden, Indian commissioner in Georgia, that he understood the Florida Indians were suffering severely from lack of food and other necessities and that they might, therefore, be amenable to discussions about removal to the West. Cass ordered Gadsden to proceed to Florida and to make a treaty with the Indians which would insure that the Seminoles would "proceed to join their countrymen the Creeks west of the Mississippi, and ... become a constituent part of that tribe." Their removal was to take place within the year and Gadsden was authorized to provide fresh beef or salt pork and corn during the negotiations for no more than three months.

Cass admonished Gadsden to make sure that the Indians understood the government's stipulations. He was to explain the matter "fully and plainly," to make the Indians see all the "disadvantages of their present position and all the benefits of removal." Having

88

done this, he was to allow the Indians to "decide freely." *But* he was to "suffer no influential persons to appropriate to themselves an undue share of the consideration to be allowed."[1] In other words, Gadsden was to permit the Indians to decide freely if they would emigrate, but he was to allow no chief or chiefs to monopolize the conversation with arguments against it!

When Gadsden arrived in Florida late in March, he was told by Micanopy, hereditary head chief of the Seminoles, that because of adverse conditions, the hunting season had been extended and that the planting was just beginning. Consequently, Micanopy would not be able to bring the warriors and their families together for some weeks. The colonel agreed to postpone the meeting until the first of May. On that day the Indians would assemble at Payne's Landing on the Ocklawaha River. While he awaited the appointed time, Gadsden went to the Apalachicola where he distributed presents to the chiefs who had put their signatures on the Treaty of Camp Moultrie nine years earlier.

When the Seminoles from the reservation began to arrive at the banks of the Ocklawaha, they were "practically naked" and they had been subsisting on roots and palmetto cabbage for three months. Their chiefs were in a truculent mood. They had heard rumors of the cold climate in Arkansas and refused to agree to remove to a land they had never seen and knew nothing about. To reassure them, Gadsden promised each person a shirt and a blanket upon arrival in the West but the chiefs were not impressed with this show of largesse on the part of the United States government. Only after arrangements were made for a delegation to journey to Arkansas to inspect the new land, did the chiefs reluctantly sign a treaty on 9 May.[2] The preamble to that document began:

> The Seminole Indians, regarding with just respect the solicitude manifested by the President of the United States for the improvement of their condition by recommending a removal to a country more suitable to their habits and wants than the one they presently occupy in Florida. . . ."

Those words may have seemed a handsome justification to the Americans for the pressure exerted on the Seminoles by the government, but the Indians did not believe that lands west of the Mississippi would be more suitable to their habits and wants.

Yet in the Treaty of Payne's Landing, the Seminoles gave up

all their Florida lands and agreed to emigrate west in a time period
from 1833 to 1836; they would take up residence within the confines
of the Creek reservation and receive their annuities through them—
an incomprehensible concession in view of the bad feelings between
the two groups. In return for their Florida land, the government
would pay the Indians $15,400, with a special fee of $200 each to
Abraham and Cudjo for their services as interpreters and for the
improvements they had made on their lands. Upon arrival in the
West, every person would receive a homespun shirt and a blanket;
the United States would support a blacksmith for ten years beyond
the time set in the Treaty of Camp Moultrie and would send an
annuity of $3,000 a year for fifteen years after removal; the United
States would buy all livestock from the Seminoles after it had been
valued by "some discreet person to be appointed by the President."
The thorniest article was number six.

> The Seminoles being anxious to be relieved from the repeated
> vexatious demands for slaves and other property, alleged to have
> been stolen and destroyed by them, so that they may remove
> unembarrassed to their new homes; the United States stipulate to
> have the same property investigated, and to liquidate such as may
> be satisfactorily established, provided the amount does not exceed
> seven thousand ($7,000) dollars.[3]

The Seminoles did not wish to "remove unembarrassed" by the
company of their Negro allies to their western lands; they did not
want to leave their homes, their lands, nor the graves of their loved
ones. But, above all, they did not, under any circumstances, wish
to be placed in the power of the Creeks whom they feared. Yet
every one of these conditions was specifically spelled out in the
treaty. Why Abraham and the chiefs consented to these terms has
puzzled historians ever since. Perhaps they hoped to put off saying
"no" until they returned from Arkansas.

After putting their marks on this paper, the Seminole chiefs
asked for time to complete their harvest and celebrate the Green
Corn Dance, which would take place some time in June. They also
asked that the annuity be paid to their people before they left for
Arkansas. Gadsden agreed to these stipulations and asked for a
company of troops to be stationed at Fort King to keep the Indians
within their reservations and prevent depredations on the settlers
until emigration could take place.[4]

In the meantime Gadsden turned his attention to those fortunate chiefs who had remained on the Apalachicola. Even they would get no consideration now; on 18 June 1832 they too ceded their lands. The treaty read:

> The undersigned Chiefs for and in behalf of themselves, and Warriors voluntarily relinquish all the privileges to which they are entitled as parties to a treaty concluded at Camp Moultrie on the 18th of September 1823, and surrender to the United States all their right, title and interest to a reservation of land made for their benefit in the additional article of the said treaty." [5]

They were to receive equal portions of land at a place designated by the president of the United States. If they left within the next three years, they would receive the same benefits as the Seminoles but if they remained in Florida, they would forfeit the protection of the United States and would have to pay their own way should they decide to move to the West.

Finally the Seminole chiefs, Ote-Emathla (Jumper), Fuchi Lusti-Hadjo (Black Dirt), Charley Emathla, Coa Hadjo, Holahte Emathla, and Chief John Hicks, were ready to set off with their interpreter, Abraham, and their agent, John Phagan. They traveled by boat to New Orleans and by river steamer up the Mississippi and Arkansas rivers to within two hundred miles of Fort Gibson. From there they went on horseback until they reached the fort in the dead of winter.

They spent five weeks examing the area that was to be their new home. They were not happy with the cold climate nor with the fact that their neighbors on the southwest would be such dangerous marauders as the Pawnee and Comanche, and they were still afraid of the Creeks. The government had, in the meantime, made another treaty with that tribe in which the Creeks had agreed to take in the Seminoles—a situation which would bring under their control both the Seminole annuities and the Seminole Negroes.

When the party returned to Fort Gibson, Montford Stokes, Henry L. Ellsworth, and John F. Schermerhorn, commissioners for the United States, awaited them. A council met on 25 March 1833. Proceedings began with Phagan reading a letter signed by all the chiefs which mainly praised their agent and asked that he be allowed to represent them and remain with them through the move if it took place. The Americans explained that they had no authority to determine who the Indian agent would be but that they would convey the chiefs' wishes to the government in Washington. Then Chief Hicks made a speech stating emphatically that the Seminoles wanted their annuity separately and would only settle on land that was separate from that of the Creeks. The commissioners decided "it was improper to agitate the question at this time," and apparently brushed the matter aside.

The second meeting called was never convened because one of the chiefs was ill and the Indians did not appear. The council met again on the twenty-eighth and this time the treaty was concluded. It is interesting to note that all the chiefs who did sign were among the first to emigrate. On the other hand, Arpeika's mark was made by John Hicks.[6] Whether Arpeika (Sam Jones), one of the last resistors, had refused to make the trip because he was unable or because he would not put himself in the power of the Americans, no one knows.

The new treaty, as placed before the chiefs for signature, contained a slight but significant word change which no one seemed to notice. Instead of stating that the people would emigrate should the Seminole nation be satisfied, the new document contained the words, "should this delegation be satisfied." Apparently the chiefs returned with the idea that their people would be given an opportunity to vote upon the issue of removal while the government assumed that the issue had been settled by the paper signed in Arkansas.

How did such a misunderstanding come about? No one knows how much English the chiefs knew; certainly they had all had years of dealing with the whites. But Abraham, with his knowledge of English, must have been crucial to the negotiations. It is conceivable that he did not know how to read well enough to spot the slight wording change in the written document. It is not unlikely that the legal jargon also confused him.

Abraham was a full-blooded Negro, supposedly born of slave parents in Pensacola some time between 1787 and 1790. He had fled from his master, Dr. Sierra, while a mere lad and had become a slave to Micanopy, hereditary chief of the Seminoles in Florida. Not much is known of his education as a boy or of his early years among the Indians. He must have prospered in his new life, for in 1826 he accompanied a Seminole delegation to Washington as Micanopy's interpreter. Upon his return to Florida, he was emancipated in consequence of his faithful services. He married the widow of the former chief of the nation (probably a younger wife of the elder Payne or Bowlegs) and was appointed Micanopy's "sense-bearer"—actually secretary, chief counsellor, and spokesman. He was even referred to as "prime minister and privy counsellor," or "high chancellor and keeper of the King's conscience." There is no doubt that he exercised great power over the Seminoles both because of his relationship with Micanopy and because of his "conspicuously polished manners," which served him well as he moved between Indians and whites to maintain the delicate negotiations that went on from 1830 until he finally emigrated with Micanopy's clan in 1839.[7]

The question of how the misunderstanding of the wording of the treaty occurred has never been cleared up. In his memoirs Ethan Allen Hitchcock blames the betrayal on Abraham who received $200 for his services as interpreter and for improvements he had made on his lands. But this seems an incredibly small handful of silver to betray lifelong friends among whom he held so much authority and respect. It is worth noting that the Indians never blamed Abraham, for he continued to represent them throughout the war and the trek west. Furthermore, since Abraham knew that his freedom was worth little once he was in Creek territory, he was not eager to emigrate. In putting the onus on Abraham, Hitchcock explained that he did so because the alternatives were unthinkable. If the Negro interpreter were not guilty of such perfidy, then one of two American army officers and gentlemen must bear the responsibility. Only Colonel Gadsden and Major Phagan were left—surely neither of them could have stooped so low![8]

Back in Florida an investigation of the finances of the tribe had been in progress. Major Phagan, unable to account to his supervisors for most of the money he should have given his charges, was replaced by Wiley Thompson of Georgia. The new agent was an able man and usually honest, but when he found how adamant the Seminoles were against living with the Creeks in the West, he tried to keep the knowledge from them that this would be their fate. He also had an unfortunate tendency to talk to the Indian chiefs as if they were naughty children whenever he was irritated by them. In any event, he never was able to create a rapport with his charges such as Gad Humphreys or even the rascal Phagan had established.

President Jackson now appointed John Eaton governor of Florida. Eaton had served as secretary of war for a short time but his wife Peggy (a tavern keeper's beautiful daughter) was so offensive to the wives of other cabinet members that they had succeeded in forcing all their husbands to resign until Mrs. Eaton was removed from the social scene in the Capital. The ladies of Florida, incidentally, would be no kinder to Peggy Eaton than the women of Washington had been. "Nor would Mr. Eaton impress the Indians. According to Florida tradition, ... when Eaton entered the governor's office for the first time, the Tallahassee Chief Tiger Tail followed him in and stood for a moment in silence, gazing earnestly at the governor, then silently withdrew ... the old days of friendly intercourse between the two races were fast drawing to an end. ... No more Indians coming and going, meeting the governor in his office or his home, gathering about the door of the council room to listen to the talk of the white man, sitting by the white man's fireside, or teaching his children wood craft."[9]

But if Eaton did not inspire confidence in the Indians, he worked hard to understand the problems of the area for which he was responsible. He reported to Jackson that there might be legal difficulties over the order to remove the Seminoles in 1833 when Congress had not gotten around to ratifying the treaty until 1834. He warned his president that "the people here want their lands on which they reside," and stated that he believed that land speculators were the greatest cause of conflict in Florida. He advised force only as a last resort and urged that the militia be forbidden under any circumstances to take part in military operations against the Indians as they would "breed mischief." He predicted that if military force of any kind were used to effect removal, the Indians would fight back. Now it was not Peggy Eaton who was embarrassing the president, it was her husband, who was doing his job as governor of Florida too well.

Jackson turned over the question of the legality of the Treaty of Payne's Landing to Attorney General B. F. Butler, who obligingly ruled that the government had a right to remove the Indians in a later span of three years than the one particularly specified in the treaty. He used the convenient argument that the United States was obliged, for all practical purposes, to be its own interpreter and judge.[10]

Armed with Butler's decision that the treaty was legal and with Jackson's determination that it should be carried out, Thompson called the chiefs together on 3 April 1835. He read aloud the document signed at Fort Gibson. The chiefs were aghast. For the first time, apparently, they learned that they had "freely and fully" assented to emigrate to the West. As Thompson laid down the paper, Colonel Clinch asked who would sign. Eight minor chiefs reluctantly put their marks on the paper but Halpatter-Tustenuggee (Alligator), Arpeika (Sam Jones), Fuchi Lusti-Hadjo (Black Dirt) and Ote-Emathla (Jumper) refused. Micanopy, "the lazy, fat, old" and senior chief whose signature was imperative, was home "sick." Thompson lost his temper. He accused Micanopy of evading his responsibilities by not attending the conference. Clinch threatened military force if the Indians continued on their "reckless course." The president had sent word promising them certain destruction if they did not comply. Even so, Jumper, Alligator, Black Dirt, and Sam Jones refused to sign for themselves or for the absent Micanopy.[11]

According to legend, a man who was not a chief but who was deeply respected for his athletic prowess, his skill as a hunter, and his intelligence, stood quietly by. He was Osceola, son of a white father and a Creek mother, who had escaped to Florida during the Creek War and had joined a group of Seminoles. For several years he had watched silently as the chiefs negotiated, but many white observers believed that he had great influence behind the scenes. On this day he waited as the American officers attempted to bully the Indian chiefs into signing away their Florida land and agreeing to be moved into the midst of their Creek enemies. At last his name was called. He stepped lightly to the table and, with a sweeping motion, drew his knife and stabbed down savagely on the treaty. "This is the only way I sign!" he cried. Chiefs and soldiers alike waited in stunned silence.

Then Thompson, frustrated by the obstinacy of the chiefs, slashed a line through the names of each man who refused to sign and declared that he was stripping them of their chiefdoms and would deal only with more amenable leaders. Since this gesture made no difference to the Indians, who would continue to revere their proper chiefs no matter what any American said, the action had little effect except to anger both the Seminoles and the secretary of war who felt it was a futile and incendiary act.[12] Thompson finally calmed down and offered a compromise. The Seminoles could have until January 1836 to prepare for emigration. The chiefs agreed, knowing this would give their warriors time to store powder and lead.

The agent finally managed to corral about four hundred Indians under Chiefs Holahte Emathla, Fuchi Lusti-Hadjo, and Charley

Emathla who agreed to emigrate. But Osceola and Jumper prevented the people from penning their cattle for selling and spread
the rumor that once aboard the ships all would be massacred. They
actually went so far as to have Charley Emathla killed when he
persisted in his determination to go West.[13]

John Lee Williams described Jumper as a Mikasuki who had
left the Creek nation to avoid signing a treaty with General Jackson.
He was married to a sister of Micanopy and was considered his
private counsellor although they parted later over differences of
opinion. Another on-the-scene observer, an army officer named
M. M. Cohen, said of him, "The crafty and designing Ote-mathla
[Jumper] is tall and well made, his face narrow but long, forehead
contracted, eyes small but keen, nose prominent, countenance
repulsive, and its expression indicative of sinister feelings. He is an
orator, and what is better, a man of sense and a brave warrior."

If Jumper was fierce and crafty-looking, Osceola was slight,
graceful, and handsome. He was usually dignified and composed—
"free from all stride and swagger." His silence had often impressed
the American negotiators more than the speeches of his companions.
But once aroused, a terrible passion would blaze forth. He understood English, having once acted as a messenger between the two
races until his sympathies with the Seminoles made him throw in
his lot with them. As all Creeks counted their kinship through the
mother and were raised by their maternal uncles rather than their
fathers, Osceola always called himself an Indian. He may have
repudiated his white blood because his white father had departed
from the scene when he was a small boy and most of his life had
consisted of running before the armies of the invading Americans.
These two men—Osceola and Jumper—were to lead the early
resistance. They had decided they would be pushed no farther.[14]

But they were not alone. In October Wiley Thompson called
the chiefs together for another meeting. He was proceeding with
plans for emigration even though he knew of the opposition. After
an introductory speech in which he reminded the chiefs of their
obligations to comply with the treaty, he asked if they wished to
travel by sea or land and how they wanted to be reimbursed for
their livestock and land improvements. They were to give him
their answer the next day.

Thompson had underestimated the resistance. All the chiefs
except Charley Emathla absolutely refused to discuss emigration.
Their speeches were short but to the point. Holatter Micco said,

"I never gave my consent to go west; the whites may say so but I never gave my consent." Jumper replied, "We are not satisfied to go until the end of twenty years. . . . We had a good deal of trouble to get there; what would it be for all our tribe?" Micanopy was brief, "I say what I said yesterday. I did not sign the treaty." Only Charley Emathla took responsibility for the treaty, "At Payne's Landing the white people forced us into the treaty. I was there. I agree to go west, and did go west; I went in a vessel and it made me sick; I undertook to go there, and think that for so many people it would be very bad."

The agent's reply was stern; the gist of it was expressed in one sentence, ". . . my talk is the same. You must go west." He then repeated all the arguments he had stressed before but Osceola, who was not a chief who could speak for the people as a rule, came forth to insist that the decision of the chiefs had been given, that they did not intend to give any other answer. Micanopy closed the meeting by saying that he did not intend to move.[15]

Micanopy's response was important for he was the legal hereditary chief of the Seminoles. He was originally called Sint Chakki or frequenter of the pond, but after the death of his brother, he took the name of Micanopy, successor to the chief. He was a large man "of sluggish, peaceable habits, and much under the control of others, more from indolence than want of good sense." He spent his early days on Black Creek below Garey's Ford but after he assumed the title of chief, he settled at Pilaklakaha in the heart of his tribe.[16]

Although Thompson appeared arrogant and insensitive to the Seminoles, he understood the situation in Florida and tried to impart his knowledge to the federal government. He accepted the fact that the Seminoles were determined not to unite with the Creeks in the West nor to part with their Negro allies in Florida. He reported to the commissioner of Indian Affairs that ". . . the Seminole Negroes were in danger of enslavement by the Creeks if they moved to Indian Territory, and in danger of enslavement by the white people if they remained in Florida." In a talk to the Seminoles at Fort King the previous October, he had promised that "the President would defend them and their Negro property against all persons," and had added that "should the negroes be so foolish as to object to removal . . . the President would compel them to go, even in irons if necessary."[17]

All too familiar with irons, the Seminole Negroes had their

own ideas about how to deal with American threats. While Thompson was bargaining with the Indians, the blacks were deep in the Florida swamps and took no overt part in the negotiations. But Sprague wrote: "The negroes exercised a wonderful control. They openly refused to follow their masters, if they removed to Arkansas. Many of them would have been reclaimed by the Creeks, to whom they belonged. Others would have been taken possession of by whites, who for some years had been urging their claims through the government and its agents.... In preparing for hostilities, they were active, and in prosecution blood-thirsty and cruel. It was not until the negroes capitulated that the Seminoles thought of emigrating."[18]

There is a lack of specific knowledge about the relationship between the Negroes and the Indians. In order to protect their allies, the Indians had to insist to white authorities that the blacks were all slaves which they intended to defend from the depredations and claims of Americans. Also, although many army officers came to sympathize with and respect their Indian enemies, they suffered from the blindness of their time; they could never see the Negro enemy as capable of the dignity and intelligence they were willing to bestow on the chiefs. Joshua Giddings, alone, saw the role of the Negro in Florida as that of an equal partner. He, alone, felt any sympathy for their plight.

He wrote that Osceola's hatred of Wiley Thompson developed out of an incident in which the agent took one of the chief's wives—a beautiful mulatto—and sold her into slavery. While intermarriage was fairly common and Osceola might have had a wife who was part Negro, no historian, including Porter, has been able to find concrete evidence of such a wife or such an event. But no one was as adamantly opposed to leaving the swamps of Florida as Osceola, and his most ardent supporters were the blacks who were equally determined to remain. If the young Seminole leader was a staunch defender of the Negro allies, it was because they shared with him a common objective—to remain on the land they called their own.

The incident which actually incurred Osceola's wrath and revenge happened when Thompson confiscated some liquor from him and refused to sell him arms. Angered at being treated like a slave—the only members of American society who could not own arms and ammunition—he flew into a rage. It took four soldiers to subdue him; then the agent had him placed in irons and thrown into the guardhouse. It is said that Osceola was carried away shouting,

"I shall remember the hour! The agent has his day. I will have mine!"[19]

As he spent the night in jail, Osceola formed a plan. He sent a messenger to Thompson offering to bring in his band to emigrate if he were freed. He actually came in some time later with seventy-nine people. Delighted at this turn of events, Thompson gave him a fine rifle which he courteously accepted.[20] At first nobody noticed that fewer and fewer Indians came near Fort Brooke or that some who had come in were no longer around. And no American knew that deep in the forests fifteen hundred Seminoles gathered to hear Osceola, Micanopy, Jumper, Alligator, and Abraham urge the people to resist any efforts to move them again. Not until Charley Emathla was killed because he insisted on emigrating did the white authorities realize the depth of the Seminole determination to remain in Florida.

Thompson was discouraged. As late as November 1835, he wrote of his worries over the deplorable conditions of Charley Emathla's people who were at Fort Brooke waiting to emigrate. "Destitute as they are, of the means of subsistence, it is feared they too will return to the nation and from necessity become disaffected." He predicted that the Seminole war faction was so large and powerful that it could bring even this group back to the forests. He urged the government to reconsider the policy of forced emigration. The secretary of war replied that the treaty must be fulfilled.[21]

As the negotiations went on, plans to organize the exodus were laid on. Lieutenant J. W. Harris, Second Artillery, USA, disbursing agent, had arrived with funds. General Duncan L. Clinch stood ready with a company of troops should the Seminoles continue to show resistance. Transports were on hand at Tampa Bay to carry the people to New Orleans while Captain Jacob Brown, USA, waited at the mouth of the Arkansas River to transport the Seminoles by wagons to Fort Gibson. All of these preparations served only to strengthen the determination of the people to resist, but they did not want to act until their crops were gathered. In the midst of all the activity, the Indian agent was uneasy. Before another month was gone, Wiley Thompson would worry no more about the fate of the Seminoles and the war he had hoped to prevent would blaze across the territory of Florida.

As the situation grew more tense, both sides prepared for the worst. Four companies of mixed artillery and infantry were ordered to Fort King under Brevet Lieutenant Colonel A. C. W. Fanning.

There was one company of infantry there under Captain W. W. Graham. General Clinch was now in charge of all the troops in Florida.

Osceola watched intently the strenthening of Fort King. He noted that cannonballs were not effective except when large numbers were confined in one spot. He realized he must train his warriors to scatter whenever they saw soldiers with big guns. He perceived that the Americans would be easy targets as they set up their big artillery. He gave orders that as soon as fighting began, certain groups were to burn bridges crossing every stream or river along military roads. Even if quickly rebuilt by the army, such damage would cause delay. He observed that on cold days the men buttoned their overcoats over their cartridge boxes and he trained his warriors to carry rifle balls in their mouths for rapid loading. As he watched the inexperienced troops practice firing their American muskets, he realized that the Spanish rifles which the Indians possessed were superior.

The Seminoles had learned from youth to slip through forests like a shadow and to make themselves invisible in seconds. They were amused as they watched the Americans blunder through the woods, stumbling over cypress knees, bedeviled by mosquitoes, chiggers, and other denizens of the swamp. The soldiers' uniforms stood out against the surrounding forest and the noise of their progress proclaimed their presence long before they could be seen. As they watched the enemy mobilize, the Seminoles could take comfort in the fact that in spite of its size and power, the American army did not have all the advantages.

Under the guise of preparing to emigrate, Osceola went back and forth between his camp and the army fort. As General Clinch reinforced the American army, the Seminoles met to make plans to face it. Scouts were instructed to note how big the guns were and how numerous the mounted men of the enemy forces were. Cattle were driven to the swamp ranges and women and children retreated there for safety and to watch over their provisions. Plans were made to capture wagon trains because, for the Seminoles, there would be no national arsenal or commissary to provide supplies.

When Abraham asked who would be the war leader, it was agreed that they, like the enemy, must be under one authority. Shortly thereafter, Osceola was named tustenuggee thlocko, head war chief, while Jumper and Alligator were made his top lieutenants. A message was sent to Coacoochee, son of King Philip and leader of all the Seminoles east of the St. Johns River, to be ready when the time came to attack. Coacoochee had about 250 warriors and the same number of blacks under arms.

The council decided to make their military headquarters in the cove of the Withlacoochee River southwest of Fort King. No one but the Seminoles could penetrate the area; it was within striking distance of the military road connecting Forts King, Drane, and Brooke. There Osceola planned his attacks and trained his men. Teaching them to obey orders and not fight as individuals was the hardest task but he kept after his men to obey without question whatever tustenuggee they were fighting under. He promised that any warrior who failed to obey orders would die. Anyone who doubted this edict had only to remember the fate of Charley Emathla.

As Seminole women and children retreated to the safety of the swamps, frightened settlers thronged to Fort Drane and to newly-built stockades such as Fort Defiance at the town of Micanopy (no longer occupied by the chief), Fort Crum (farther northwest), Fort Gilleland at Newnansville on the St. Augustine-Pensacola highway near modern Gainesville, and into the city of St. Augustine. General Clinch was desperately short of supplies but he looked forward to the help he had been promised. General Joseph Hernandez was sending several companies of Florida militia under Colonel John Warren to Fort Crum. General Richard K. Call was in the field with five hundred more militia. However, by December the volunteers would have served out their terms.[22] Whether either side was ready or not, the conflict on the diplomatic front was over. The action would now move onto the battle field.[23]

*Part Three*

# THE SECOND FLORIDA WAR

*Armed Resistance to Emigration*

*1835–1842*

# 7

# Osceola's Campaign

## The Indians and Blacks Strike on Three Fronts

"... a heart bold enough to strike the first blow."

CAPTAIN JOHN T. SPRAGUE

THE SECOND SEMINOLE WAR began with a mild skirmish on 18 December 1835. Osceola lay in wait near the town of Micanopy when a wagon train escorted by thirty mounted militia under Captain John McLemore came by. Eighty Seminoles began to plunder the wagons. When McLemore ordered a charge, only twelve of his men responded. He was forced to retire with eight killed and six wounded. Osceola, having replenished his stores, was ready for the real attacks.[1]

On 23 December, Major Francis L. Dade left Fort Brooke with two companies (110 men) to relieve Fort King. They had a six-pounder drawn by oxen and one wagon holding ten days' provisions. They passed through the Seminole stronghold and crossed the Withlacoochee River without incident. On the night of the twenty-seventh they were only twelve-five miles from their destination.

The twenty-eighth dawned cold and miserable. The major allowed the men to button their overcoats outside their belts and cartridges; he even neglected to send out flankers or skirmishers because he felt so secure. The party moved out early in the morning with an advance guard of only six men, followed by major Dade and

Captain Upton S. Fraser. The men walked in double file behind the cannon in a line that straggled over a hundred yards.

At eight o'clock in the morning the troops were marching through a growth of low palmetto with a lake on their right. The major turned to his men and said, "We have now got through all danger—keep up good heart, and when we get to Fort King, I'll give you three days for Christmas." His words were scarcely uttered when the Seminoles leapt from their hiding places, pouring a sheet of fire into the American force. Dade, Fraser, and the advance guard fell in a cluster and many others dropped too; the rest took shelter behind small trees as they were able. The fighting continued for three or four hours before the Indians withdrew. Only thirty-five Americans were alive and many of them were mortally wounded.

The survivors soon realized that the enemy formed a half-moon around their company with each end touching the lake. Dade and his men had walked into a trap which had closed around them; they were surrounded without hope of escape. They built a triangular barricade like a rail fence and waited for the Indians to return. As soon as the warriors had disposed of their wounded and obtained more ammunition, they came back to attack again. The battle continued fiercely for some time until there were only four Americans left. Two survived by climbing trees and hiding. On the ground, the last man able to fire a shot was Ransome Clark. He had been shot in one arm and thigh; then a bullet entered his shoulder and penetrated a lung. He coughed blood but continued to fire from a prone position.

At last the Indians breached the barricade; they took all the arms and ammunition, but for some strange reason, they left the scalping of the victims to about fifty blacks who also took some clothing for the day was bitter. One of them put another bullet into Clark and left him for dead. As soon as everyone had gone, Clark began to climb over the bodies of his comrades toward the path. Suddenly he felt one that was different; this was Private Edwin DeCourcy, a Canadian, only slightly wounded and very much alive. Since he could walk, he supported Clark until they became aware that an armed and mounted Indian was watching them. They took off in opposite directions, knowing that the enemy could not pursue them both. The horseman chose to follow DeCourcy; in a few moments Clark heard a shot signalling the end of his comrade. He lay motionless in a hummock while the Indian searched for him in vain. At last his pursuer rode away and Clark began the painful trek toward Fort Brooke.

For five days he dragged himself along with no sustenance but spring water. When he reached the fort, he found that the other two soldiers had also arrived there in spite of their wounds. They both died shortly afterward from their injuries; only Ransome Clark lingered on, a helpless invalid. He was awarded a pension of eight dollars a month.[2]

There was one other survivor of the engagement, the Negro guide Louis Pacheco. He was a slave who had been hired out by his master to lead the detachment through the Florida countryside. He spoke, wrote, and read not only English, but also Spanish and French. He was so highly trusted by his master that he was allowed to move about quite freely. When the attack began, he disappeared and is said to have escaped to the Seminoles by prearrangement. In any event, he carried with him military dispatches which he read to the warriors, giving them useful information about future plans of the Americans. As an old man, he swore that he was captured but he remained with the Seminoles until he was deported with them to the West.[3]

Jumper and Alligator had been in charge of the attack on Dade. Osceola was occupied elsewhere. He lay in wait just beyond the compound of the Seminole agency. While other citizens had huddled behind barricades and in forts ever since the attack on McLemore's train, Wiley Thompson went about his work as openly as ever. On 28 December Erastus Rogers, the sutler, was moving his stores into the fort in case of attack. Helping him were a clerk named Kitzler, a boy, Robert Suggs, and several Negroes. They all stopped to eat lunch at the sutler's while Thompson went to the fort to eat. About 3:00 p.m. Thompson and Lieutenant Constantine Smith decided to walk over to see how Rogers was progressing with his move.

Inside the fort, Captain Landrum heard an Indian war whoop. Before he could decide how to deploy his tiny force, a sentry announced that some Negroes had escaped from the sutler's kitchen. They reported that Osceola and his men had shot Rogers and his helpers. The bodies of Thompson and Smith were found about three hundred yards from the fort. Thompson had fourteen bullets in him and Smith had only two. Osceola had had his day![4]

Meanwhile the victors of the Dade ambush had returned to camp to wait for Osceola and his party and to celebrate—to rejoice over the arms, ammunition, and warm clothing they had acquired that day. The scalps had been turned over to the medicine man who placed them on a tall pole around which a victory dance began. The warriors were still in their war paint but now a few wore army coats and caps. As the elated warriors danced and whooped, a messenger announced that Osceola was back. He rode into the circle of light on a tired, muddy horse. He was carrying his new rifle and the bloody scalp of the man who had given it to him. He tossed his bit of scalp to the medicine man and announced that the agent was dead.[5] Humphreys had left the post of Seminole agent in disgrace; Thompson had paid for it with his life.

In the meantime, on the nights of December 26 and 27, the St. Johns River Indians and Negroes under King Philip and John Caesar, a black advisor, fell upon the plantations of the region. Brigadier General Hernandez, in command of the troops in East Florida, was taken unawares. He had detached some of his troops to help General Clinch who was desperately short of men and supplies. Others had been deployed north of the St. Johns. Thus, when the assault came, Hernandez was virtually helpless.

He reported to Brigudier General Abraham Eustis that homes had been burned and pillaged and slaves "carried off." But to the military, the frightening element of the attack was that all granaries had been spared. The general felt sure the Seminole allies meant to come back for the corn. He begged for troops and supplies. The citizens, however, were most upset over the disappearance of their slaves.[6] From plantation after plantation came word of defections and of fears that slaves were in league with the Seminoles. *The Charleston Courier* reported that at least 250 slaves had joined the Seminole allies and were "more desperate than the Indians." Hernandez estimated the number of missing slaves as three hundred.

Cooperation between free and slave blacks had not been left to chance. Yaha Hadjo, a war chief, and Abraham had visited St. Augustine and the sugar plantations in East Florida. It was believed that they had worked out an agreement between the Negroes in bondage and those under arms. Abraham had succeeded in recruiting the slaves by holding out the inducement of freedom—the right to possess their own homes, families, fields and herds.[7]

The Florida citizens had hoped for an Indian attack which would give them a reason to remove the Seminoles by force. By the end of 1835 they had more than they had bargained for. They were stunned by the unexpected allied victories.

Did even the army understand the genius of Osceola's three-pronged attack? In an act of personal revenge for humiliation suffered, he had killed Thompson, and the sutler and his white assistants (sparing only the Negro servants). He had planned the ambush of Major Dade's party in a spot ideal for surprise attack and strategic withdrawal to the safety of the Withlacoochee swamps. Finally, he had ordered an attack by King Philip and John Caesar that had terrified the St. Johns planters. The Seminole chiefs and warriors wholeheartedly endorsed him as their tustenuggee thlacko —their commanding officer in charge of defending the life and lands of the Seminoles. He had spread panic among the settlers across the entire northern half of Florida. Now he planned to lead his people to final victory.

In response to the lightning attacks by the Seminole allies, the American army, under General Duncan L. Clinch, set out to right matters by attacking Osceola's town in the swamps near the With-lacoochee River. Progress was slow as the supply wagons bogged down in the mud and turgid water; horses neighed, dogs barked, and soldiers groaned and swore as they struggled to pull their supplies through the swamps. Indian scouts watched every move they made and reported to the Indian leadership. Osceola and Alligator, with 250 warriors (of whom 30 were blacks), waited to intercept the Americans at the ford. For some reason General Clinch moved on down several miles below the spot he was expected to cross. He sent two scouts to examine the river; they came back with one canoe which could hold no more than six to eight men. In this frail craft all the regulars crossed the river.

The Indians, who had followed them, were entrenched in scrub and hummock where they could observe without being seen. General Clinch stationed his men on an open plain with their ammunition and arms at the ready, then told them to rest until further orders.

The militia, under General Richard Keith Call, began to build a bridge over which they were to cross the river in order to support the regulars. But while they were still on the opposite side of the stream, Osceola placed his warriors on three sides of the plain on which Clinch and his men were waiting and attacked suddenly from all directions. With his back to the river, Clinch was trapped. The forces under Call could not fire without hurting their comrades. When the Indians attacked, their fire was murderous, but even more frightening to the inexperienced troops were the grotesquely painted bodies and the wild war cries of the Seminole allies.

Overwhelmed by the bullets and the sounds and sights of the savages, Clinch and his men fell back, but they quickly regrouped and came back firing. This time Osceola ordered his men to aim at the officers. Although General Clinch had one hole in the sleeve of his jacket and one in his cap, he continued to ride among his men, urging them on. The Indians tried an attack on the left flank but Colonel A. C. W. Fanning was there with a company of regulars to hold the line. Suddenly Osceola took a wound in his arm. Alligator later told army officers that this caused their leader to order a retreat. At any rate, the Seminoles melted back into the swamps and the battle was over. The army claimed thirty dead Indians; the Seminoles insisted they lost only five dead and five wounded. Official records listed five American soldiers killed and fifty-one injured.[8] The battle was a standoff; Osceola had stopped General Clinch before the army could inflict serious injury to the Seminoles. The general's troops struggled back across the bridge and returned to Fort Drane. The Florida volunteers went home the next day, their enlistments over.

John Lee Williams wrote bitterly that had General Call and the volunteers fought as hard as Clinch and his regulars, the war might have been over. He complained, "General Call who had refused to fight was now placed in charge of the army of Florida while General Clinch, with one hundred and fifty tired men, was ordered to protect Forts Drane, Micanopy and Oakland and to guard wagon trains from Garey's Ferry sixty miles away."[9] In defense of Call, it does seem that he was caught behind Clinch in a position where he could hit no one but his allies had he entered the fray.

From this time forward, Florida was a scene of devastation, murder, and sorrow; plantations were abandoned and villages swollen with destitute and unemployed citizens. The fifteen years of government efforts to avoid a war had aggravated the hate and mistrust between the two groups fighting for possession of the land. The Indians, exasperated by years of mistreatment, needed only "a heart bold enough to strike the first blow." They found it in Osceola. The women, driven from their homes and fatigued by constant flight, gathered in remote places to supply food and clothing for warriors as they came and went to battle. Boys practiced daily in the use of arms and old men did what they could to teach the young and to supply their embattled warriors. The contest had become inevitable. If the Seminoles were determined to stay, the citizens were as resolved to be rid of them.[10]

# 8

# The United States Army
# Strikes Back

*Generals Clinch, Scott, Gaines, and Call Take Turns
at Confronting the Seminole Allies, 1836*

"Another such victory would be more than any one general
could stand. . . . "                                    M. M. COHEN

AS THE YEAR 1836 DAWNED, the Seminoles were in control of Florida.
They had small parties dispersed across the country covering all lines
of communication between the different stations of troops and their
resources. It became a great hazard to transport provisions or to
communicate from one part of the country to another. Troops were
returning from the battle of Withlacoochee with all their provisions
gone; volunteers whose terms were up were hurrying home after a
taste of war; commanders from every area of the territory were
imploring the local government and Washington for supplies and
reinforcements.[1]

When the government tried to answer the calls for help, it
became clear that logistics through virgin forests and swamps would
be a nightmare. Everywhere, civilians and military were running out
of provisions. Unable, like the Indians, to subsist on palmetto cabbage
and coonti, they demanded supplies from outside the territory. Major

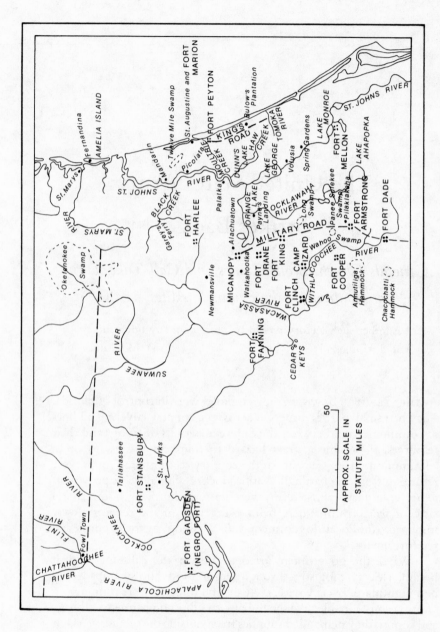

4. *Seat of the Florida Wars, Upper Florida. By E. Glendon Moore, based on maps in the National Archives Collection.*

Putnam, coming down the St. Johns River with three boatloads of corn from Georgia, was attacked; seventeen of his men were wounded, two mortally. When wagons laden with supplies began to come in to the beleaguered Floridians, much was captured by the Indians and blacks who hid in the lush growth, struck with lightning speed, and disappeared into the impenetrable jungle. It was a new tactic of war that had never been taught at West Point.

Into this environment came General Winfield Scott, the man sent by Washington to assume command of all military operations in Florida. He was ordered to round up the recalcitrant Seminoles and transport them to the Indian territory west of the Mississippi. Not a West Pointer himself, he was, even so, such a stickler for military protocol that he was known as "Old Fuss and Feathers." He arrived at his new theater of operations on 13 March 1836 with a fine military band and three wagons full of furniture and other household amenities, such as a good supply of fine wines, without which he could not exist. General Scott's training had been in the best European tradition. His formal parades and marching bands would be somewhat unsuitable in the swamps of the Withlacoochee.[2]

As General Scott made his deliberate way to Fort Drane, General Edmund Pendleton Gaines, commander of the Western Division of the army, heard of the troubles in Florida. Since the western part of the territory lay within his command, he picked up a body of volunteers in Louisiana and proceeded from New Orleans to Pensacola. Here he obtained the support of Commodore Alexander Dallas, commander of the West Indian Squadron, who sent some marines down the coast with what ammunition he could spare. At Tampa Bay, Gaines was joined by Colonel David E. Twiggs and eight companies of volunteers who proceeded together in three steamboats to Tampa. From there they marched into Indian territory on 13 February.

On the twentieth, the expedition arrived at the site of the Dade battlefield. Captain Ethan Allen Hitchcock described the scene in a letter to the adjutant general as the most appalling sight he had ever seen. Within the breastwork were thirty bodies—mostly mere skeletons but fully clothed with many personal possessions untouched. They were lying in combat position, their heads next to the logs over which they had fired, their bodies stretched uniformly parallel to each other. They had evidently died at their posts. Other bodies lay scattered along the road and in some nearby woods. The horror for the living soldiers was to recognize many of the bodies as those

of friends and acquaintances. The officers were identified by "un-
doubted means" and buried in one grave. A six-pounder cannon,
recovered from the swamp, was placed over it as a marker. All non-
commissioned officers and privates were likewise identified and
placed in two graves.[3] This grisly task completed, a sobered army
marched on to Fort King.

In January, Florida military commanders had begged for reinforcements but the arrival of eleven hundred troops on 22 February
caused consternation at General Clinch's headquarters for he had no
extra supplies. Gaines had brought so large a force into this remote
area without adequate provisions on the strength of a letter from the
quartermaster general saying that 120,000 rations had been ordered
on 21 January from New York. Gaines apparently had no idea how
long it would take to fill such a request and put those supplies in
the hands of troops in the field. Clinch finally procured eight days'
rations for him but with no more in sight, Gaines was forced to
about face and march his men back to Tampa Bay. He reasoned
that although he would not be able to engage the enemy his excursion
would not have been in vain, for the mere presence of his large force
marching through the countryside would reassure the citizens and
daunt the enemy. He had never been more wrong.

It was the wet season and the heavy wagons cut so deeply into
the muddy roads that horses could scarcely pull them empty. More-
over there was no forage for the overworked animals. Gaines had
seventy friendly Indians who acted as guides, but as he and his huge
party floundered through the wilderness, they met not one hostile
native. His "friendly" Indians said they would show him where he
could ford the Withlacoochee but on reaching the spot two days
later, they discovered they were mistaken. They advised the general
to move downstream about three miles. Here they found the river
completely impassable and ran into heavy enemy fire. Today's
historian can only speculate on whether the "friendlies" were as
inept as they appeared to be or if perchance they were less friendly
than they claimed.

With no supplies, Gaines could not retreat but neither could he
cross the river in the face of the strong opposition. On 27 February
he ordered his men to build makeshift barricades; they were pinned
down behind these until 5 March, with no provisions and low on
ammunition. The Indians yelled and whooped, set tall grass aflame,
and fired intermittently at the helpless Americans.

Actually, Osceola was awaiting reinforcements too and was

using every means at his disposal to occupy the attention of his opponents until help arrived. To show that Indians could be disciplined in warfare he had his men hold a "dress parade" just out of reach of the army's gunfire.

On the night of the twenty-eighth a messenger slipped away to inform Scott at Fort Drane that the enemy had been found and to ask that another force cross the river higher up and approach the Seminoles from the rear. On the morning of the 29th, the barricade was attacked from three sides. There were several casualties and General Gaines was wounded. Since the Indians had crossed the river and surrounded his force, Gaines sent another messenger that night to beg for reinforcements at his camp. He named the place Camp Izard after a young officer killed in the day's attack. The Americans managed to mount some artillery which killed one Indian and frightened his comrades so that they finally left him on the field after dragging him some distance. The dead warrior was carrying sixty bullets on him, indicating that for the present the Seminoles had adequate ammunition.

As the soldiers lay behind their breastwork, they tried to fire only when they saw a target, for their ammunition was running low. They also began to inquire "into the virtues of roots and the comparative excellence of horse meat." At the point where they were reduced to eating their horses, the Negro John Caesar appeared carrying a white flag of truce.

Apparently some of the chiefs were furious at this act, but Osceola urged his men to hold their scorn of Caesar and go out to talk to General Gaines. Late that afternoon Abraham, Jumper, Osceola, Alligator, and Caesar appeared to say that they would agree to a cease-fire if they were permitted to remain unmolested on the west side of the Withlacoochee. Captain Hitchcock, who led a delegation of officers from General Gaines, warned the Seminoles that they had better surrender because the United States Army was even then bringing up its hordes of men and its big guns to subdue the Seminoles if they persisted in their war. As the talk went on, Clinch, unaware of the peace talks, arrived and began firing at a line of warriors watching the negotiations. The leaders of the Seminole allies went back to their men and disappeared with them into an area the army could not penetrate.[4]

Rescued by Clinch, Gaines went back to the western front claiming he had won the war! But when Mobile and New Orleans wanted to honor him with public testimonial dinners, he declined.

M. M. Cohen, a contemporary observer, wrote of Gaines' campaign, "Another such victory would be more than the reputation of any one General could stand."

When the secretary of war ordered General Scott to take over the Florida command, he assured him that he need not be concerned about the fact that his and Gaines' commands would overlap. Gaines' arrival on the scene before him belied that assurance and Scott was deeply offended by the intrusion. He stayed at Fort Drane preparing for his own campaign and even cautioned Clinch against wasting supplies to help the western commander. As soon as Gaines returned to Texas, Scott proceeded in his deliberate way to carry out a campaign that he felt would win the war in Florida. With ample provisions, he set out to converge on the Withlacoochee from three directions.

The left wing of Scott's army was gathered at St. Augustine under Brigadier General Abraham Eustis; it consisted of four artillery companies and a group of South Carolina volunteers numbering fourteen hundred in all.[5] Eustis took his men across the St. Johns to Pilatkilaha village near the Dade battleground. The terrain he had to cover was difficult but the force reached Volusia on 17 March. Here they were ambushed by a band of warriors—probably attached to King Philip whose Negro allies had once lived in the town. Cohen wrote that Eustis' men became so confused when attacked that they fired on their own men.[6] They lost three killed and six wounded. They claimed they had killed six Indians but one of their casualties, Chief Euchee Billy, turned up alive later. In any event, the left wing saw little action in the major battle. One of Eustis' officers met and killed Yaha Hadjo, a signer of the Payne's Landing Treaty and co-worker with Abraham in recruiting slaves for the East Florida Seminoles. Then he and his troops went on to burn Pilatkilaha before straggling on to Fort Brooke.

On 26 March the right wing, consisting of two thousand regulars, led by Scott with Clinch assisting, marched the short distance from Fort Drane to Camp Izard in two days. Scott had two six-pounder cannons on carriages that kept bogging down in the mud. When he reached the Withlacoochee he put his supplies on two flatboats that were slow and unwieldy. Just in case the Indian scouts had failed to note this armada's ponderous approach, Scott ordered his band to entertain the tired men one night. The Indians responded with a volley of shots that killed two soldiers. Then they withdrew, allowing the expedition to pass unopposed. As soon as the Americans were over the river and into the swamps, the Indians attacked them from the rear. But the battle was short, for the Seminoles could save their men and ammunition by letting the terrain do battle for them.

Scott chose to press on but decided to abandon his supplies. He left three hundred men to guard the wagons while the others moved forward through the swamp. The water was dark and murky, filled with rotted tree stumps, tangled vines, and nameless living creatures. The soldiers walked in the muddy water up to their knees and at times to their arm pits, carrying their guns and ammunition above their heads. They were wet, muddy, and exhausted. The Indians were nowhere to be seen. Sometimes they screamed their war whoop from an unseen position or felled a soldier with a sniper's shot, but the pursuing army could never catch sight of its quarry.

When the Americans stopped for the night, they could not make a decent fire from the wet wood which smoked and stank. Unable to procure hard tack and bacon which kept edible for longer periods, they were reduced to eating flour cakes and pork—both half raw because of the poor fires. They slept in their wet clothes and dreamed of the unseen enemies—the hidden warriors, the unfamiliar animals, and the treacherous bogs.[7]

Scott knew he had met his match. He could not follow Osceola and his men in a territory they knew so well and he knew not at all. Even his friendly Indians were always getting lost in this labyrinth of tree stumps, moss, and vines above dark and menacing water. He turned his men about and marched to Fort Brooke.

The center of Scott's invading force was under the command of Colonel William Lindsay. He had about 1,250 Alabama and Louisiana volunteers at Fort Brooke who were to approach the Withlacoochee from the south. As Colonel Lindsay began to march, "... the Indians lay concealed in the numerous hammocks and thickets and harassed the flanks and rear of his wing."[8] He had built a stockade on the Hillsborough River and called it Fort Alabama. On 27 March his garrison of seventy men was attacked by the Seminoles and lost one man; the next day another battle occurred and another Alabaman was killed and two wounded before the Indians were driven off. Unable to find Scott, Lindsay returned to Camp Brooke without accomplishing anything.

Scott was called to account by an ungrateful government for his failure to subdue the Seminoles but his white paper paints a vivid picture of the thankless job he failed to do. He had set out to take Osceola's stronghold with 4,650 men; he claimed the Seminole fighting force numbered no more than 1,200 in all and that he personally never saw more than 130 men together at one time. Furthermore, he added, "No Indian woman, child, or negro, nor trace of one has been seen in that time." Scott would gladly have fought the Seminoles but he was never able to find them! It was obviously the policy of the Indian leadership to retreat deep into the wilderness and allow the Americans to be defeated by the swampy terrain, the unbearable climate, and tropical disease.

Scott said of the parley for peace begun by Caesar and brought to an abrupt halt with the arrival of Clinch's firing force:

> Was this the language of a subdued people, humbly suing for peace? ... Sooner than quit their native soil, they had appealed to arms; they had massacred a detachment of one hundred men; they had held their country notwithstanding the gallantry of Clinch and his handful of troops on the 31st of December; they had even held General Gaines himself, with his strong and excellent column, penned up under fire from the 27th of February; they had, in short, glutted their revenge, conquered the country up to the left bank of the Withlacoochee, gained all they wanted, and felt themselves in strength to dictate the terms of peace.[9]

The general explained that in contrast to the confident Indians, his men were dressed in winter clothes because the sutler's goods had not reached Tampa from New Orleans. They were ill from the heat and bad water. Many sinkholes or ponds on which both men and horses had to rely were dried up, while in others the water was tepid, filled with vegetables matter and "animalculae." The swamps and hummocks across which they moved were often literally impenetrable, the unsuitable food was often raw or half-cooked on the smoky fires. The men were frightened of their surroundings and many were too ill to either march or ride. Scott had crowded them into wagons for he dared not leave them behind in so savage a country. Forage for horses was poor along the way for there was almost no grassland in the thick growth and since the cavalrymen refused to carry more than three pecks of grain each, General Eustis had been forced to order every cavalry horse led by his owner the last sixteen miles of the march from Volusia to Tampa.

The American army had brought almost five thousand men and a thousand horses into the swamps of Florida in pursuit of from twelve to sixteen hundred warriors. In spite of the heavy odds in men and materials, three generals had retired in defeat. No wonder the Seminoles watched and chuckled to themselves at the misfortunes of the powerful government forces! Outnumbered and outweighed, the Seminoles had found their secret weapon—the United States Army—and they meant to make the most of it. Among the officers and men sent to Florida, their ignorance of their foe was matched only by their inability to cope with the terrain of the battlefield and the unsuitability of their equipment. The Seminole allies had merely to keep out of sight and let the colossus of the north destroy itself!

On 16 March 1836, President Jackson appointed Richard Keith Call governor of Florida and sent John Eaton to Europe as minister to Spain.[10] When General Clinch, whose son had been ill with scarlet fever and whose wife had died of it, resigned,[11] General Thomas Sidney Jesup was designated the next commander in Florida. Since other commitments kept the new commander from reporting for duty for several months, Call begged to take the field himself during the hot summer season.

Although the Seminoles would not come out and fight the large government forces, they were a constant menace to the general population. Settlers barraged the territorial government and Washington with pleas for protection against actual or imminent raids. In May the Seminoles attacked the plantation of Judge Randal and that of Colonel McIntosh. Frightened citizens took up arms but only to defend their property. The army spent the month conveying provisions to Forts King, Drane, and Defiance but the weather was so bad that sickness broke out and spread among the troops until Drane had to be abandoned. Then Fort Defiance, untrue to its name, lost heart and requested evacuation of the garrison. As the men moved out with twenty-two wagons of stores and many ill men, they were harassed all the way. At one point the unseen enemy "poured galling fire on the front and right of the train," until at last a military escort came and led the party to safety.[12]

Some of the casualties of war died not from wounds or fevers but from despair. A Major Wheelock had been among the troops that pursued the destroyers of Colonel McIntosh's plantation. He had helped to burn granaries full of stores to keep food out of the hands of the Indians. When the job was completed, he went back to Fort Drane, locked himself in his room and shot himself. All the army could do for him and his family was to bury him with military honors.[13]

If the Indians were deprived of the corn at Colonel McIntosh's plantation, they gained a windfall because soldiers, abandoning such forts as Defiance, were too ill to harvest the crops they had planted. It was estimated the enemy garnered between ten and twelve thousand bushels, enough to feed them for another season. Osceola and his people built huts near Clinch's abandoned plantation and lived off his corn. After the Green Corn Festival[14] the warriors went out to "distinguish themselves by some bold exploit" and destroyed Colonel Hallowe's plantation. The volunteers had already killed his stock, and "thus sank in flames the fortunes of a man ... who ... deserved a better fate."

Small battles continued through the summer. In one engagement, Osceola rallied three hundred men, marshalled them into a line half a mile long and sustained heavy fire for nearly an hour with "perfect steadiness and bravery."[15] During the harvest, Indians fired on some men gathering corn in a field. The warriors, pursued by three columns and a twenty-four-pound howitzer, sustained the attack with "desperate obstinacy." Several Indians were seen to fall but none was left on the field. Only a large quantity of fresh blood attested to their casualties. A tall man on horseback rode to and fro giving orders. It is interesting to note that the only time warriors fought desperately enough to sustain serious losses was when a supply of food was involved. Unable to plant corn in peace and often forced to abandon their possessions as they fled before the advancing army, they looked to enemy stocks as their only quartermaster. They may also have hoped to drive the Americans from Florida by starving them out.

By August all the posts between Tampa Bay and Black Creek could not muster one hundred and fifty Americans fit for duty. Many forts stood empty because of lack of provisions, bad weather, and sickness. If the Seminole blacks and Indians were acclimated to the intense heat, high humidity, and fever-bearing insects, the American soldier was so susceptible that several years would pass before the army could continue the war through the summer months.

In spite of the enervating weather and illness of the troops, Governor Call spent the summer preparing for an early fall campaign. He planned to use volunteers and friendly Creeks while the regular army recuperated in order to take the field again the next winter. Actually Call hoped to have the war won before December for he was confident that he could succeed where Gaines and Scott had failed. He knew the area better and thought he understood the enemy. He had fought with Andrew Jackson in the Creek War of

1813 and had been with him during the 1818 campaign in Florida, had been a protege of the general's and had served as his aide for a time. He had assisted in turning West Florida from Spanish to American authority in 1821 and had represented the territory in Congress in 1824–1825. He was a brigadier general in the Florida militia.[16]

Call hoped to capture Osceola and thus take the heart out of enemy resistance. He planned to go after him at his headquarters which were still at the cove of the Withlacoochee. If he found him at abandoned Fort Drane—where his band was reportedly spending the summer—so much the better. Toward this end he worked assiduously all through the summer. What happened to the governor, as he set his plans in motion, is a good example of how the most energetic and forceful of men came a cropper in this baffling war.

Call did not mean to suffer defeat because of a lack of provisions as Gaines had done. His arrangements to provide rations for his men, forage for the horses, and arms and ammunition were detailed and massive. Hoping to launch a three-pronged assault on the cove in September, he planned to have one supply depot at Fort Micanopy for the center flank, one at Volusia for the left column, and one in the heart of the battlefield along the Withlacoochee with back-up supplies at Tampa Bay and the mouth of the Suwanee for his right wing. He had 1,350 men. Major Benjamin K. Pierce was to march from the east with a contingent of Creeks, some volunteers, and a few regulars; Colonel John Warren would lead the center column of regulars while Call, at the head of the Tennessee volunteers, would approach from the west.

Before he led his troops to the field, the general ordered Lieutenant Colonel Ichabod Bennett Crane, commanding the forces in East Florida, to be prepared to send the entire transport train at Black Creek to Micanopy with supplies. He arranged for two steamboats and several schooners, loaded with forage and other provisions, to sail down the St. Johns to Lake George and there await a signal to move on to Volusia when the action began. He chartered the steamship *Miranda*, lying at anchor on the Apalachicola, to bring supplies to the mouth of the Withlacoochee and then to sail them up the river. He arranged to have naval logistics support.

On 19 September 1836, he moved out from Tallahassee with the Tennessee Brigade. When he arrived at Suwanee Old Town on the twenty-fourth, he had his first taste of how his well-laid plans would go awry. Of the three ships promised him by the navy and awaiting him at the river, only one was operable. The other two were in need of major repairs and manned by crews so debilitated by illness that they were useless. Furthermore, their draft was too deep to be navigable on the Withlacoochee. Commodore Dallas had ordered the other, the *Izard*, to return to Pensacola, but Call countermanded the order and commandeered the ship.

On 29 September, General Leigh Read, a native of Florida who knew the river well, led a small detachment of soldiers to escort the *Izard* and two barges as they moved up the Withlacoochee. Read had orders to establish a depot at Graham's Camp about twenty miles above the mouth of the river.

Thus prepared, Call and his Tennessee Brigade left the Suwanee the same day without a wagon train but carrying a ten-day supply of provisions on riding and pack horses. The night before he left, he sent an express to Major Pierce at Black Creek to bring the wagon train with all supplies available there and meet him at Fort Drane after depositing the extra provisions at Micanopy. He sent another messenger to the ships on Lake George to move to Volusia.

About ten miles west of Fort Drane, Call's detachment surprised a body of Seminoles and gave battle, capturing most of them. However, one warrior escaped and spread the alarm to a large camp near Fort Drane. When the advance scouts reached it, they found food cooking on the fire, pigs and fowls tied, everything indicating sudden flight. Wagon tracks even pointed to the direction of the fleeing Indians. But instead of following the trail, the general halted his men to wait for Major Pierce and more provisions. John Lee Williams was incensed. He declared the troops were prepared to live on half-rations of weevil-eaten biscuit and ride their favorite horse without forage, if only they could overtake the enemy and end the war at once. Instead the warriors were permitted to fly, taking their women and children, their corn, and their baggage in carts to the stronghold of the Withlacoochee.[17]

The partial failure of his naval support at Suwanee was only the beginning of logistics problems for General Call. He learned, to his embarrassment, that Fort Micanopy had been abandoned during the summer without his knowledge and that the enemy was "in undisputed possession of the country for forty miles further north," than he had anticipated. Colonel Warren had engaged the Seminoles bravely several times but, by himself, did not have the strength to dislodge them. The fact that the warriors were fending off the central column probably explains why Call, with his large contingent, could surprise the main camp.

The express Call had sent to Black Creek was three days late arriving so that Pierce did not reach the rendezvous until 8 October. When he finally brought up the wagon train, Call estimated that there were enough provisions to last the entire force seven days. Accordingly, he notified Washington that he planned to follow the Indians to their stronghold and defeat them within that time.

The entire army moved out from Fort Drane on the evening of the ninth, following the trail of the enemy which led straight to the cove of the Withlacoochee. When the Americans reached the river on the thirteenth, it was so wide that Call thought he had discovered an unknown lake. As the advance guard and a company of mounted militia began to ford the stream, clinging to their swimming horses, the Seminoles poured a volley of heavy fire on them from the opposite side. They were forced to turn back. Then a detachment of foot soldiers tried to cross at another location only to meet an even heavier barrage. Since Call had no boats, he considered the possibility of making rafts on the spot. However, he soon found that he was not carrying axes or other necessary tools and he knew that rafts made of heavy swamp wood tended to sink. He was sure they would founder under the weight of troops loaded with gear. He could not find a place near the river for his men to work where they would not be subject to constant attacks from the unseen Seminoles. After a final attempt to cross was thwarted when the party under Colonel Guild ran into a swift current that nearly swept away both men and horses, the general had to give up.

By the fourteenth, his men were nearly out of rations. Call had miscalculated the amount of Pierce's rations so that there had been only enough for five days. He had also misjudged the distance to Volusia. He realized that to resupply his troops there would involve six or seven days of marching rather than two or three as he had planned. He decided to send a detachment to Graham's Camp where he was sure General Read awaited him with ships and supplies. Major Goff with two hundred Tennessee volunteers set out and reached the place on 15 October. He spent several hours setting off signal guns and searching in vain for Read before returning empty-handed on the sixteenth. There was nothing the general could do but take his troops back to Fort Drane where he could get beef from the abandoned cattle there and sugar cane for the horses. He sent an express to Black Creek to bring a new supply of provisions to Fort Drane and retreated.

Later Call learned that Read had been at the mouth of the Withlacoochee on 5 October, that he had ordered the commander of the *Izard* to examine the entrance of the river to find a suitable lane for ascending to the point designated for the depot. The naval officer, familiar with ocean navigation, did not know how to cope with a tricky river channel. His ship went aground "at bow and stern on full tide and when the water fell, she broke in two and sank." Read had subsequently managed to load a barge with supplies when the *Miranda* arrived—a week late as she had been on an unscheduled mission for General Jesup. He had then proceeded upstream with two vessels and had established a depot by 22 October.

Unaware of this fact, Call went back to the Withlacoochee on the nineteenth with fresh provisions from Black Creek. He established a camp four miles from the river and then moved up to attack. The Indians had chosen the spot on which they meant to make a stand. They were behind a deep creek and flanked by two boggy ponds. Artillery was brought up and shelling went on most of the day but with little effect as the Indians had dispersed at the sight of the big guns. The enemy contented themselves with sniping at any group that tried to cross the stream. Call decided to withdraw before dark and brought his troops back to camp. That night the Indians slipped into Call's bivouac and slit the throats of twenty horses!

Call was ill with a lung ailment; he and his troops were exhausted from all their activity in the excessive heat. The disaster of the horses was the last straw. The general again retreated to Fort Drane and from there marched his summer army to Volusia where the men boarded seven schooners and four steamboats which took them to Lake George.

Although quick to keep Washington informed of his plans to win the war, Call waited a month to report the sad outcome of his campaign. In the meantime, newspaper stories, reports from officers in his command, and letters from outraged citizens who feared his retreat would leave them open to attacks, reached President Jackson. Secretary of War B. F. Butler wrote Call to say that he and the president were withholding judgment until they had an official report from him. Call was hurt to the quick by this implied disapproval from his idol. He blamed Commodore Dallas and his inept naval officers for forcing him to retreat on 16 October. He demanded a court of inquiry to clear his name and insisted it be held in Florida as his lung condition would not allow him to travel north in the winter.

Butler sent General Call a cool letter in reply stating that he was being replaced by Jesup because of his ill health and that after receiving the official report of the campaign, the president did not question his courage or competence.[18] When he turned over the Florida forces to General Jesup in December 1836, it could be said that another general had bit the dust.

Sprague summed up the year 1836 with dismay. He said that the progress of the war had been attended with "large expenditures of money and serious embarrassments." He felt that the climate, ignorance of swamps and hummocks, and the skill and treachery of the enemy had baffled the most intelligent and zealous officers. The Seminoles had retreated and disappeared before the massed armies of the Americans, they had stood to fight only when they were in impregnable positions, and they had struck when the Americans least expected it or were most vulnerable.

Sprague estimated that there were 1,600 warriors with 250 blacks capable of bearing arms. He noted: "This force was divided into various bands, comprising Seminoles, Mickasukies, Tallahassees, and Creeks, and led by youthful, sagacious chieftans. In resisting the encroachment of the whites, and the Treaty of Payne's Landing, the most perfect harmony [among the various tribes] prevailed."[19]

It had been just a year since Osceola had called Abraham to him and asked him to send a message to General Clinch. Abraham had written for the Seminole tustenuggee a letter to the commander of the American forces in Florida in which he said, "You have guns and so do we; you have powder and lead and so do we; you have men and so have we; your men will fight, and so will ours until the last drop of blood has moistened the dust of his hunting grounds." He had gone on to give notice to the invaders that he and his people could hold out as long as five years against any force sent to conquer them.[20] He had repulsed Clinch, Gaines, Scott, and Call. How long could he continue to repel the armed might of the United States?

A Lieutenant Colonel Cauldfield reported that while on a scouting party he had killed two chiefs—the Indian We-a-Charley and the Negro Cooper. Cauldfield's party had captured three hundred Indian ponies, some loaded with dried beef and coonti root. Skirmishes between the Seminoles and the army often resulted in the Indians escaping with nothing but their lives, leaving all their baggage to be appropriated or destroyed by the soldiers. Seeing this, Cauldfield predicted that there would be hunger in some enemy camps during 1837. Yet, he wrote, "Osceola and the Mickasuki have declared their determination to die on the soil that has for centuries furnished places of sepulcher for the bones of their fathers; and where every hill and valley bears upon its breast the recollections of childhood and the attachments of early life; where their first-born has been nourished, and where the wives of their youth have followed them through all the windings of the dark forest."[21] Only the last half of that statement was true, for the Seminoles and Mikasukies were themselves relative newcomers to Florida. But they felt the land was theirs and they meant to stay.

Prior to the arrival of the white men, the Indians had never experienced total war. In almost every tribe and nation, wars were a matter of lightning raids and ambushes. When one or two warriors died, the victorious went home to celebrate and those who had lost a brave returned to mourn. Their regard for life took precedence over any need to exterminate whole societies. Now Osceola wondered if he could keep his warriors in the field against the Americans for months or even years.

The Seminoles—Indian and Negro—really wanted only to be left alone on enough land to plant their gardens, to hunt and fish to provide for their families. They would take any part of Florida and make the best of it. But every peace talk had begun with American demands that all of them emigrate to the West, live under control of their enemies, the Creeks, and turn over Negroes to the whites who claimed them. These were three conditions which the Seminoles could not accept. Osceola need not have worried; the unreasonable demands at the peace table and the constant assaults on their camps and persons would keep the Seminoles angry enough to go on fighting.

# 9

# Emigration, the Alternative to Resistance

## Holahte Emathla Finds Going West
## a Poor Alternative to Resistance

"Those people have been humored, petted and pampered. . . ."
LIEUTENANT JEFFERSON VAN HORNE

IF OSCEOLA AND ARPEIKA (Sam Jones) had decided to fight for the
right to die on Florida soil, it may have been because that course was
safer than the process of emigration. The first chief to go west was
John Blunt, head of an Apalachicola band. He was one of several
chiefs who had been given fertile farms along that river for putting
their marks on the Treaty of Camp Moultrie in 1823. Now, only a
decade later, whites were pressing for all the good land in Florida.
All the Indians would have to go.

After completing the Treaty of Payne's Landing in May 1833,
Gadsden went on to negotiate another with the Apalachicola bands.
The arrangement with Blunt was that if he left in November, he
would receive three thousand dollars in Florida and ten thousand
more when his people were settled in the West. They would be paid
for their livestock and ponies aboard ship. Having always cooperated
with the Americans—even to helping General Jackson in his cam-

paign against the Seminoles—Blunt decided to take the money and leave.

In the spring of 1834, after a delay caused by an outbreak of sickness, Blunt gathered his own band and those of Davey and Yellow Hair and set off down the Apalachicola to the bay. Here his people were transferred from their canoes to a large vessel bound for New Orleans.

As they were about to embark, word came to Wiley Thompson that a man named William Beattie from Columbus, Georgia, was stalking the party. The agent ordered the emigrants to disembark fifty miles from New Orleans, took the chiefs to a bank and personally paid them eight thousand dollars with the admonition to leave at once. Then he returned to Florida. However, the transfer to the river boats took a few days. Before they could get away, Beattie (whom Thompson believed was a scoundrel operating under an alias),[1] filed suit against the group, secured an attachment for their persons and had them thrown in jail. To gain their freedom, the Indians gave Beattie two thousand dollars and two slaves worth a thousand more.[2] The case of William Beattie was not exceptional for wherever there were Indians in possession of an annuity from the United States government, there were unscrupulous adventurers scheming to relieve them of it.

Having lost the equivalent of nearly half their payment, Blunt and his people were allowed to proceed up the Mississippi and hence to the Trinity River in Texas where the chief's uncle, Red Moccasin, had settled his band many years earlier. Blunt's party consisted of 276 persons of whom 35 died along the route. Since a large number deserted along the way, only 152 of his people reached Texas. Blunt himself died soon after he arrived there.[3]

During the summer and fall of 1835, extensive plans were made to remove all the Seminoles. Lieutenant Joseph W. Harris was sent to Florida, as the disbursing officer for the tribes, with authority to plan all details of the emigration.

Because Wiley Thompson, Indian agent, sensed the deep reluctance to remove among many leading chiefs, he concluded that instead of sending the people out in three annual evacuations, it would be wiser to deport them all in one year before the resistance could gain momentum. He wrote Secretary of War Cass that "malcontent" Indians were spreading the rumor that he was personally planning to secure their Negroes for himself. To make matters worse, citizens had approached him with what they considered

permission from the War Department to buy slaves from the Seminoles. Thompson warned that any such action would confirm
the Indians' fears and prevent plans for emigration from going
forward. He also reported that large numbers were slipping into
the Everglades where they would be inaccessible.[4]

The Seminole allies had not been cooperative in giving information to make an accurate census but Thompson estimated
that they did not number more than three thousand, including
blacks. Harris used that number in making his plans. He hoped to
send west a group of fifteen hundred whom he felt would go willingly. He suggested that two or three of the reluctant chiefs be brought
in at bayonet point to serve as an example to others who were
dragging their feet on the matter of removal. Little did he know!

Harris and Thompson decided that instead of embarking during
the fall of 1835, it would be wiser to wait until January 1836. This
would give the Seminoles time to gather their livestock and crops;
it would assure that the waters of the western rivers would be high
enough to accommodate their boats on the second stage of the
journey; and it would bring the Seminoles to Arkansas in the spring,
thus minimizing the shock of adjustment to a much colder climate.

Harris established two points of assemblage—Tampa Bay and
the Seminole agency at Fort King. He planned to send out runners
in December with bundles of sticks for each band indicating the
number of days remaining before they must appear at a point of
assemblage. At each site he established pens for the livestock and a
springhouse where all could find water. In order to receive subsistence while arrangements were made, each family must report
at the springhouse for ration coupons. This procedure would also
give the government a chance to take a census.

The people were to round up their livestock, pack their personal belongings on their ponies, and move with their chiefs to
their point of assembly. Here they would be issued rations and
provided with one wagon per fifty people to carry the very young,
the aged, and the infirm. The others would walk or ride their horses
to the point of embarkation about twenty-five miles below Tampa
Bay. Upon their arrival at the ships, their cattle and ponies would
be branded, counted, assessed as to value, and then driven to a
designated location to be sold. Each family would receive payment
for its property and its share of the annuity after embarking.[5]

In October Harris went to New York to hire transports to take
the emigrants to New Orleans. Because ships often traveled with

ballast when they went south to pick up cargo, he hoped they would
carry his charges for a reasonable fee. He finally signed a contract
with a firm that agreed to carry a number of passengers per ship
that seemed humane. Several had insisted on packing them in at
twice the usual number.

Then Harris turned his attention to providing a warm blanket
and a garment for each emigrant. He selected gaily colored woolsey
and interesting border trim which he hoped would appeal to the
Indians' love of color. He had a pattern for the mens' "frocks"
which he ordered made up in three sizes but the New York garment
makers could not understand the principle of the "wrapper and
skirts" worn by the women. Harris decided to bring back the
material in bolts and let the women sew their own. The government
had planned to hand out the clothing in Arkansas but Harris prevailed on the commissary to send the clothing to Tampa Bay so
that the people, who were literally naked and in rags, would have
protection on the journey.[6] Had the original plan prevailed, the
Seminole allies would not have gone back to the wilderness warmly
clothed at the outbreak of the war in December.

From New York Harris traveled west to Chicago and then
down the Mississippi to New Orleans. Here he arranged to have
steamboats suitable for river traffic meet him at Balize, outside the
city, where he could transfer the people directly from one ship to
another and thus avoid such a castrophe as had befallen John Blunt.

His plan was as comprehensive, as detailed and as thoroughly
thought out as those of General Scott or General Call for their
military campaigns. It was also as expensive although he had worked
diligently to keep the cost down without depriving the Seminoles of
a comfortable journey. When he left New Orleans, Harris felt that
he had prepared for every exigency. All was now in order for a 15
January departure.

Harris arrived in Florida late in December and hastened to Fort
King. He was approaching the Indian agency on a spent horse when
he heard the shots that signaled the death of Thompson and the
wild whoop so characteristic of Osceola in battle.[7] By the day set
for the embarkation, northern Florida was a shambles of gutted
buildings, wasted plantations, and terrified citizens. The army had
been soundly beaten at the Withlacoochee in the west and the St.
Johns in the east.

In spite of the military disasters of December 1835, indicating
the implacable resistance of large numbers of the Seminoles allies to

removal, Harris managed to collect five hundred—almost a third of the number he planned to send out originally—who were willing to go. These were members of the bands of Holahte Emathla, Fuchi Lusti-Hadjo and two other chiefs. Holahte Emathla and Fuchi Lusti-Hadjo had signed the treaty of Fort Gibson and felt obliged to honor it. When they had written Thompson in the spring asking for compensation for their land in Florida and requesting permission to settle in Texas near John Blunt, they had begged the agent to keep their request secret lest they suffer reprisals for their choice.[8] Since then they had lived in fear of the leaders of the resistance and had suffered at the hands of whites who tried to take advantage of them while they waited to depart. Yet they persisted in keeping their promise to move.

Of the five hundred who started for Fort Brooke, some defected and over fifty died on the way as illness broke out. Three hundred and ninety-nine reached the fort but one baby died as Harris was taking the roll. Just before they embarked for New Orleans, the chiefs made a speech to commemorate the occasion. They said in part: "Could our father now see us, he would see us with all our people around us, at the place where we were told to come; and from whence the big canoes were to carry us to our new country; we are here and we are ready to go. If we did not mean to go we would not have been here, but with our mad brothers in the red path. We believe that our great father is our best friend. General [sic] Thompson has always told us so, and he always told us the truth."

Although they might believe that the president of the United States was their best friend, they were not so naive about some of his citizens. They asked to be protected from people who might try to claim some or even all of their annuity through fraudulent claims and they asked that once they were in their new land, they might have "a paper from our father giving us a right to our country." They had learned the value of those incomprehensible but magic pieces of paper that meant the difference between having or losing ones property. They concluded on this sad note, "Our father, we have seen much trouble since this division came amongst our people; our lives have been constantly threatened, and we have lived unquiet and unsafe in our towns; and we have felt as if we had, and indeed, for some moons past, have had no home; and this because we have been your fast and true friends. . . . Our father, we have said our talk; we wished to say it whilst we lived, for in these times we know not how soon we may be amongst the dead. We hope that our father will find our talk good." [9]

Harris got his 398 friendly Seminoles aboard transports for New Orleans and safely transferred to riverboats at Balize. Here he picked up a few more so that he left Louisiana with 407 souls. Many were ill and Harris himself was too sick to go farther than Little Rock with them.[10] He sent them on with Lieutenant Meade who took them to a spot just below Fort Smith, Arkansas. When they left the boats on 9 May, 78 were ill (56 with measles). Lieutenant Meade waited there to start the journey overland. He hoped that the epidemic would run its course and that the people would be in better condition to travel if he delayed their departure for a few days.

Lieutenant Jefferson Van Horne, sent to relieve Meade, arrived on 13 May. He was not as compassionate toward the ill. In his journal[11] he observed that the Indians were treating the patients by bathing them in the icy river—a prescription that usually caused death, that the camp was filthy and a source of reinfection, that every day on the journey was costing the government huge sums of money, and that local inhabitants were unhappy about the wood being cut down for the camp. He therefore decided to move the people out in spite of the illness and managed to procure eleven wagons to carry the ill. Those who were able had to walk. He issued four days' rations of corn before starting his caravan across the plains of Arkansas on 14 May 1836.

The next morning dawned to a steady, cold rain; more were ill and two had died in the night but Van Horne placed the sick in the wagons and proceeded over bad roads and through driving rain for a distance of six miles that day. His diary reveals that he was angry because he had to contend with the weather, with illness, and with bad roads. He complained that "those people have been humored, petted and pampered . . ." until now they refused to move farther with their sick.

It was still raining on the seventeenth when he managed to procure one more wagon for the growing number of ill. Van Horne noted, the people "begged not to be moved in the rain. A principal man was very low, they begged me to let them stay till he died and was buried. He died and was buried."

The rain never stopped. On the nineteenth, Van Horne had to halt again while another chief was buried. By the twenty-second, the party was at the Poteau River which he found they could not ford. Here it was necessary to ferry the wagons across and to repair the axletree of one of the vehicles. That night Van Horne found a Choctaw Indian among his emigrants who had brought three gallons of whisky into camp. The irate lieutenant promptly confiscated the liquor. The next day his party reached the Choctaw agency.

The rain continued without letup and, on the morning of the twenty-fourth, Black Dirt's wife and daughter and his principle warrior died. Again the people begged to be allowed to remain long enough to bury their dead, but Van Horne continued to urge them on. He felt very ill-used when the Choctaw agent supported the Indians. He confided to his journal that "someone ready to breed trouble had put Black Dirt up to require of me Coffins and burial for his wife and daughter.... myself and Mr. Chase were obliged to expose ourselves to a soaking rain to effect this."

The next day they all plodded through a "constant Torrent." The wagons mired so deep that each one had to be pulled in succession by ten or twelve yoke of oxen. That night Van Horne wrote, "...every soul soaked with rain; some of the Teamsters shivering with Ague, the poor Indians suffering intensely. Some of our wagons broke down, the Oxen exhausted by floundering in the mud. The whole country one Quagmire." Holahte Emathla lay seriously ill in one of the wagons, helpness to do anything for his sick and dying people. As he contemplated the misery and suffering all about him, did he ever recall the preamble to the Treaty of Payne's Landing? Did he ponder the words:

> The Seminole Indians, regarding with just respect the solicitude manifested by the President of the United States for the improvement of their condition by recommending a removal to a country more suitable to their habits and wants than the one they presently occupy in Florida....[12]

Did he question whether or not the president of the United States really was his best friend?

On the 26 May, the party was forced to halt while the oxen and people rested. The sun must have been shining for the Indians dried their clothes. But there was no meat. The cattle were still on the other side of the Poteau; three cows had drowned as the drovers tried to bring them across the river. The Indians were still sick and dying; they refused to move and Van Horne had to go back to buy beef from the Choctaw agency at "exorbitant prices."

On the twenty-eighth, the sick were lifted into the wagons and the journey continued but the lieutenant reported that instead of the usual two or three deaths, four had expired that day: "The effluvia and pestilential atmosphere in the Waggons, where some twenty sick or dying lay in their own filth, and even tainted the air in their camps, is almost insupportable, and affects more or less those exposed to it."

The next day they reached the San Bois River but it was so high they had to wait for the waters to subside. They finally forded the swollen stream but two wagons overturned in the process. Although no one drowned in these mishaps, a woman died in the night and there was another delay for a burial. The roads were miserable. On the thirty-first the chiefs came to beg Van Horne to buy them horses but he declined because he didn't know what funds to use in their purchase.

On the first of June, Holahte Emathla was dying and the people refused to go any farther. Moved by the piteous condition of all the sick, Van Horne halted and issued beef and corn. The next day he tried to press on but the Indians were so "willful" and displayed some arms and ammunition so ostentatiously that he dared not resort to force. On the third they moved eleven miles until they came to a creek that was so deep that all wagons had to be unloaded and hauled over empty. As the teamsters struggled to bring the provisions and sick across the water, Holahte Emathla died.

The next morning he was buried by his people on a "handsome eminence" overlooking the stream. His body and personal effects were encased in a sturdy wooden pile which stood five feet high. The ground around it was cleared of leaves and grass and a fire was left burning near his head. He had declared from his first attack that he would never survive to see the new land. His title, Emathla, meant leader and as such he had decided that it was best for his people to obey the United States government and remove. It was a choice that cost him and many of his people their lives. Van Horne assessed him as a man of "pleasing manners, . . . a good person, cool and crafty and politic." But he also found him "wanting in decision" and undependable.

With broken wagons and bedeviled by swarms of flies, always the plague of the prairies, the band of Indians and their escorts struggled on across the plain and over a mountain until they came to the Canadian River. The people and their possessions were ferried over in two canoes. As they waited their turn to cross, they voted to make Eneah Thlocco, son of Holahte, their new chief even though he, too, was seriously ill. Van Horne felt that Chief Fuchi Lusti-Hadjo (Black Dirt) would have been a better choice but he left the decision to the Indians.

When the band of emigrant finally reached their destination, 87 of the 407 who embarked from New Orleans had died in less than two months. One hundred and forty-two souls had succumbed to disease, overexposure, and despair. Osceola and Arpeika had good reason to believe that the odds for themselves and their people were better if they stayed in Florida.

Lieutenant Harris, another casualty of the emigration, who would die in 1837 at the age of thirty-two, appeared sensitive to the way of life of his charges. He wrote Secretary of War Lewis Cass in July, attempting to explain to the powers in Washington what he had learned. He reported that Holahte Emathla's people had lost everything because the wealth of the Seminoles consisted of ponies, hogs, poultry, and a few pelts along with a scanty store of corn, rice, and roots gathered in the fall. The greatest loss to the men was their horses. The band had left Florida with nothing but the clothes on their backs and the few personal possessions which each could carry.[13]

Harris urged that Congress appropriate money to pay the interpreter Cudjo fifteen hundred dollars for back pay and livestock losses, four thousand dollars to the friendly Seminoles for property losses, regular army pay for warriors serving General Gaines, and about three thousand dollars for loss of livestock.[14] He had seen that those who chose to honor their treaties had suffered even more than those who resisted, and urged the government to remedy this injustice.

Harris wrote to Secretary of War Lewis Cass that Holahte Emathla, as the spirit who directed and controlled his band, and as a leader who gave his life in that endeavor, deserved to be honored as a patriot—his name long and reverently cherished.[15]

Holahte Emathla was the first of many Seminole chiefs to inspire the greatest admiration in the army officer who saw him die tragically but heroically after a bitter struggle. There would be many other such defeated leaders of a defeated people who would face disaster with courage and dignity. It was a strange war with a peculiar bond growing up between the two enemy groups that faced each other over the swampy battlefields of Florida or along the "trail of tears" to the western lands. One army officer who had been present at the death of We-a-Charley and Cooper wrote: "My heart bled for two of the recent widows, when I saw them prisoners; they were on horseback, each with a little child on her back, and another at her breast; and when I remembered that the sun rose upon them with peace in their cabins, and in company of the husbands of their youth; but ere the noon arrived, they were bereft and desolate, and their children fatherless. The grief and distress of these two female inhabitants of the forest were apparent to the slightest observation, and few could look upon them without pity and commisseration." [16]

There were widows and orphans of the American soldiers as there were families destroyed in attacks on citizens. The price in human suffering paid for one race to displace another in Florida was high indeed. And the bloodshed was far from over in the summer of 1836.

# 10

# General Thomas S. Jesup's
# Campaign, 1836–1837

*The Status of Seminole Blacks Becomes Crucial to Peace*

"I concluded to die, if I must, like a man."
ABRAHAM, *Negro Interpreter and Diplomat*

AS A CHASTENED GOVERNOR CALL went back to his civilian duties at Tallahassee, General T. S. Jesup took command of all the United States forces in Florida. He had been born in Virginia, grown up in Ohio, been commissioned a lieutenant at twenty, gained battle experience in the War of 1812, served as quartermaster, and made rank of major general in 1828. Since he had induced the Creeks to emigrate, he was sent to Florida with the hope that he would have similar success with the Seminoles.

Although he was not as brilliant as either Gaines or Scott, Jesup had learned from the experiences of his predecessors. He defended Call and planned to use the governor's Tennessee volunteers until their enlistment was up to go against Osceola whom he thought to be thirty miles of the Ocklawaha River. He hoped to go another twenty miles to pick up Micanopy and then capture Osuchee (Cooper) on the way back.

Determined to have enough troops to end the war quickly and

137

sure he would never get what he requested, he wrote the surrounding states asking for volunteers. To his surprise, four thousand showed up. With an equal number of regulars, he had a force of nearly eight thousand men. As usual, the number of troops on the roster gave no indication of those fit for duty. There was much sickness among the Creeks who were begging to go home to prepare to accompany their tribe West, one-third of the Alabama mounted were sick, and measles had broken out among the garrison at Fort Brooke.

Nevertheless, on 27 December 1836, Jesup started south from Lake George toward Fort Brooke with the Tennesseans. He stopped twice along the way to build forts from which men and materials could more easily reach the Indian country. The first he placed at a crossing of the Withlacoochee and called Camp Dade. The second he erected on the site of the Dade battlefield and named Fort Armstrong.

In the meantime, he had General Hernandez scouring the area east of the St. Johns, a company of dragoons covering the territory between that river and the Suwanee, one unit scouting the south and another the north bank of the Withlacoochee. They found no Indians but one mounted unit surprised a camp of Seminole Negroes near the mouth of the Withlacoochee and took sixteen prisoners. Two days later they found the village and captured thirty-six more. This was Osceola's town and the prisoners reported that although the chief was seriously ill, he had escaped with three other warriors. A few days later another mounted unit overtook a party, killing the chiefs Osuchee and We-a-Charley and capturing eleven Indians and nine Negroes. Suddenly, Jesup's mounted troops had secured seventy-seven blacks. While most of these were civilians, a number were warriors of Osceola's band.[1] The records show no reason for the apprehension of so many Negroes. It may be they were overtaken because they had delayed to support their ailing Indian leader.

By 22 January, Jesup was ready to mount a major offensive. From prisoners taken, he learned that as a result of Call's campaign the main body of the Seminole allies had retired from the Ocklawaha southeast toward the head of the Caloosahatchee River. He had no guides but followed the tracks of the Seminole ponies and cattle. On the way he was forced to cross the Thlau-hatkee (White mountain) which he felt sure no one but natives knew existed. On the morning of the twenty-seventh, scouts found livestock tracks going in several directions and a herd of cattle grazing on the prairie.

A reconnaissance party reported that the enemy was on the Hatchee-Lustee near Great Cypress Swamp. Colonel Henderson was sent to pursue them. He drove them over the river in the face of a fierce crossfire and followed them into a dense swamp where they dispersed. The Americans simply couldn't follow them any farther. Jesup then sent Brigadier General Walker K. Armistead with a volunteer brigade, supported by an infantry unit under Major Graham, and a force of warriors under Tustenuggee Hadjo, to assist Henderson. But as Armistead was on the point of entering the dense swamp, he received word that Henderson was in rapid pursuit of the enemy and quite able to manage alone. At the same time, Indian scouts reported a large force of hostiles in a camp about two miles to the right. Graham found a large encampment with fires burning and cooking provisions hastily abandoned. However, since it was dusk, both Graham and Armistead withdrew to their camps for the night.

The enemy was surely within their grasp as they had been forced to leave pots of coonti and cabbage boiling on the fire, with wooden spoons and bowls indicating the preparation of a meal. The Seminole allies had left behind a rifle, bows and arrows, shot pouches and powder horns, tomahawks, axes, and scalping knives. They had fled without their blankets, skins, and even ornaments in the face of the advancing army. Yet they had escaped.[2]

During January and February 1837, Jesup's left wing burned villages and camps and destroyed or captured 24 saddles, several canoes, 24 ponies, 306 head of cattle, 6 horses, and 24 mules.[3] One soldier in the outfit wrote: "Thus it is the poor devils are driven into the swamps and must die next summer, if not before, from the effects of being constantly in the damp, low, foggy ground. *And yet they will not go.* [author's italics] There is a charm, a magic . . . in the land of one's birth.[4]

On the morning of the 28 January a messenger was sent to Jumper and the other hostile chiefs with a peace offering provided the Seminoles promised strict fulfillment of the treaty which spelled out plans for removal. The army moved forward to a strong position on Tohopi-ka-liga Lake to await the reply. Here they corralled several hundred head of cattle.

The hostiles must have been very near for the messenger returned on the twenty-nineth with "pacific messages" from Alligator and Abraham. On the thirty-first, Abraham arrived in Jesup's camp; after being reassured that no one would be taken prisoner, he went out and returned with Jumper, Alligator, a nephew of Micanopy, and one other subchief. They agreed to return with other chiefs on 18

February to talk peace and promised to send runners to ask their warriors to refrain from attacks until after the talks.

But as he waited, Jesup wrote General Jones in Washington that he planned to use the interim to prepare himself for the next battle in case his terms were rejected at the conference. He had to report that he had no victories to claim but he suggested that opening a road of almost seventy miles into the interior of the enemy's country where white men had never been was no small feat. He went on to say that the difficulties attending military operations in Florida could be properly appreciated only by those acquainted with them. He expressed appreciation for what the commanders before him had done to prepare the way and concluded with these words. "This is a service which no man would seek with any other view than the mere performance of his duty; distinction, or increase of reputation is out of the question; and the difficulties are such that the best concerted plans may result in absolute failure, and the best established reputation be lost without a fault." [5]

As the general had feared, no chiefs showed up on the appointed day. Instead, they sent a messenger to say that the warriors were so widely scattered that they could not be brought together in such a short time. Jesup set a new date for a conference to began on 4 March.

In the meantime, on 8 February King Philip and Coacoochee, probably with Louis Pacheco (the Negro guide who had led Dade into ambush) attacked Fort Mellon, a stockade near Lake Monroe on the east coast. The Seminoles from the St Johns area had not been at the peace talks and may not have known about them. Seventeen soldiers were wounded and Captain Mellon died in the battle. (He had fought in the War of 1812 and he left a widow and four children who would receive a pension of $25 a month for five years!) The fort night have been overcome had not a young lieutenant slipped aboard one of two steamboats nearby and fired a six-pounder with such accuracy that he drove off the nearly two hundred warriors.

After this engagement, Lieutenant Colonel Fanning, commanding at Fort Mellon, wrote to Adjutant General R. Jones commending Captains Brooks and Peck who had "unhesitatingly pushed their boats through the difficult channels and unknown waters, into the heart of the enemy's country." [7] These men with their vessels were part of a special navy unit patrolling the coasts of southern Florida with the intention of pressing the Seminole allies from the south as the army pursued them from the north. As all branches of the service were becoming more adept at dealing with an alien environment and were learning to support each other, they were pressing the enemy ever more relentlessly from all sides.

Indeed, suddenly the war was not going too well for the Seminoles. Several of their towns had been destroyed and those brought to bay in the January campaign had abandoned all their possessions, including cattle and draft animals.[8]

Osceola was so seriously ill with a fever that he could no longer take an active role in the fighting. He had narrowly escaped capture by Colonel Cauldfield but Primus, a Negro who had been with him since the battle with General Gaines, claimed he could still raise a hundred warriors if the need arose. Coacoochee appeared to assume leadership and he would continue to use Osceola's method of warfare for some time to come. But in the spring of 1837, General Jesup had the Seminoles on the run. They had not had time to plant crops and were short of war materials.

Jumper and Abraham sent word by a black named Ben that they would come in as agreed if they could be assured of their lives for they feared reprisals after the attack on Fort Mellon. Jesup, hoping to achieve emigration without another costly campaign, promised protection. Only Abraham came in. The Negro's appearance in the camp of the enemy to negotiate for the Seminoles is best described by an eye-witness:

> Abraham who is sometimes dignified with the title of Prophet . . . is the prime minister and privy counsellor of Micanopy, and has, through his master, who is somewhat imbecile, ruled all the councils and actions of the Indians in this region.
>
> Abraham is a non-committal man, with a countenance which none can read, a person erect and active and in stature over six feet. He was a principal agent in bringing about the peace, having been a commander of the Negroes during the war, and an enemy by no means to be despised.
>
> When sent for by General Jesup, Abraham made his appearance, by bearing a white flag on a small stick which he had cut in the woods, and walked up to the tent of General Jesup with perfect dignity and composure. He stuck the staff of his flag in the ground, made a salute or bow with his hand, without bending his body, and then waited for the advance of the general with the most complete self-possession. He has since stated that he expected to be hung, but had concluded to die, if he must, like a man, but that he would make one last effort to save his people.[9]

In raid after raid, the Seminoles had been forced to leave their provisions and belongings behind as they fled for their lives before Jesup's troops. There were rumors that Spanish-speaking Indians supplied the Florida tribes with arms and other necessities from Cuba but no direct evidence of this ever came to light. Thus, with no arsenal or quartermaster, the Seminole allies were forced to negotiate to survive. Over and over again the Seminoles entrusted these delicate discussions with army officers and Indian agents to this huge black man. Only "a non-committal man with a countenance which none could read" could, for years, have walked the tight rope as Abraham did.

Later that year Jesup wrote Commissioner of Indian Affairs C. A. Harris, "I have promised Abraham the freedom of his family if he be faithful to us; and I shall certainly hang him if he be not faithful." [10] Actually, it was said that an agent had taken Abraham's emancipation papers from him in order to force him to become a go-between with the Seminoles. Abraham had learned how to keep the respect and confidence of the Indians and the American army while he sought to protect his family and the Seminole Negroes from the constant importunings of the slave owners. One wrong step and he could lose his life and bring down his family and his people.

On this occasion Abraham did not lose his life. As a result of the Negro's careful negotiations, General Jesup put his signature on a document for the United States on 6 March which promised that the Seminoles and their allies who came in to emigrate should be secure in their lives and property; that their Negroes should accompany them West and that their cattle should be paid for by the United States government. [11]

Jesup's fear for the fate of Seminole blacks was so great that on 5 April, he issued an order forbidding any whites not in the service of the United States government to enter any part of the territory between the St. Johns River and the Gulf of Mexico. He ordered a watch of all ships entering ports in this area to prevent anyone coming ashore who was not on official business. To placate whites, he promised that all Negroes determined to be property of citizens would be sent to St. Marks to be returned to their owners. Floridians held a "very temperate" meeting to remonstrate against the order but the general replied that the reason for his order was that "unprincipled white men will tamper with the negroes of the Indians, and thus lead to a renewal of hostilities."

By May, Osceola and King Philip talked of emigrating; then even the implacable Arpeika came in to confer with Colonel William Harney, commanding officer at Fort Mellon. The colonel reported to Jesup that there were about twenty-five hundred warriors camped nearby, "good warriors, and not including lads, etc., or Negroes who fight as well as the best of them." All portents seemed hopeful except for the fact that the chiefs refused to tell how many free Negroes were among them.[12]

The Indians gathered in two large camps near Tampa Bay where they drew rations and articles of clothing from the government. The warriors collected arms and ammunition in order to go hunting and to collect their cattle. The women and children were apprehensive but an army officer stayed in the camps to allay their misgivings about emigration. General Jesup's policy was to ease their fears and gain their confidence. He planned to give them time and means to make their preparations for removal. A citizen whose family had been killed on Indian River by Indians he had deemed friendly did not trust the promises to emigrate. He viewed the kegs of powder and food rations being carried to the forests with suspicion. But Jesup and most of the Americans felt that the Seminoles were sincerely preparing to leave.

Then measles broke out and twenty died. At the same time whites, some with legitimate complaints and others without, began clamoring to go among the Seminoles to look for missing slaves. Jesup, unable to withstand the pressure, let them go. All the Negroes disappeared at once and the Indians followed them into the swamps.[13]

The Seminoles were accused of coming in to acquire arms and other supplies in order to prepare for another campaign. This may have been the case, but it is also likely that many of them really planned to emigrate until fear of death from the white man's disease and of having their Negro allies reenslaved frightened them back into the forest. Surely news of the tribulations of John Blunt, Holahte Emathla, and Black Dirt filtered back to their brothers in Florida. The Seminoles could survive the rigors of life in the wilderness but they were defenseless when attacked by the white man's diseases.

Later it came out that not all the Indians went into the swamps willingly. On the night of 5 June, Micanopy, Jumper, Cloud and their families were carried off by a party of warriors opposed to emigration.[14]

Jesup was forced to write Indian Commissioner Harris that his plan to have the Seminoles emigrate had failed. The Seminoles had returned to their hideouts well supplied with food, clothing, and ammunition for another battle with the United States Army.

A newsman who observed the conference between Jesup and the Seminole chiefs described the men who had fled back to the swamps in order to fight another day.

> Halpatter Tustenuggee (Alligator): "... a sensible, shrewd, active jocose man—worth all the Indians I have seen."

> Onselmatche [Ote-Emathla] (Jumper): "... In a decline from pulmonary infection ... a sensible man but from state of health and low spirits is much disposed to peace."

> Micanopy: "... not the fat old fool we thought him, but possessing good sense, and actually exercising regal powers ... respectable in appearance with the council, his remarks evincing judgment, and his deportment suitable and comporting with his nominal rank."

> Coacoochee (Wild Cat): "... son of King Philip, principal chief of St. Johns River ... the most talented man among the Seminoles [who] will no doubt be chief of the nation."[15] (Not present at the meeting.)

It was Abraham, "a cunning negro of good consideration with the Seminoles, and who can do more than any other,"[16] who had moved between the chiefs and the general to keep negotiations open until the Seminole allies slipped back to the forest.

With all hope of a peaceful emigration gone, the war had to be continued. Jesup decided to use local militia through the summer while the regular army prepared for the fall campaign. He asked Governor Call for four hundred mounted militia to patrol the area east of the Suwanee River. In his request to the secretary of war for northern Indians to assist him, he wrote, "... if the war be carried on, it must necessarily be one of extermination. We have at no former period in our history, had to contend with so formidable an enemy. No Seminole proves false to his country, nor has a single instance ever occurred of a first rate warrior having surrendered."[17]

It is interesting to note that Jesup had written Colonel John Warren, commander of the Florida militia and volunteers, in March that he saw no disposition on the part of the majority of the Seminoles to renew hostilities, but he had warned that "any attempt to seize their negroes or other property would be followed by instant resort to arms."[18]

In April he wrote Governor Call that "if the citizens of the Territory be prudent, the war may well be at an end; but any attempt to interfere with the Indian negroes, or to arrest any of the chiefs or warriors, either as criminals or debtors, could cause an immediate resort to hostilities." He added that thirty Seminole Negroes who had been ready to emigrate had disappeared as soon as three Florida citizens came searching for slaves. In a letter to Colonel James Gadsden he wrote in June, ". . . all is lost, and principally, I fear, by the influence of the negroes."

Harried by citizens who came to his office asking to look for blacks and barraged by letters from citizens demanding that he secure lost slaves, Jesup had given in and allowed the very circumstances he knew would cause trouble. Yet when the inevitable happened, he turned on the victims rather than on those who had caused the problem. In July he wrote Colonel Warren. "There is now no obligation to spare the property of the Indians—they have not spared that of the citizens; their negroes, cattle and horses as well as other property which they possess, will belong to the corps by which they may be captured. The property of citizens which may be captured will be restored to them."[19]

Jesup repeated this offer in a letter to Lieutenant Colonel W. J. Mills in command of Florida troops at Newnansville and to Captain David S. Walker at Talladega, Alabama. In other words, although it was quite obviously the settlers' designs on their Negroes that had sent the Seminoles back to the forests, Jesup's frustration at not persuading them to emigrate caused him to offer American volunteers and militia as well as the Creek Indians the right to keep any property, including Negroes, which they might capture if they went against the Florida Indians.

From time to time since the war began, blacks had been captured and held while their fate was being determined. Six slaves had died in captivity; the rest Jesup determined to dispose of. He kept sixteen at Fort Mellon and Tampa Bay to be used by the army. He sent off to New Orleans ninety Seminole Negroes to be held as prisoners of war until they could be moved west. Another ninety blacks he classified as the property of citizens and sent either to St. Augustine or St. Marks to be returned to their masters.

Having disposed of the captives, he turned back to the problem of subduing those yet free. In his determination to fulfill his mission to remove the Seminoles, General Jesup was ready to use every means at his command. He asked for northern Indians and in July the secretary of war sent out orders to recruit one thousand warriors, including Shawnee, Delaware, Kickapoo, Sioux, Foxes, and Choctaw. Jesup wrote to Captain William Armstrong on 17 September, promising the Choctaw Indians who went against the Seminoles that they could have everything they captured—Negroes, horses, cattle, and other wealth. He held out as bait the fact that the Creeks who had helped in earlier campaigns had collected between fourteen and fifteen thousand dollars.[20]

In fact, the Creeks were not enjoying the fruits of their battles. They were at Pass Christian, Louisiana, dying of disease and despair as they awaited deportation to the West. Jesup sent Lieutenant Frederick Searle, acting assistant inspector general of the Army of the South at Tampa Bay, to Louisiana to muster the Creek warriors out of the army and pay those who had been active for the slaves they had captured. In order to be sure the Creeks were rewarded for their services, Jesup was prepared to give them eight thousand dollars for the Seminole Negroes taken and the stipulated twenty dollars per head for a list of thirty-five blacks designated as runaway slaves belonging to the citizens.[21]

The problem of finding the money for this enterprise was a delicate one since Congress might ask uncomfortable questions if asked to vote an appropriation, however modest, to put the United States government in the slave-buying business. After giving the matter careful thought, General Jesup wrote Commissioner Harris on 24 September, suggesting that the money come out of the Seminole annuity! The government was obliged by a series of treaties to reimburse the Creeks for all Negroes captured. If Jesup's plan were carried out, that same government would force the Seminoles to pay for property taken from them in war! However, the Creeks refused to sell for eight thousand dollars and did, in fact, get fifteen thousand dollars from private individuals.[22]

Although Jesup was a government official charged with implementing an impossible law, he did the best he could. He ordered that all captured blacks not held in New Orleans be kept at Tampa Bay under control of the military. At least he was keeping them out of the hands of unscrupulous men who were hoping to speculate in the buying and selling of Seminole Negroes.

On 31 July 1837, Colonel Zachary Taylor, aged fifty-three, was directed by Jesup to take charge of the troops in Florida and given freedom to plan his own strategy so long as it achieved the objective of destroying or capturing the Seminoles. Colonel Taylor had thirty-one years service in the army. He had been active in the War of 1812 and had experience in frontier duty in the West.

With a seasoned officer in charge of military operations, General Jesup continued to work on the diplomatic front. But he didn't remain diplomatic for long. When a group of chiefs came in to Fort King for a talk in August, he lost his temper. He refused to recognize Arpeika as their spokesman. Arpeika was described as "a well set, neatly formed and perfectly finished small man, with locks white as the driven snow—aged and venerable, yet active as a hind, and intrepid as a lion, struggling for the home of his childhood and the grave of his forefathers." He was also represented by those who knew him as a great rascal who claimed to his people that the horses of American troops that died along the road were killed by his incantations.[23] His people, the Mikasukis, had been in Florida when the Seminoles came and he had been consistently and adamantly opposed to emigration. In fact, he had earned the nickname of "Sam Jones, Be Damned" for his staunch resistance to removal but Jesup was prepared to be as adamant as Arpeika and threatened that if Indians spilled even a drop of blood, he would execute Seminole prisoners man for man.[24]

Unable to deal with any of the more powerful chiefs, he made an agreement with Coa Hadjo which provided for a cease-fire if the Indians would remain in the area south of Fort Mellon between the St. Johns River and the Fort King Road. Coa Hadjo promised to call a council of warriors but he warned that Arpeika, Osceola, and the young warriors were so opposed to emigration that they were threatening to kill any who agreed to move. Coa Hadjo promised to bring in runaway slaves but this pledge could not have been worth much as long as Osceola and a number of Negro troops were yet free.

Porter suggests that the close ties between Osceola and the Seminole blacks stemmed from the fact that they were all outsiders. As a Creek, Osceola did not rank as the hereditary chief of any clan but had been forced to build a band of warriors from among the young "hawks" of the various Florida tribes and from the Seminole Negroes. By the fall of 1837 he had recruited a new band to replace the one decimated by Cauldfield's attack in January.[25]

When Coa Hadjo returned with his treaty to the Seminole

council, the stipulation to return runaway blacks drew a strong protest from Osceola. He declared that such a policy would never prevail
as long as he was in the nation but some of the chiefs were ready to
sacrifice captured Negroes as their own situation grew more precarious. Soon thereafter the army began to send detachments into
pacified areas to collect small groups of blacks that were being turned
over.

Some blacks who had suffered severe privation in the wilderness,
chose to return to slavery as a lesser of two evils. A dozen who
surrendered during the summer came in dressed in nothing but
muddy breechcloths. They complained that they had been forced to
live on coonti roots and alligator tails (probably the same menu as
their allies), and that the Indians vented their ill temper at being
defeated in battle by beating them. Others had been sent to remote
hummocks to raise corn—a fate little better than working in sugar
plantations on the St. Johns.[26]

In September some Negroes came to Fort Peyton on Moultrie
Creek just south of St. Augustine and reported that King Philip was
camped with a party of warriors near Bulow's plantation (an estate
abandoned during the war). General Joseph M. Hernandez, a native
of Florida, took a force of over 150 men and went after him. To
catch the man who was the leader of the Indians in the St. Johns
region would be a coup for anyone; for Hernandez it would be a
sweet revenge for the attacks on the plantations in 1835. King Philip
was not at the site but Hernandez and his troops made camp there
for the night. The next morning one of the chief's slaves, searching
for his wife who had run away, came upon the camp and agreed
to guide the army to his master's hiding place.

It was a remote area requiring a difficult march with horses
bogged down to their bellies at times but the party finally reached
its destination about sunset. Hernandez halted his troops and moved
forward cautiously. He saw some Indians moving about the ruins of
another deserted plantation. When they left, Hernandez followed
with a few men until he saw the fires of their camp a mile away.

The troops must have learned a great deal about swamp fighting
since the beginning of the war for the Indians never realized they
had arrived. In a dawn attack, Hernandez captured King Philip and
twenty other warriors without bloodshed. He learned from his
captives that Euchee Billy (reported dead by General Gaines in an
earlier battle) was actually in a camp nearby and set off to find him.

Late that afternoon, Hernandez came to a dense stand of cabbage palm. Here he left the horses and all but one hundred men. Those chosen moved forward on foot through wilderness never before seen by white men. At midnight they reached Euchee Billy's camp and quietly surrounded it. The battle began just before dawn when the barking of Seminole dogs aroused the warriors. They leaped up, whooping and firing, but were soon overcome. One Indian was killed and Lieutenant John McNeil was mortally wounded. General Hernandez brought his prisoners back to St. Augustine amid general rejoicing.

When word of the coup reached Jesup, he wrote to Lieutenant J. C. Casey, Assistant Agent to the Seminoles at Tampa Bay: "General Hernandez' operations have resulted in the capture of forty-seven Indians and negroes, and the killing of two Indians; and among the prisoners are Philip, and his negro John; Euchee Billy and his brother Euchee Jack. These four prisoners are worth fifty common Indians and negroes." [27] Hernandez had, indeed, achieved a great victory and Coacoochee must have heard the news with a sinking heart. A short time later he learned that his father had asked to have his immediate family join him in prison.

On 26 September Coacoochee arrived, under a white flag of truce, at the Bulow plantation where he was met by General Hernandez and a mounted guard who escorted him to St. Augustine. He entered the city on a spirited horse, riding with "a great deal of savage grace and majesty." He was dressed in "all the pomp of scarlet and burnished silver," his gaudy turban trimmed with white crane feathers in a silver band. His leather leggings had been replaced by some of scarlet cloth. The handsome young chief appeared to ride through the city in triumph but he was virtually a prisoner. He was taken to Fort Marion and incarcerated there with a companion, Blue Snake.[28] In an audacious move, Coacoochee had ridden into the jaws of the enemy to consult with authorities over the fate of his father. Would he be permitted to come out?

In a few days, he was temporarily released to carry messages to his people. He returned on 16 October, bringing with him an uncle and his youngest brother. He gave himself up and promised that Osceola, with a hundred warriors, would be in for a conference. There can be no doubt that the reason Osceola and Coacoochee were willing to risk their freedom in order to talk was that they hoped to negotiate the release of King Philip and to establish peace on terms that would allow them some land in Florida.

When Philip's band began to drift in, Hernandez went out to

Hewitt's Mill with provisions for them. The people expected to eat, drink, play ball, and talk; Jesup wanted to get them close enough in and close enough together to lay hands on them.

Osceola and Coa Hadjo came in and camped about a mile from Fort Peyton. They sent word to Hernandez that they wanted a conference, that he was to come to the Indian camp without military escort. Hernandez set out from St. Augustine to meet the chiefs but at Fort Peyton he picked up 250 dragoons commanded by Major James A. Ashby. On the way he met Lieutenant John M. Hanson coming in with seventy-four Negroes. The Seminoles may have planned to turn them over as part of the fulfillment of the Coa Hadjo treaty with Jesup or, more likely, they hoped to trade them for King Philip. The fact that Coa Hadjo and Osceola appeared together suggests that they had reconciled their differences over the issue of returning runaways.

But it is a measure of the desperation the Seminoles must have felt if they were willing to turn over such a large number of blacks to the army. True, King Philip, like Micanopy in the West, was the principal chief on the east coast. He had to be rescued if there was any way to do it, but one wonders how much this unusual act stemmed from the fact that Philip's capture had occurred because of his betrayal by an unhappy slave. We may never know what lay behind the arrival of blacks at Fort Peyton with the news of Philip's whereabouts. Were they seeking revenge for friends turned over to the army? Why was the slave looking for his wife? Had she suffered at the hands of the chief some injury that made her husband willing to betray him? Was she, perhaps, slated for return to a white master? At any rate, blacks were falling into the hands of Jesup's army in alarming numbers in 1837.

Hernandez arrived at the Indian camp on 21 October and approached the chiefs. Osceola awaited him beneath a white flag of truce. As Hernandez began to read a message from General Jesup, Major Ashby and his dragoons deployed quietly about the camp.

"What is your object in coming here at this time, what do you expect?" asked the general. There is no record that the chief replied. Hernandez pressed on. "Why haven't you delivered up the negroes taken from the citizens? Why haven't you surrendered them as Coa Hadjo promised at Fort King?" At the reference to surrendering Negroes, Osceola answered merely that he was too "choked" to speak and asked Coa Hadjo to answer for him. Osceola may have been speaking the literal truth as he was known to suffer from quinsy, but if he knew of the seventy-four blacks turned over to Lieutenant Hanson—for he must surely have been in on that decision—he may have been choking on his own betrayal.

However, it appeared the general's question was purely rhetorical. (He had, after all, met Lieutenant Hanson on the road.) He went on to another grievance. "Why haven't the principal chiefs, Micanopy, Jumper, Cloud and Alligator, come in?" Coa Hadjo's answers were vague. The general felt he could interpret the chief's responses as uncooperative. He had his orders from Jesup and, at a given signal, the soldiers seized the Seminoles.

There were only six women in the party and the warriors had over forty loaded rifles, but they seemed too stunned to resist. For the second time an Indian chief had been captured under a white flag of truce. Jesup became the center of a storm of criticism for his lack of good sportsmanship but he felt his actions were justified. He pointed out that the Indians had deceived army officers many times to gain an advantage and that the only way to conquer them was to beat them at their own game. He was positive in his own mind that the only reason Osceola had come in was to rescue King Philip and Coacoochee by storming the fort or by taking officers hostage in order to effect an exchange of prisoners.[29]

General Jesup might not be winning any popularity contests but he was slowly and painfully achieving his objective of rounding up the Seminoles and deporting them. He had captured over seventy Mikasuki warriors and now held such Seminole leaders as King Philip, Coacoochee, Osceola, Coa Hadjo, Euchee Billy, and Holata Tustenuggee.

With the most formidable chiefs behind bars, Jesup set in motion his next campaign. He ordered a two-pronged mopping-up operation that pushed most of the Indians south of Tampa Bay. Brigadier General C. H. Nelson, with a brigade of Georgia volunteers, swept the swamps from the Fort King Road to the Gulf of Mexico, killing six and taking four prisoners. This action apparently cleared the western coast down to Fort Brooke. Colonel Snodgrass, with a battalion of Alabama volunteers, destroyed several villages in the country between the St. Johns River, the Ocklawaha, and the swamps around Orange Lake but he found no Seminoles.[30]

In the meantime, although the Cherokees were having troubles of their own, they were so moved by the suffering of the Seminoles that they offered to mediate between them and General Jesup. A United States agent, Colonel John H. Sherbourne, suggested a meeting which took place on 10 November 1837 in Fort Marion where the Seminole chiefs were imprisoned.

The Cherokees arrived in full costume and were brought into the courtyard of the fort. The greetings between the peace delegation and the prisoners were formal and courteous. The Cherokees sat down in a row and the Seminoles sat opposite them. Colonel Sherbourne and Captain Brown, Jesup's aide, were also present. The speech from Chief John Ross of the visitors was read by a Negro interpreter.[31] Coa Hadjo replied for the Seminoles. The peace pipe was handed round.

Although the imprisoned chiefs asked Ross to go into the Indian country to talk to leaders who were still free, Coacoochee warned it would be dangerous, for those who had not given up never intended to capitulate. The ailing Osceola stated simply that he was tired of fighting and too ill to say more.

On 28 November, the Cherokee delegation set out for a meeting with Micanopy and other chiefs. They struggled through sixty miles of swamps and hummocks until they arrived at Chickasaw Creek. Here they delivered Ross' speech to a council of Mikasuki and Seminole warriors and chiefs. Again they smoked the pipe of peace. Then Micanopy, Cloud, and eleven other chiefs, with a handful of warriors, accompanied the Cherokees to General Jesup's headquarters under a flag of truce.

While Jesup was dealing in diplomacy with the Cherokees, the imprisoned chiefs were plotting escape. Osceola was too ill for much activity and he was waiting for his wives and children but Coacoochee intended to fight again.

The night of 29 November was dark. Inside the prison a Negro chief, John Cavallo, hoisted one of his companions onto a high ledge. Above it was a loophole (a slit in the wall of a fort through which small arms could be fired) which had either lost a bar through neglect and corrosion or at the hands of an expert with a knife or saw. A rope made from the sacks which covered the prisoners' beds was lowered through this opening. Then silently, one by one, as Cavallo hoisted them up, the Seminoles began to squeeze through the narrow aperture and slide down the makeshift rope into a muddy ditch outside the prison walls. Among those who escaped were King Philip's brother, Coacoochee and his brother, Cavallo, and two women.[32]

News of the escape hardened Jesup further in his resolve to take the Seminoles by any means he could devise. He awaited the return of the Cherokees with five Seminole chiefs. Micanopy declared that he wanted peace and was even ready for removal but that the war had scattered his people so that it would take some time to reassemble them. Whether it was anger at the old excuse for delay or at the recent prison break, Jesup gave the people ten days to come in and took Micanopy's entire delegation hostage. He had written to Secretary of War Poinsett the day before, stating, "If the council have no other effect, it will cause the Indians, who are much dispersed, to reassemble, when they can be more readily attacked."[33]

Now Jesup had his hands full. Both civilians and military men attacked him for his ungentlemanly behavior in repeatedly capturing enemy leaders who appeared under a flag of truce. The Cherokees were furious at being used to implement Jesup's perfidy. Ross protested to the secretary of war against this "unprecedented violation of that sacred rule which has ever been recognized by every nation, civilized or uncivilized, of treating with all due respect those who had ever presented themselves under a flag of truce before the enemy."[34] Those who had not fought in Florida couldn't understand that here was a game being played without benefit of Marquis of Queensberry rules!

Jesup made one more attempt at diplomacy. He gave Colonel Sherbourne a proposal which he wanted him to read to the Seminoles in front of the Cherokees before they left. It offered the Indians all the land south of Tampa Bay between the Gulf of Mexico and the Atlantic if they would defend it against all foreign invasion and if they would return runaway Negroes who entered it. Naturally the chiefs agreed as they had hoped all along that they might keep the swamps of southern Florida if they gave the good land in the north to the Americans. Only King Philip mistrusted the offer. He was right, for Jesup had offered it before obtaining approval from Washington.[35]

Early in December, Colonel Zachary Taylor set out with eight hundred regulars, two hundred Missouri volunteers, and some Delaware Indians for the heart of Florida Indian country. He moved down the west side of the Kissimmee River where he built a fort near Lake Istopoga. On the way he met Jumper with a band of sixty-three persons (including some Negroes) who gave themselves up. Remember that Jumper was "in a decline from pulmonary infection" and "from state of health and low spirits ... much disposed to peace." Another twenty-two Seminoles were picked up in an encampment at Isotopoga Outlet. The captives, with eighty-five sick and disabled soldiers, were left at the newly built stockade. Taylor moved on to Alligator's camp which was located in a nearby hummock. Here he secured a few more who were ready to come in.

Taylor then proceeded after the redoubtable Arpeika who was supposed to be entrenched about twelve miles farther on. He finally found the camp of the Seminoles on the border of another cypress swamp near Lake Okeechobee. The Indians had fled, leaving their hot food on the fires. They had crossed to the other side of an impassable swamp, covered with tall saw grass growing in deep water.

Taylor ordered his troops to dismount and leave their horses and baggage under guard. The volunteers, under Colonel Gentry, were to lead the assault, followed by the Fourth and Sixth Infantry under Colonel Thompson. The Seminoles had chosen their battleground carefully. Arpeika and his Mikasukies formed the right wing; Halpatter Tustenuggee (Alligator), with his warriors, held the center while Coacoochee, just escaped from prison, made up the left wing with eighty-five men.

Ten men, wrapped in moss, lay hidden in the tall saw grass to spy on the approaching army and warn their comrades. Some awaited the soldiers from hiding places in the treetops; others were hidden behind trees on the ground with their rifles wedged in notched branches for steadier aim. When the army came within range of their guns, they let fly a murderous barrage.

The volunteers, undone by a lethal enemy they couldn't even see, fled back to their horses and baggage but the infantry under Colonel Thompson held fast. The battle went on for about three hours with heavy casualties among the Americans. When Colonel Thompson fell, mortally wounded, Colonel Foster of the Fourth Infantry rallied the remnants of all the troops and charged with bayonets. The Seminoles had to leave the field to superior forces but they kept firing as they retreated. When the smoke of battle cleared, Taylor found he had lost 26 killed and 112 wounded. He buried his dead and then began the return to the Withlacoochee River. His troops carried the wounded on "rude litters made from poles and dry hides found in the Indian camp and conveyed on the backs of weak and tottering horses" over a distance of 145 miles. They reached their destination on New Year's Eve.

Taylor reported of his December campaign that he had penetrated 150 miles into the enemy's country, opened roads, and constructed bridges and causeways when necessary along the route. He had built two depots with necessary defenses for each. He claimed

150 allied prisoners taken along with six hundred cattle and one hundred horses. He professed a thorough knowledge of the previously unexplored country through which he and his troops had marched.[36]

Perhaps the last item represented the greatest accomplishment. For Jesup would say of his tour of duty in Florida that if the public felt that his results seemed trifling by comparison with their expectations, it was because everything had to be done in a theater of operations and over terrain that was completely unknown.[37]

Alligator later told Lieutenant Sprague that the Seminoles had about 380 warriors, that Arpeika fled at the first fire but that Halleck-Tustenuggee rallied the braves who would have followed him. The Prophet sang and danced and prepared magic medicines to remove danger. Coacoochee reported that as they retreated they broke into bands of ten to fifteen men and scattered so as to make pursuit more difficult. But Taylor was too busy burying his dead and tending his wounded to push the enemy further. The Seminoles lost eleven Indians and one Negro killed and nine wounded.[38]

A letter from Captain John C. Casey, Fourth Artillery, to his brother appeared in the *South Carolina Courier* in January 1838. In it Casey wrote that the Battle of Okeechobee "was the hardest yet fought in Florida since Dade's."[39]

Bruised as they were from defeats at the hands of Hernandez and Jesup, the Seminoles needed a victory. Surely they felt better after this battle. For while Taylor had claimed he had defeated them, he had sustained much higher casualties among his own men and the Seminoles had survived to fight another day.

But during 1837 the Seminole allies had suffered genuine reverses. Their homes, fields, and livestock were gone. They would have to live on swamp cabbage and coonti if they continued to hold out against emigration. In addition to those hundreds who had emigrated voluntarily, there were now scores more held captive awaiting deportation. Osceola, their symbol of resistance, was ill and, with several other chiefs and many warriors, imprisoned.

The ranks of free blacks had been decimated. Many who joined the Seminole allies during the raids on the St. Johns plantations in 1835 had known nothing but danger and privation in freedom. Some had welcomed the security of slavery after the fear and confusion of constant flight before the American army through a land filled with its own terrors. While some who had enjoyed freedom and prosperity before the war were still implacable, others were reassured by Jesup's promise to Abraham in March 1837 that they could safely move west with their Indian "masters." From the date of that guarantee, those chiefs closely allied with blacks began to consider emigration. Others, like Micanopy, had been captured and their Negro associates would follow them.

The battle at Okeechobee was the last in which large numbers of Negroes participated. From now on the number and influence of Seminole blacks on the battlefield would decline.[40] In fact, there would be no more battles involving hundreds of troops on both sides even though the second Florida war would drag on for five more years.

Jesup deplored the long, expensive process of capturing or destroying a people who could melt into the landscape with barely a trace and he repeatedly urged alternative methods when he wrote to Washington. However, the orders from the secretary of war never changed. Jesup and Taylor must go on fighting.

In the summer of 1837, Poinsett had written a long letter to Jesup laying out the logic of the government's position. He stated that the choice lay between allowing the Seminoles to remain in the south where they and their free black allies would be a constant threat to the peace of mind of the American settlers or removing them—by force, if necessary. "Every consideration of sound policy required" the government to adopt the latter.

Poinsett reminded Jesup that for three years the Seminoles were allowed to prepare for removal and "every indulgence they asked promptly and kindly granted." Only when it became manifest that they did not intend to fulfill their treaty obligation, did it become the imperative duty of the executive to compel them to do so. He pointed out: ". . . the conduct and courage of the enemy do not alter the nature of the war, nor diminish our obligation to subdue them and to compel them to fulfill their engagements. To abandon the settled policy of the government because the Seminoles have proved themselves to be good warriors and rely for the protection of our frontiers upon the faith of treaties with a people who have given such repeated proofs of treachery, would be unwise and impolitic."[41]

There was truth in Poinsett's argument—if one granted the premise that the treaty was honestly negotiated. Furthermore, frontier troubles never ceased as long as whites and Indians lived side by side. But Poinsett revealed the heart of the matter when he argued that to remove the Seminoles to the West was imperative for, as long as they remained in Florida, they invited "the resistance of all those who remain east of the Mississippi." This was even more crucial in the matter of free blacks on the border of slave states.

Poinsett's remarks implying that Jesup could not face the skill and courage of the Seminole warriors must have pierced the general's armor—already battered by criticism of his capture of Osceola, Coacoochee and Micanopy. He asked to stay on for another campaign which he hoped would finally win the war.

# 11

# General Thomas S. Jesup's
# Second Campaign, 1838

## Osceola Dies Defeated but Unvanquished

"Can any Christian in this republic ... still pray for the
continuance of blessings when he is about to wrest from the
unhappy Seminole all that the Great Spirit ever conferred
upon him?"                                                    *A soldier*

AFTER COACOOCHEE AND JOHN CAVALLO escaped, General Jesup decided that Fort Marion was not secure enough. He had the Indian
prisoners moved to Fort Moultrie on Sullivan's Island. That
stockade, built of palmetto logs during the Revolution, had been
attacked by the British in 1776. It was named after Colonel William
Moultrie who had defended it then. In 1811 a new brick structure
had been imposed on the foundation of the old log fort. When the
S. S. *Poinsett* arrived with its load of prisoners on 1 January 1838,
the modern stronghold was the most important harbor defense for
Charleston, South Carolina. There would be no escape from it.

Osceola's quarters were spacious and comfortable for his two
wives and two children. The rooms boasted a fire for the ailing
chief who was allowed to keep his scalping knife and to move freely

about the fort. He lay near the fire to ease the chills and when he broke into a sweat, his wives gently bathed his face.[1]

On 16 January, George Catlin arrived to paint the Seminole chiefs in captivity. The painter described the prisoners as Seminoles, a group of runaway Creeks, and Euchees—a remnant of a native Florida tribe invaded and then absorbed by the Seminoles. The artist quickly summed up the situation.

> With this tribe the government have been engaged in deadly and disastrous warfare for four or five years; endeavouring to remove them from their lands, in compliance with a Treaty stipulation, which the Government claims to have been justly made, and which the Seminoles aver, was not. Many millions of money, and some hundreds of lives of officers and men have already been expended in the attempt to dislodge them; and much more will doubtless be yet spent before they can be removed from their almost impenetrable swamps and hiding places, to which they can, for years to come, retreat; and from which they will be enabled in their exasperated state, to make continual sallies upon the unsuspecting and defenceless inhabitants of the country; carrying their relentless feelings to be reeked in cruel vengeance on the unoffending and the innocent.[2]

Catlin found 250 Seminoles in the fort. Each day he painted the chiefs, Osceola, King Philip, and Coa Hadjo, and every evening he sat by the fire and listened to their tales of suffering and betrayal. He wrote that he was convinced from what he had heard and from personal observation that Osceola was "a most extraordinary man, and one entitled to a better fate." He observed, "In his manners, and all movements in company, he is polite and gentlemanly, though all his conversation is entirely in his own tongue; and his general appearance and actions those of a full-blooded and wild Indian."[3] Catlin painted Osceola in full costume. "He wore three ostrich feathers in his head and a turban made of vari-coloured cotton shawl—and his dress was chiefly of calicoes, with a handsome bead sash or belt around his waist and his rifle in his hand." The painter felt that his subject manifestly revealed a childhood molded by running and hiding and a short manhood spent in relentless warfare against those who meant to take his land. He saw him as "... this gallant fellow [who] is grieving with a broken spirit and ready to die, cursing white man, no doubt to the end of his breath."[4]

While Catlin was still at Fort Moultrie, he noted that Osceola had an attack of quinsy—"... putrid sore throat, which will probably end his career in a few days." Dr. Frederick Weedon, brother-in-law of Wiley Thompson, was at the fort and hastened to the chief's quarters. He found the patient laboring to breathe and in danger of suffocating because of his inflamed and swollen tonsils. As Weedon was attempting to take steps to relieve the pain and pressure, a Seminole prophet or healer arrived. He refused any and all ministrations from the doctor. Not wanting the responsibility for allowing Osceola to die, Weedon called in Dr. B. B. Strobel, professor of anatomy at the Medical School, College of South Carolina. Dr. Strobel confirmed Dr. Weedon's diagnosis and begged to be allowed to lance the tonsils or to bleed the patient at the throat or behind his ears, but the "conjurer" flatly refused any medical treatment.

Shortly before his death, Osceola signed (he could not talk) to his wives to bring his full dress. When all his paraphernalia was brought to him, he rose from his pallet and donned his shirt, leggings, and moccasins. He girded on his war belt, bullet pouch, and powder horn and laid his knife on the floor beside him. Then he called for his looking glass and paint. He covered one half of his face, neck, and throat with vermillion, "a custom practiced when the irrevocable oath of war is taken." He arranged his turban with the three ostrich plumes and sheathed his knife. After this exertion he was forced to lie down to rest a few moments; when he had recovered his strength, he arose and "smiling sweetly," he shook hands with the doctors, the army officers and chiefs in the room, then with his wives and children. There wasn't a sound in the room as he "made a signal for them to lower him down upon his bed ... he then slowly drew from his war-belt his scalping knife, which he firmly grasped in his right hand, laying it across the other on his breast, and in a moment smiled away his last breath without a struggle or a groan."[5]

Officers and chiefs wept. Osceola was given a military funeral the next day and his body was buried near the main entrance to Fort Moultrie. Mr. Patton, a sympathetic Charleston resident, provided a marble slab with the inscription:

Osceola
Patriot and Warrior
Died at Fort Moultrie
January 30th, 1838

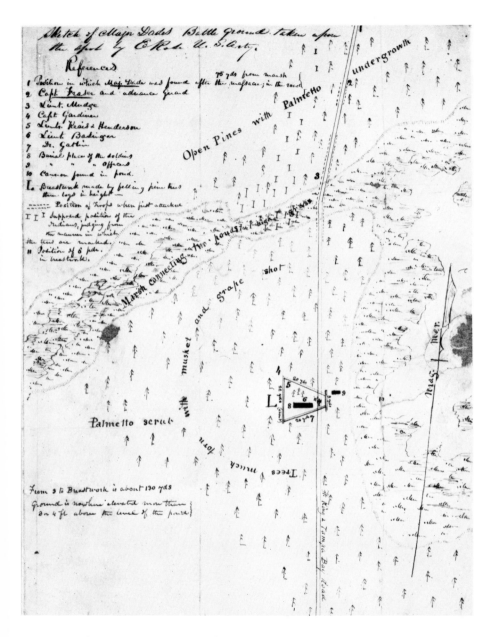

SKETCH OF MAJOR DADE'S BATTLEGROUND (*Civil Works Map File, National Archives*)

COACOOCHEE (Wild Cat). A Seminole leader who with Osceola chose to resist. Portrait from The Exiles of Florida, Josiah R. Giddings. (*National Anthropological Archives, Smithsonian Institution*)

[Top] MICANOPY. Hereditary
    Chief of all Seminoles.
    Captured under a flag of
    truce and deported.
    (*National Anthropological
    Archives, Smithsonian
    Institution*)

[Bottom] FOKE-LUSTE-HAJO
    (Fuchi-Lusti-Hadjo).
    Seminole Chief who
    chose to emigrate.
    (*National Anthropological
    Archives, Smithsonian
    Institution*)

[Top] GOPHER JOHN (John Cavallo). Seminole Negro leader, government interpreter. (*Moorland-Spingarn Research Center, Howard University*)

[Bottom] ABRAHAM. Seminole Negro negotiator and interpreter. (*Moorland-Spingarn Research Center, Howard University*)

SEMINOLE WOMAN. One of many anonymous heroines of the
Florida Wars. Portrait by George Catlin. (*National Collection of Fine Arts, Smithsonian Institution*)

[Top] GENERAL WINFIELD SCOTT
(*U. S. Signal Corps Photo,*
*National Archives*)

Two prominent generals who
met defeat in the Florida
Wars.

[Bottom] GENERAL EDMUND P.
GAINES. (*U. S. Signal Corps*
*Photo, National Archives*)

[Top] GENERAL THOMAS S.
JESUP. (*U. S. Signal Corps
Photo, National Archives*)

Two military leaders who did
most to implement
national policy in Florida.

[Bottom] GENERAL WILLIAM
JENKINS WORTH.
(*Engraving, Library of
Congress*)

HOLATTER MICCO (Billy Bowlegs). Seminole leader in the
Third Florida War. (*National Anthropological Archives,
Smithsonian Institution*)

Osceola, who had rejected completely his white ancestry in life, was buried in the tradition of his father. He had lost his battle against the white man but he had gained his respect. Coe wrote:

> The fearless bravery and manly qualities of this chief, his unusual knowledge of scientific warfare, and above all his unswerving determination to defend to the last his chosen home, had spread his fame throughout the length and breadth of the country, and won for him respect and admiration even in the hearts of his bitterest enemies. The fame of Osceola was well earned ... for true patriotism and determined effort, against the combined armies of a great and powerful nation, in one of the most remarkable struggles known to history. His fame will never die; centuries will come and go, but the name of Osceola will remain as long as the earth is peopled.[6]

Coe wrote in the extravagant prose of the nineteenth century but he was right in a sense, for the charisma of Osceola seems as powerful today as it was almost a century and a half ago.

An editorial on 2 February 1838 paid tribute to the fallen hero of the Seminole in more restrained terms.

> He made himself—no man owed less to accident. Bold and decisive in action, deadly but consistent in hatred, dark in revenge, cool, subtle, and sagacious in council, he established gradually and surely a resistless ascendancy over his adoptive tribe, by the daring of his deeds, and the consistency of his hostility to the whites, and the profound craft of his policy. Such was Osceola who will long be remembered as the man that with the feeblest means produced the most terrible effects.[7]

Osceola was dead. Many Seminoles had given themselves up, been captured in battle or by ruse when they came to an army camp to negotiate, but a few chiefs were still free. Coacoochee, especially, would carry on the spirit and methods of Osceola in battles to come.

Had Osceola met his end cursing the white man as George Catlin had predicted? According to those who were present, he died smiling and offering the hand of friendship. For whom then, or what, was the red war paint applied? Was it to face the Grim Reaper that he girded himself for war or was it to show his captors that, ill and defenseless, he could still face military defeat and fatal illness with dignity and grace. Only the silent, enigmatic chief would ever know.[8]

While Osceola was dying at Fort Moultrie, Jesup took command of a force that encountered the Seminoles at Locha Hatchee, a crossing on the Jupiter River. He left Fort Lloyd, at the head of the St. Johns, on 20 January and arrived at the Indian ford at noon on the twenty-fourth.

As usual the enemy was entrenched in an almost impregnable position—on a hummock covered with dense foliage and surrounded by a deep creek. As usual the Americans had too many troops. Ten companies of the Third and Fourth Artillery attacked from the left, the Second Battalion bore the brunt of fire in the center but the North Alabama volunteers on the right couldn't get near enough to the battle to enter the fray. Lieutenant Colonel William Harney took a detachment of dragoons around to the rear of the Seminole allies. Fifteen men with two junior officers crossed the creek and penetrated the hummock. The warriors were so startled at seeing the enemy approach from the rear that they dispersed.

That ended the battle, for Harney's men found most of their ammunition had been destroyed while crossing the creek and they were so exhausted from their exertions in reaching the rear that Harney "contented [himself] with having dispersed the enemy." It was often true that American troops were too worn out when they finally caught up with the Seminoles to fight or follow them! The dragoons estimated that there were sixty warriors on the hummock but the exchange had been heated. Seven Americans died and twenty-nine were wounded. Jesup was severely injured in the arm. The Seminole allies apparently suffered no casualties.

In spite of his wound, the general moved his force to a point below Okeechobee where he built a fort called Jupiter. He wrote the adjutant general that he intended to pursue the enemy as soon as he had four or five days' rations.[9]

It was Jesup's plan that with Taylor operating west of the Kissimmee and his own force along the coast, they would push the Seminole allies south into the Everglades. Here the enemy would be met by a special naval force that would operate along the coast and in the rivers and inlets, pushing north toward the army. Jesup hoped to encircle the Seminoles in a ring of military units through which they could not escape. It was a good plan and it reflected a knowledge of the country gained after two years of trial and error.

The use of the navy in the Seminole War was not a new development. As early as General Gaines' abortive campaign, Indians had begun to move south in the face of massive military advances. To prevent this, Colonel William Lindsay, in charge of approaching the Withlacoochee from the south, had requested a naval patrol. Although the unit never caught up with the Seminoles, it did establish that some Indians were moving south and officers involved began to understand the nature of the terrain on which the Seminoles might choose to fight. Scott also sent Colonel P. F. Smith with his Louisiana volunteers to proceed up Pease Creek from Charlotte Harbor.

Lieutenant Levin M. Powell, USN, was ordered to escort the column. Supplies were placed aboard cutters while Powell with his sailors and marines walked on one side of the stream and Colonel Smith and his soldiers marched on the other. As the creek narrowed, the ships grounded. Smith sent the cutters with most of the supplies back to the harbor while he and Powell took ninety-one volunteers with forty-one sailors and marines and proceeded to the head of Pease Creek. Here they found nothing but a deserted village. Since they dared not enter the swamp without guides, they returned without finding any Seminoles. However, Colonel Smith was very impressed with the behavior of the sailors and the value of using boats to pursue the Indians in the swamps.[10] Powell, a young naval officer not too entrenched in navy tradition, also saw the significance of a new and special kind of warfare, especially suited to the coast of Florida with its tiny keys and numerous inlets. He suspected that it might be the only method of reaching the enemy when they retreated into swamps where the army could not follow.

Powell asked to be put in charge of a group of sailors and marines who would operate in small boats to explore the rivers and swamps of southern Florida and to seek out the enemy in its secret recesses. After receiving approval from both services, he set out in October 1836 from Key West to Cape Florida (Key Biscayne).

He had a crew of fifty sailors and ninety-five marines, manning a fleet of two schooners, the *Carolina* and the *Firefly*, the revenue cutter, *Washington*, and scores of small boats. He had under him Lieutenant William Smith, USN, as well as Lieutenant Waldron and Second Lieutenant McNeill, USMC. Stephen R. Mallory, a civilian from Key West, and Dr. Frederick Leitner, a physician and scientist who knew the area well through his study of local fauna and flora, served as volunteer paramilitary guides. Working in small groups, they probed inlets and small keys all the way to Cape Florida and pushed their boats up the Miami, Little, Indian, Ratones and New

Rivers. While they found no enemy, they learned much about the area. From time to time they came across deserted camps and villages where they destroyed everything that might be useful to the enemy.

At one time, Powell took four of his lightest boats, a scanty allowance of provisions, and a party consisting of Dr. Hassler, Dr. Leitner, Mr. Mallory, Mr. Hunter, and an "old resident," Mr. Cooley, as guide into the Everglades. Powell described their experience.

> We anchored our boats that night in the great inland basin of South Florida, known as the Everglades. We had now a night view of the coast that encircles the glades. Forests of pines and cypress enclosed us on one side like a black wall; while on the other, the grass, which covers the whole surface of this shallow lake, offered no obstruction to the eye as it wandered over the dreary waste. . . . With the dawn we pushed into the grassy sea before us, and endeavored to approach an island seen in the distance. Several other islands were above the horizon as we progressed; but the boats, although the smallest of our little fleet, could not get near either of them. The matted saw-grass, which wounds like a razor, and the deep sluices, which intersect the glades, prevented access to them on foot. I found it impracticable to navigate the glades, at this stage of water, in keel boats, though no labor had been spared; and we reluctantly commenced our return to the camp.[11]

By 15 November, all units of his organization rendezvoused at Cape Sable. The next day the whole fleet sailed south. Powell wrote:

> The entire coast seems to be formed of a mass of mangrove islands, packed in upon each other, and separated from the water of the everglades by a lagoon, fresh or salt, by turns, as the tide or waters of the glades prevail. To Snake River it would be difficult to find an acre of dry land on which to encamp.

From the mouth of the Snake to Cape Romano, the islands presented a sandy beach with patches of dry land. Powell's crews continued south along the coast, stopping to explore inlets and rivers, until the end of November when cold, stormy weather, leaking boats and illness among the crew, forced him to abandon his search. He and his command reached Key West on 8 December, having covered more than a thousand miles of the South Florida coast.[12]

Convinced that Powell's methods would eventually succeed,

Jesup put both army and navy men in boats during January 1838. The troops stowed their guns and ammunition, their pork, bread, and coffee and their blankets in boats which they pushed before them through mud and dense growth in the swamps. One officer described their lives at this time: "... often barefooted, and their pantaloons cut off as high as the knee with the saw palmetto, [they] press forward in defense of their country and in checking the depredations of the savage upon the inhabitants of this region whose presses teem with abuse upon the army now serving in the Territory. The officers are alienated from home, kindred, and friends, and compelled to remain in this inglorious war, defending a domain which can never be densely populated, and protecting some of its inhabitants who would suffer much by comparison with the savages."[13]

Thus the men lived in mud and slime, rarely ate hot food, slept in their wet clothes, let their beards grow and their faces become black from the smoke of fires they used to drive away the hordes of mosquitoes. If they ever saw a newspaper, it was to read articles about their ineptness and failures or their mistreatment of the Indians or their gullibility regarding them—according to the philosophy of the paper. If they had leave and entered a border town, it was to grow disgusted with the whites whose interests they were protecting.

In January, Powell was patrolling along the coast while Taylor pushed down the Kissimmee and Colonel Smith again operated in the west with his Louisiana volunteers. On the tenth, the lieutenant reached the headwaters of the Jupiter River and was about to return to the coast when he saw evidence of a large band of Seminoles in the area. Following the trail, he came upon a woman whom he forced to escort them to her camp. With fifty-five sailors and twenty-five soldiers, he approached the Seminole stronghold. The warriors moved back into the brush, firing as they went, but the Americans pressed on. Dr. Leitner was killed and both Powell and an officer named Harrison were injured. As darkness fell, they decided to return to their boats. This time the Indians pursued; the sailors, unaccustomed to this type of warfare, were frightened and confused. Powell and Harrison, in spite of their injuries, managed to rally the sailors to effect an orderly retreat while the army fought a creditable rearguard action. At the end of this skirmish, there were five Americans dead and twenty-two wounded.[14] Powell had little to show for his losses but his men had experienced their baptism of fire; they would be better prepared next time.

Jesup hoped there would not need to be a next time. Both he

and Powell had suffered defeat because they had engaged an enemy securely entrenched in territory alien and well-nigh impassable to the Americans. To continue such costly battles without capturing a single Seminole seemed senseless.

In February a group of officers met with General Jesup to discuss ending the war by truce. After a conference with General Abraham Eustis, Colonel David E. Twiggs, and others, Jesup sent word by a Seminole Negro for the allies to come in for a conference.

Soon he received the message that a group of them were waiting for him with a flag of truce near Cypress Swamp. A young chief, Hallec Hadjo, spoke of the wretched condition of his people and of their desire for peace. He begged the American government to give them a piece of land—however small and miserable—which would be their own. Jesup asked the Indians to assemble outside Fort Jupiter in ten days while he asked the president if he could comply with their request.

Jesup warned his superiors that unless emigration plans were abandoned the war would continue at an ever-increasing cost. He pointed out that the swamps of lower Florida were not needed for agricultural purposes and that the army was fighting in territory as alien to the men as "the interior of China." He wrote, "We exhibit in our present contest the first instance, perhaps, since the commencement of authentic history, of a Nation employing an army to explore a country (for we can do little more than explore it) or attempting to remove a band of savages from one unexplored wilderness to another."

Secretary of War Poinsett replied that it was the stated policy of the president and Congress that all Indians, including the Seminoles, should be shipped west of the Mississippi. He went on to give the beleaguered general a gentle slap, "The Department indulged the hope that, with the extensive means placed at your disposal, the war by a vigorous effort might be brought to a close this campaign." He concluded that if the safety of the settlements could be secured by a "temporary" agreement to let the Seminoles have some land in Florida, the general was free to make the offer.[15]

The citizens of Florida wanted no compromise and the *Tallahassee Floridian* took General Jesup to task.

> From the confidence with which General Jesup expresses his views of the policy to be pursued toward the Indians, we should suppose he had entirely mistaken the nature of his mission to Florida. We

presume the General Government will feel no obligations to him for spending their money in constant negotiations with the enemy whom he is sent to subdue whilst an army of 10,000 men is kept in pay merely to witness his rare talents for diplomacy. And we are sure the people of Florida will not thank him for his assiduous efforts to barter away their lands to savage enemies. . . . In whatever light the proposition is received, it is abhorrent to every man endowed with common feelings of humanity.[16]

Angered by the elusive Indians, by his unrelenting superiors, and by public condemnation, Jesup read the letter from the secretary of war and sent out a messenger to call in the Indians who had been waiting for his reply from the Great Father. They had become suspicious of his "Flag of Truce" conferences and had begun to slip away but he was ahead of them. He had deployed troops who managed to detain all who were still in camp and to catch those who had left.

By March 1838, Jesup could report to Poinsett that 642 Indians and Negroes were at a camp near Fort Jupiter waiting to emigrate, and that 100 more were on their way from Okeechobee to give themselves up. But in spite of his success, Jesup was not satisfied. He estimated that the Seminole allies had lost 500 warriors since the beginning of the war, that those remaining were without a home or resting place. He warned that 50 such fugitives could cause as much trouble to the frontier as a whole army and would be much more difficult to find.

Again Jesup urged that a new treaty be presented which would forbid the Seminoles to purchase arms or ammunition but would allow them land on which to plant crops and build homes for two years while they prepared to emigrate. He advised that under no circumstances should anyone again assemble a large army in Florida; he suggested that two, or at most three, regiments could concentrate the remnants of the Seminoles in one area and protect the citizens.[17]

However, the citizens would have no part of a compromise. They had another argument for winning the war—the honor of the United States. An editorial in the *St. Augustine Herald* declared, "The people of Florida will not submit to it [Jesup's plan to allow the Seminoles to remain in the Everglades]. . . . The national honor and dignity are too deeply concerned for it to listen for one moment to the proposed arrangement."[18]

To this argument, Jesup replied in his letter to Poinsett:

It has been said that the national honor forbids any compromise with them—can there be a point of honor between a great nation and a band of naked savages, now beaten, broken, dispirited and dispersed? I think those who believe so form a very low estimate of national honor. But admit that our national honor could be tarnished by giving up the contest entirely, and forming a new treaty with different provisions from those of the existing treaty— we are surely at liberty, without compromising our honor, to adopt those measures whether of direct hostility or of policy which shall promise the greater probability of ultimate success.[19]

An army officer stationed at Fort Jupiter wrote to a journal called *The Political Arena*, "It is no cause for triumph to beat and drive the poor miserable Indians who are desperately and obstinately contending for their natural rights and possessions, against most unequal numbers."[20]

That journal carried an editorial along the same vein.

It is too late in the day to contemn [*sic*] an enemy, who, seconded by the peculiar characteristics of the country, has baffled the military operations of successful generals, and virtually defeated our troops in every skirmish. The fact is, we are inclined to believe that the Seminoles are impregnable in their fastness, and are not to be sub- dued by military force. Soft words and the persuasive force of gold, may induce them to emigrate. Otherwise, we believe that they will maintain their footing in spite of all the efforts we can make to dislodge them. The country to which they might be confined is uninhabitable for the white man, and the question seriously presents itself, whether the design of forcibly expelling them had not better be relinquished. It is idle to suppose that the national honor requires their subjugation. No credit will accrue from the most successful termination of the war.[21]

Jesup protested to Poinsett that to continue the war was folly for while six hundred regular troops could have bested the Seminole allies in any battle yet fought in Florida were it not for the terrain, twenty thousand would not be able to catch those remaining. He did not claim he had won the war but he argued that he had beaten the Seminoles as completely as they were beaten by General Jackson in 1818; they had been pursued and dispersed farther, more had been killed and more taken prisoner. Of course, it must be said that

General Jackson only beat the Spanish in that war, not the Seminoles! Jesup maintained that the allies in Florida had been beaten as completely as the western Indians had been by General Wayne or General Harrison. Were he allowed to make a treaty on the terms on which those generals had treated, he promised that permanent peace could be secured in a week. With almost reckless courage, he defied the secretary of war in the closing lines of his report: ". . . To persevere in the course we have been pursuing for three years past would be a reckless waste of blood and treasure; and I sincerely hope that I may soon receive instructions to adopt the course I have recommended, or if I should act without instructions, that my measures be approved." [22]

A soldier of the Fourth Artillery, under General Jesup's command, wrote of the enemy to the Charleston, South Carolina *Courier*: ". . . At length after much suffering, they have been driven into the swamps and unwholesome places of their country, and they are now clinging with the last efforts of desperation to their beloved home. Can any Christian in this republic know this and still pray for the continuance of blessings, when he is about to wrest from the unhappy Seminole all that the Great Spirit ever conferred upon him?" [23]

Even his own soldiers were appalled at the task they were ordered to perform. Yet Jesup had no choice but to carry out his orders. This he did with a stubborn thoroughness that brought the first success the army had achieved in three years of warfare in Forida. His methods earned him the displeasure of some who thought he was too soft when he tried to negotiate and of others who condemned him when he used force. Each time he captured a sizable number of the enemy it was through guile rather than military might but this too brought recriminations upon him. Disappointed because he had not succeeded in convincing the Seminoles to emigrate peaceful and disheartened by criticism from the press, the citizens, and his own men and military colleagues, General Jesup left Florida. He carried away with him not only his physical wound but one of the spirit as well.

# 12

# The Second Emigration

## Jumper and King Philip Die on the "Trail of Tears"

"... the honors of war were bestowed upon him...."
LIEUTENANT JOHN G. REYNOLDS

IN THE SPRING OF 1838, over 1,000 Indians and Negroes were assembled at Tampa Bay ready for shipment to Arkansas. Three weeks after the death of Osceola, his family and those of Micanopy, King Philip, Coa Hadjo, and Cloud—including 116 warriors and 82 women and children—were taken, with about 40 others, aboard the brig *Homer* to New Orleans under supervision of Captain Pitcairn Morrison.[1]

That spring was a time of special sadness for the Indians. Osceola's desecrated body lay in a white man's grave in far-off Charleston, South Carolina. Chief after chief had been captured and his people taken into custody for deportation. By the end of the summer, two more great Seminole leaders would be buried in alien soil.

On 18 April, Jumper (Ote-Emathla) succumbed after a long bout with tuberculosis. He and his people were confined at Fort Pike near New Orleans. The *Arkansas Gazette* reported: "The distinguished Seminole Chief, Jumper, died at New Orleans Barracks on 18th ult., and was buried in the afternoon. In his coffin were placed his tobacco, pipe, rifle and other equipment, according to his people's custom. The military, and a number of citizens, attended his funeral, which was conducted with all the honors of war."[2]

Jumper had been one of the chiefs to sign the Treaty of Payne's Landing. He had gone on the ill-fated expedition to examine the Arkansas Territory and signed the paper used by the government to demand immediate removal. Once a leader in the resistance, his illness had disposed him to compromise and peaceful emigration. Then he and his people had been kidnapped in June 1837, on the eve of their departure West, by the hawks of the Seminole nation. Now after another year of negotiation, hiding, and suffering, he died in a refugee camp far from his beloved Florida. Perhaps he was lucky that he never reached "The Promised Land" of Arkansas.

By May, most of the prisoners had been moved from Tampa to New Orleans and were confined in New Barracks, awaiting transportation to their western homes. Although half of them were ill and the number of indisposed was increasing daily, ships began to steam up the Mississippi with their loads of dispossessed. On the nineteenth, the *Renown* embarked with 453 aboard and the *South Alabama* followed on the twenty-second with 674 more, of which over 200 were blacks.

Lieutenant John G. Reynolds, USMC, was in charge.[3] He was uneasy as he set off because he had with him sixty-seven Seminole Negroes who were still alive of the ninety whom the Creeks had captured in battles with the Seminole allies. To protect them from being returned to slavery, General Jesup had sought to buy them in the name of the United States government but the Creeks had turned down the eight thousand dollars he offered and sold them to a slave trader, James C. Watson, from Georgia for between fourteen and fifteen thousand dollars. Watson had commissioned his brother-in-law, Nathaniel F. Collins, to go to New Orleans to pick them up.

Since this transaction had the approval of both Secretary of War Poinsett and Indian Commissioner Harris, Collins expected no difficulties when he arrived to take possession of his property. However, Lieutenant Reynolds had received orders on 31 March that he was to meet the Micanopy-King Philip party at New Orleans and there pick up the Seminole Negroes and escort them all safety to the West. Edmund P. Gaines, now a major general of the army and commander of the Western Division, ordered Major Zantzinger, commander of Fort Pike, to turn over the "slaves or servants belonging to, or claimed by, or lately in the possession of, the said

Seminole Indians to be conducted by him [Lieutenant Reynolds] . . .
to [where] the said Indians and their slaves or servants are to be
permanently located. . . ."[4]

The Creeks wrote to Washington, asking Commissioner Harris
to turn over the blacks to Collins who had paid for them.[5] Collins
obtained a restraining order forbidding the Negroes to be moved
and General Gaines went to court, claiming that both Indians and
blacks were prisoners of war and under army control. The Louisiana
court decreed that only the Indians were prisoners of war; the Negroes
were property which could be attached by claimants. But after a
series of legal manuevers, Lieutenant Reynolds finally got the
beleaguered blacks aboard a ship with their Indian allies. Undaunted,
Collins followed them.

At Vicksburg, he boarded the ship with an order from Commissioner Harris to turn the Negroes over to him. Lieutenant Reynolds
invited Collins to face the angry Indians and blacks. He convinced
him that nothing short of physical force would get the Negroes off
the ship. Since Reynolds did not have enough troops aboard his
transports to effect the transfer, he sent word to General Matthew
Arbuckle in Arkansas asking for help to carry out the commissioner's
order. Arkansas permitted slavery but the general did not want to
anger his new inhabitants by interfering in their affairs before they
had even set foot on the territory. He declined, giving as his reason
the fact that there was no one competent to identify the Negroes and
it would be madness to irritate the Indians.[6]

Reynolds brought his refugee ships up the Mississippi to a spot
where the passengers had to be reloaded onto smaller vessels because
of low water and through the Arkansas River to Fort Gibson. He
discharged his passengers on 12 June. Fifty-four had died along the
way. The rest proceeded on foot to their final destination. Many, too
ill to walk, were moved in wagons.[7]

In spite of their hardships along the way, nearly sixty of the
ninety Negroes captured by the Creeks reached freedom in the West
because four military men had doggedly done their duty. General
Jesup had failed to buy the freedom of the Seminole blacks but he
had held the line against all attempts to reenslave them. Lieutenant
Reynolds had successfully fended off excessive pressure from private
citizens and powerful officials in Washington. General Gaines had
gone to court to protect the rights of Negroes to be treated as people
rather than part of the spoils of war and when the judge ruled against

him, he had brought them safely aboard transports by the use of military and legal technicalities. General Arbuckle had refused to use military force to take blacks from their Indian allies and protectors. Whether the officers' motives had been purely altruistic or not, the Negroes were now nominally safe from the kind of thralldom to which Collins would have returned them. Although they were free, their troubles were far from over. But that is another story.

Besides the terror the Negroes had sustained as Collins stalked them from New Orleans to Arkansas, there was misery for the Indians too. King Philip had been ill back at Fort Moultrie. Now the hardships of the journey and his grief at being transported became too much for him. He died on 7 June only sixty miles from Fort Gibson. The morning of the eighth, both ships anchored at a spot suitable for burial. The troops of the two transports joined to form an honor guard which led a procession of all the emigrants to the grave. There his captors rendered the chief a one hundred-gun salute. He, too, was buried with all the honors of war.[8]

Through the summer and fall, the Florida Indians continued to arrive in the West. Another 445 disembarked in June; Alligator and his band of 66 in August. On 22 November, 300 Apalachicolas and 22 Creeks reached Little Rock. Those who were not ill had walked from the river. Unaccustomed to the cold, they had suffered intensely.[9]

Alligator and his people had been taken to Tampa after they gave themselves up to General Taylor. As they waited for transportation to New Orleans, they decided to hold a "White Feather" dance. The celebration lasted all day and into the night. Scouts sent out to investigate found Alligator and his band trying to slip away under cover of the festivities. Only thirty managed to escape. A hastily alerted guard surrounded the others, brought them back and put them aboard ships for New Orleans. The chief, one of those who got away, surrendered in order to lead his people on the trek to Arkansas.[10]

The Fort Gibson treaty had assigned the Seminoles a tract of land between the Canadian River and the north fork of that stream west to the fork of Little River. When they arrived, they found that much of the territory had been settled by Creeks. A meeting between the two groups broke up when the Seminoles flatly refused to move in among their traditional enemies. That left two thousand Seminoles camping around Fort Gibson and refusing to move; they felt certain the Creeks would try to take their Negroes. Shivering and wretched they waited for their promised supplies and a bit of land they could call their own.[11]

Predatory opportunists lurked about their camps, hoping to take advantage of them or to lay hands on the Negroes. One such slave dealer, R. D. Mitchell, wrote his fellow-Tennessean, Secretary of War John Bell, asking for help in dealing with the agent, Colonel Logan, who was not cooperating with him as he sought to gain possession of some Seminole Negroes. He also requested a contract to feed the Seminoles at thirteen cents a ration. He hoped to make a profit from providing their subsistence while he negotiated to obtain their blacks.[12]

In Arkansas the Seminole allies endured their misery and stubbornly demanded land of their own while in Florida the war of resistance went on. At Tampa Bay, General Taylor continued to assemble small groups for emigration. In February 1839 he shipped out 166 captives to New Orleans. Among the prisoners were women who had fought so long that they were more defiant than the men. They boarded the transport taunting their husbands for "cowardice in refusing to die upon their native soil." One of the Negroes in this shipment was Abraham, "interpreter and a wily and treacherous rascal."[13] Whether he followed his chief, Micanopy, freely or under duress, he had probably recognized that life in Florida would continue to grow ever more precarious for the hostiles. The time had come to make the best of it in Arkansas.

For each allied leader the moment of truth came at some time of confrontation—either through death, capture or a decision made in the face of events. Neither Charley Emathla, Holahte Emathla, nor Fuchi Luste-Hadjo wanted to leave Florida but chose to do so as a lesser of two evils. Osceola, Coacoochee, and Arpeika represent those who always preferred to die in Florida rather than to live in Arkansas.

The blacks; too, assessed their options before deciding where their honor or best interests lay. Among both races circumstances may have tipped the scale one way or the other but, in the end, each man had to throw in his lot with the hostiles or the Americans and accept the consequences. For the Negroes it was often Hobson's Choice with catastrophe at the end of the road in either case. Nevertheless, Pacheco, Primus, John Caesar, and John Cavallo (to name a few) became leaders of the resistance while Toney, Pompey, and Gopher

John gained reputations as loyal defenders of Americans—not only as interpreters and guides but also as valuable informers.[14]

Two of the most competent and prominent Negroes whose paths diverged when the break came in 1835 were Abraham and Cudjo. They had both made the trip to Arkansas as interpreters in the conferences that produced the Treaty of Fort Gibson.

When the Seminoles decided to fight rather than submit to removal, Abraham cast his lot with the hostiles. Later accused by Hitchcock of betraying his allies, he had nonetheless chosen to fight with them and negotiate for them. For some months in that fateful year, he had appeared to work for the Americans while he secretly recruited slaves from the St. Johns plantations and helped to stockpile arms and ammunition for the Indians. His plantation, his family, and his loyalties were with Micanopy who chose to resist.

Cudjo's property lay near the Seminole agency. Whites with whom he associated soon came to appreciate his intelligence, industry, and good will. His knowledge of both English and Indian languages as well as of the land and the natives made him a natural as an interpreter, advisor, and guide for the Indian agent. He served Phagan and Thompson, General Clinch of the army, and Lieutenant Harris, Seminole emigration officer, with such distinction that Clinch and Harris contended over who was to retain his services. Harris had to make do with someone else as the general naturally won this small battle with his rank.

Unfortunately, Cudjo's industry and loyalty won him little but praise from his employers. His plantation was destroyed by the hostiles who drove off 15 horses and 150 cattle. In addition, he apparently received only a portion of the salary promised him for his services. Over a period of three years, Phagan and Thompson had paid him only $150 when he should have had $300 a year. It appears that Phagan had deliberately withheld his salary while Thompson died before he could set things right. Harris asked for $525 in back pay and $1500 for the loss of the Negro's horses, cattle, and land improvements.[15] There was no immediate response but as long as the young emigration officer lived he continued to seek some remuneration for the interpreter. In pleading Cudjo's cause, he wrote: "Cudjoe is really so worthy & deserving a man; & has exerted himself so efficiently to advance the views of the government that I feel a great desire to see justice done him ... In faithfully & efficiently rendering his services as an interpreter, & in imparting his knowledge of the

Country & of the Enemy, to the Troops actively engaged in Florida he advances the several interests of our Indian Relations, Indian Emigration & the suppression of Seminole hostilities." [16]

When funds were finally sent to Major Julius Heilman at Fort Drane to pay the interpreter's salary, that officer had died of malaria. The money was returned to Washington as no one else seemed authorized to reimburse Cudjo. As late as 1841 correspondence still floated between the field and the commissary general of subsistence regarding the Negro's pay. In the end he was described as old and poor. [17]

# 13

# General Zachary Taylor's

# Campaign, 1838–1839

## New Methods Bring Old Failures

"Could the enemy be brought to battle, even in his strong-
holds, the war would soon be closed. . . . "

GENERAL ZACHARY TAYLOR

ALTHOUGH TWO THOUSAND SEMINOLES were now safely removed to
the West, Florida was far from free of their presence. When Colonel
Zachary Taylor had arrived in Florida at the end of July 1837,
military operations were in the hands of local militia and volunteers
while General Jesup was working to bring about the removal of the
Indians through a series of conferences. By seizing chief after chief
who came in under a flag of truce—Osceola, Coacoochee, Micanopy,
and others—the general had put out of circulation the most presti-
gious leaders of the enemy. But although the people had been pursued,
found, killed, or captured in greater numbers than ever before, those
remaining were not yet subdued nor willing to leave Florida peaceably.

Like others before him, Taylor had planned a sweeping assault
to dislodge the remaining Seminole allies. His encounter with them
at Lake Okeechobee in December had been as costly to him in men

and materials as that of any predecessor, the results as unsatisfactory —even though he received a promotion on the strength of it. Although the results of his campaign were inconclusive, he had hurt the Seminoles too. They had lost cattle, ponies, and precious supplies; they had been driven deeper into the unhealthy swamps. In self-defense they had dispersed into small groups that could not be found by a large army unit. Yet they could strike a settlement, an unprotected fort, or a supply train to replenish their dwindling resources and retreat with impunity. A new method for protecting the frontier settlements and for capturing the remaining Seminoles had to be devised. Taylor thought he had just such a scheme.

Early in 1838 he began to carry out his plan to win the Seminole War. He placed a grid over the entire state, laying it out in small, square districts. Each square was protected by a guard house, manned by a garrison, and all were linked by a network of wagon roads. For several months the army was engaged in building these simple forts and clearing the roads which connected them. There were no more massed armies floundering through jungle wilds with straining horses and mired supply wagons. Each square was patrolled by its own garrison whose modest needs could be provided quite easily over the newly-built transportation lines. From time to time, the soldiers brought in, without violence, small parties of Indians who agreed to emigrate. Citizens were protected by the fort nearest each plantation.[1]

But just as Taylor began to feel that his plan was working, General Alexander Macomb arrived suddenly from Washington with authority from President Van Buren to negotiate with the Indians. In May 1838, he set up his headquarters at Fort King and sent word for the chiefs to come in. Not a leader responded to his messengers; in fact, depredations against the settlers broke out in every part of the territory. One of Taylor's trusted "friendly" Indians sent to bring in his brothers defected to the enemy and the prognosis for successful negotiations was exceedingly gloomy.

Macomb refused to be discouraged. He finally corralled one family. Indian John, his wife and children were given presents and provisions; then he was sent out into the hummocks with instructions not to return until he had made contact with the hostiles. This was no easy task for the Indians were convinced that Macomb meant to lure them in under a white flag, capture, and deport them. Anyone who even sought contact with them put his life in jeopardy. But Indian John came in a few days later with the information that a party of eight Mikasuki warriors were camped nearby and would be in for a talk.

Halleck-Tustenuggee, bearing a white flag and accompanied by seven warriors, appeared the next morning. He was about thirty years old, well dressed, tall, a commanding person with a "manly, prepossessing countenance." He was an "expressive and fluent speaker." His followers were young, remarkable for their "hideous and repulsive faces and their fine, well-proportioned, athletic" bodies. Some of them had had no contact with whites for at least three years; they were dressed in nothing but rough buckskin shirts. They were disconcerted by the number of officers and men which flanked the general but Macomb assured them that his large military guard was there simply as a tribute to the importance of the Great Father who had sent him to deal with them. He then proceeded to welcome them with "much form and ceremony, and with every mark of friendship and kindness."

Macomb promised the Indians a piece of land on the peninsula if they would agree to gather there and refrain from attacks on the settlers. The territory to be ceded to them was an area in the center of Florida below Pease Creek. It did not include any coastline for the government hoped to prevent their preying on shipwrecked sailors. He offered them peace if they accepted his proposals or relentless war if they did not.

As the talks went on Colonel Harney and the Negro interpreter Sandy came in with a reluctant Chitto-Tustenuggee. When they had first met the chief near the Everglades where he was returning from a fishing expedition, he had said merely, "I suppose you have come with more lies," but Sandy had prevailed on him to come and hear what Macomb had to say.

The delegation departed for the wilderness to call their people together and returned eight days later with about fifty warriors.[2] The leaders who came to negotiate this time were a whole new cast of characters. The old chiefs had been designated as micco (king), emathla (hereditary leader), and hadjo (sub-chief) but the new ones were mainly tustenuggee (warrior). They had emerged as leaders in the heat of battle.[3]

Halleck-Tustenuggee's second-in-command was a Seminole, Thlocko-Tustenuggee (Tiger Tail).[4] At the beginning of the war, he was living in the home of Colonel Robert Gamble of Tallahassee and all his life remained loyal to that family and a friend of many Americans. He knew English and his manners were like the white man's. He treated his wife and children as companions rather than as "beasts of burden and domestics."[5] He was "intelligent, artful and politic" enough to gain the confidence of all the tribes around him. "His conversation was sprightly, at times witty and humorous:" He kept a stick in his girdle which he notched every day to remind him when the Sabbath occurred. On this day, he bathed and dressed in his best and abstained from "amusements and dissipation. . . . In council he was quick and comprehensive, condensing and arranging his ideas with conciseness and judgment." He had acquired the name Tiger Tail at the signing of the Treaty of Camp Moultrie. At the ball game held during the ceremonies, he attached the skin of a tiger to his belt which "hanging down some distance between his legs when running, made an amusing and ridiculous figure."[6] With many of the traditional chiefs dead or in bondage, Tiger Tail would now assume a leadership role among his people.

Chitto-Tustenuggee represented Arpeika (Sam Jones), now old and unwilling to travel. It may have been the wily old chief's fear of putting himself within reach of American generals that made him send an agent to every conference. Chitto-Tustenuggee was "about forty years of age—remarkably pleasant and affable when spoken to, but at other times very dignified and reserved." In his conversation and conduct in and out of council he displayed intelligence and a keen sense of observation. "The Indians paid him great respect and seemed gratified in having so able a counsellor."[7]

At the first conference Halleck-Tustenuggee spoke for the group; he vowed to bring the people to a specified location. Macomb, in turn, promised they would be given clothes, food, and liquor while they waited for the warriors to assemble. About 150 came in to collect what they could from a generous government. The women and children, dressed in garments made from forage bags abandoned by the army, were in pitiful condition.

On 22 May the chiefs, with forty-five Seminole and Mikasuki warriors, met with General Macomb, who welcomed them with a ceremony designed to impress and flatter the Indians.[8] A large chamber had been erected from which white flags flew from tall masts at regular intervals. In the center of the chamber a large fire burned. The Indians sat around it in profound silence. Then the general and his staff appeared, escorted by all the officers and men on the post in full uniform, advancing to the cadence of a military march played by a band of the Seventh Infantry. When all were seated, pipes and tobacco were given to the Indians; then amid a cloud of smoke, the chiefs passed round shaking hands with all present.

General Macomb spoke first. "To your Great Father at Washington his red children are as dear as his white; he loves them both alike; he regrets what has taken place ... Lay down the scalping knife, rifle and tomahawk; go south of Little Pease Creek, and your Great Father will see that you are left tranquil and undisturbed. He will establish neutral ground and shield you from disturbance by the protection of his troops." [9]

What the Indians thought of this fulsome address has not been recorded; they responded in kind. "We are alike desirous of peace; the war has originated from a misunderstanding with our white brethren; we will gladly lay down our rifles, but we want time to gather our crops before crossing the line; we will cease all hostilities and send runners to all our people to let them know the treaty." [10]

The general gave them until 15 July to harvest their crops and assemble within the designated area in which they must remain according to the agreement. The boundary ran from Charlotte Harbor up Pease Creek to Little Pease Creek, then west to the Kissimmee River, down to Lake Okeechobee and from there south to where the Shark River empties into the gulf near Cape Sable. The area from Tampa Bay to Fort Mellon and down the St. Johns to its source was to be neutral ground.

Chitto-Tustenuggee replied that he felt great pleasure at once more being friends with the other inhabitants of Florida; that he and all his people would abide by the stipulations laid down. He promised the most vigorous measures to spread the word of the peace to all the Indians wherever they were and to assemble them within the prescribed area at the date agreed. He asked, however, for assurance that posts be established near the boundaries of their territory to keep whites from intruding on them and to insure a neutral ground where neither Indians nor citizens might enter.

The council broke up after four hours. A newsman reported that "every act and expression on the part of the Indians evinced the utmost sincerity and friendship." He continued, "No deception has been practiced; nothing has been disguised and to Gen. Macomb's candor and frankness, his generous attentions to their wants and wishes, and to his knowledge of their habits and manners, may be attributed his success in the present undertaking." [11] An editorial in the *St Augustine News* for 23 May 1839 commended General

Macomb for doing what Generals Clinch, Scott, Gaines, Call, Jesup, and Taylor had failed to do.[12]

The correspondent who praised Macomb's lack of deceit had been too optimistic for the government never intended the arrangement to be permanent. However, the chiefs never asked a direct question about the length of time involved and the general thought it prudent not to mention the word "temporary." Macomb left Florida convinced he had won the war. From Fort King he issued a statement, "The Major-General, commanding in chief, has the satisfaction of announcing to the army in Florida, to the authorities of the Territory, and the citizens generally, that he has this day terminated the war with the Seminole Indians by an agreement entered into with Chitto-Tustenuggee, principal chief of the Seminoles and successor to Arpeika."[13]

Although the initial press reaction was one of elation that the war was over at last, the citizens were irate because peace had been bought at the price of allowing the Seminoles to remain in Florida where they would always be a threat, treaty or no. The government tried to placate the settlers by pointing out that there had never been any intention of letting the Indians remain permanently on the land ceded to them. The treaty had been a stratagem to make plans for a peaceful emigration. When this news broke, the press and many people around the country were furious at the deceit practiced against the Indians. Amid all the furor, a prominent white man was found murdered and the Indians were blamed. Before the real culprit—another white man—was caught, old passions had been inflamed.[14]

Even so, the Indians, who had gone back to their hummocks to gather their corn, were generally quiet. They seemed satisfied with their land although nearly all of it was completely inundated for most of the year. Nor could the Indians harvest the rich sources of seafood along the coast as their territory had been carefully designed to prevent their access to it.[15]

Taylor, although nominally superseded by Macomb, had remained in Tampa, collecting prisoners while he supervised the clearing of swamps and hummocks around the Istenhachee, the Finihalloaway, and the Econofinny rivers. He sent Colonel Fanning to search and clear the area along the St. Johns River and he dispatched Colonel Davenport to make sure there were no Indians left about the headwaters of the Withlacoochee. He was planning to proceed to the Everglades himself when trouble began.

There were a series of raids on trains and travelers during the month of July; some plantations were overrun. On the twenty-third, a group of Spanish Indians under Chekaika fell upon Colonel William Harney and a party of troops while they slept. They were on their way to Charlotte Harbor to set up a trading post for the Indians. Reassured by the new peace, the soldiers were encamped on the Caloosahatchee River without guards when the attack came just before dawn. Colonel Harney and a few of his men escaped but most of the troops were killed.

The Spanish Indians had lived deep in the peninsula without taking part in the war. They were a mixture of Spanish and Indian who had stayed on, relatively untouched by the activity farther north, until the Seminoles were pushed into their territory. They had not been a party to General Macomb's treaty and felt no obligation to honor it. The Americans apparently didn't know the difference between the Spanish Indians and the others or didn't want to differentiate. When word of the attack reached Lieutenant Hanson at Charlotte Harbor, he was so incensed that he seized forty-six innocent Seminoles who were visiting the post and shipped them forthwith to Arkansas.[16]

Macomb's peace had lasted little more than a month. The Indians had obtained food, clothing, and ammunition and had been given time to harvest much of their corn. Scouting expeditions through the summer and fall of 1839 brought few results; then yellow fever struck, causing havoc in the military ranks. Although soldiers able to perform duties could not find all the Indian fields which were skillfully hidden, they did report that they destroyed fifteen hundred acres of corn and pumpkins and burned hundreds of skimpy shelters. But they could not find the people, much less kill or capture them. The soldiers in their blue and white uniforms were easily seen at a distance while the Indians with their dark skins and dirty clothes could stand stock still in the shrubbery within view of the army without being seen. Taylor reported to his superiors at the end of his campaign: "Could the enemy be brought to battle, even in his strong-holds, the war would soon be closed, no matter at what sacrifice of life on the part of the soldiers. Fortunately for them . . . concealment is found to be more efficacious than opposition, and they leave the climate to fight their battles, which certainly has proven more destructive to our troops than the rifle or scalping knife. . . . Should the war be renewed, (which I sincerely hope may never be the case) the only way to bring it to a successful issue, in my opinion, is to cover the whole country so as to prevent the enemy from hunting and fishing." [17]

General Taylor informed the adjutant general that the enemy could only be starved into submission. The secretary of war warned the president that in the future the subduing of the Seminoles would "require exertions, and probably other than those hitherto tried." Governor Read of Florida, in a speech to an outraged legislative council, expressed the mood of the citizens. "It is high time that sickly sentimentality should cease. 'Lo, the poor Indian!' is the exclamation of the fanatic pseudo-philanthropist; 'Lo, the poor white man!' is the ejaculation which all will utter who have witnessed the human butchery of women and children and the massacres that have drenched this territory in blood." [18]

A lieutenant of the Second Artillery, who wrote anonymously, declared, "Within our limits, there does not live, nor ever has lived, a race of Indians so little entitled to our sympathy or forbearance, as those with whom we war at present." [19]

The citizens were baffled because the Indians could survive in the wilderness and because they could, as General Taylor had reported, let the climate and terrain of Florida do their fighting for them—except for lightning raids at opportune moments. The citizens wanted to get on with their business, unhampered by the troublesome presence of the native peoples. But the Indians wouldn't come out and fight fair in open battles! What were the Americans to do?

The Florida legislature decided to use a method employed in Cuba for tracking slaves. They authorized one Colonel Fitzpatrick to go to Havana and obtain thirty-three bloodhounds, at a price of $151.72, and five Spaniards trained to handle them. This method of finding the enemy had been threatened by General Jesup but he had never used it. When Secretary of War Poinsett approved the plan, he suggested in his gentlemanly way that, perhaps, the dogs should be muzzled before being sent after the hapless Seminoles.

The hounds arrived on 20 December 1839 but, alas, they did not prove to be the ideal solution for ending the Seminole War. Taught to pursue Negroes, they paid no attention at all to the scent of Indians. They apparently failed to scent any of the few remaining black Seminoles either. Giddings suggests that Negro interpreters had warned their brothers in the wilderness to hide deep in the swamps. At any rate, the method of finding the hard core remnant of the Seminoles by tracking them with dogs only succeeded in outraging Americans across the country, "Thus one more sure thing for ending the war in Florida failed." [20]

Suddenly the American nation awoke to the realization that a long, costly, and brutal war had been going on in a remote part of their country. When Mr. Collins failed to collect the Negroes at New Orleans, Mr. Watson introduced a bill into congress asking the federal government to reimburse him for his loss. Joshua R. Giddings, congressman from Ohio, who was asked to support the bill, felt that he needed more knowledge about the circumstances before he cast his vote. The subject had not been discussed on the floor because in 1836 the House of Representatives had adopted a resolution suppressing all discussion of slavery and "all agitation of questions relating to the institution." This resolution prevented open debate of any question dealing with slaves or slavery although there was apparently much negotiation and pressure applied behind the scenes. Giddings was instrumental in putting forth a resolution which was passed on 28 January 1839. It requested the secretary of war to compile a document containing all of the correspondence "respecting the disposition of Negroes and other Property captured from hostile Indians during the present war in Florida." Poinsett duly sent this material to congress where it was labeled House Document Number 225.

From the correspondence therein and other material, it became obvious that the Florida war had not been exclusively an Indian one. Fear of the free Negroes or maroons who lived among the Seminoles had instigated the attacks on the Indians in the first Florida war. Black leaders and warriors had fought as bravely and tenaciously as their Indian brothers until most of them were captured and enslaved or sent West. The refusal of the Indians to give in to demands that they turn over blacks had kept the war going over several dreary, painful, and expensive years.

Gad Humphreys had explained the situation very clearly in a series of letters to his superiors in Tallahassee and Washington as early as 1825. Every military commander in charge of the Florida forces except Andrew Jackson had warned his superiors in the nation's capital that only the thorny question of the disposition of Negroes and the determination of the federal government to relocate the Seminoles in the midst of their slave-hunting enemies, the Creeks, prevented a peaceful emigration of the Florida Indians.

The military leaders in the field and such visitors as the artist, George Catlin, as well as many newspapermen saw the problem but the federal government seemed sadly myopic if not downright blind to the true issues. Part of this was, no doubt, due to the strong pressure from citizens of Florida and the surrounding states and part of it to the fact that such powerful decision makers as Secretary of War J. R. Poinsett and Indian Commissioner C. A. Harris were slave owners or sympathetic towards them.

How many congressmen from nonslave states voted to perpetuate the Florida war out of ignorance of underlying pressures and how many voted to support it in return for help on projects important to their own local regions is debatable but suddenly that body was seized with an attack of moral indignation. It took President Van Buren to task for extravagances in expenditures and for the ineptness of the men he appointed to deal with the problem. Congressman Giddings claimed that "every honorable means was resorted to for the purpose of exposing errors in the administration during the previous four years."[21] It is not improbable that a few dishonorable motives impelled the opposition to take political advantage of a situation that was becoming more and more burdensome to everyone concerned.

The honorable William Jay of New York published a book showing the strong influence of the slave owners in prosecuting a war that was nominally Indian and in prolonging that war by demanding that the Seminoles give up their Negroes to whites on the flimsiest of evidence. General Jesup had separated the hundred blacks which he sent to New Orleans to await deportation from about eighty which he returned to whites by the simple test of language. Those who could not speak the Seminole or Mikasuki language were considered fugitives. Those who could speak only an Indian tongue were considered maroons or Seminoles and those who knew both went with the emigrants. It was a simple and practical test, yet it was seldom allowed as a criteria in disputes over the unfortunate blacks. In spite of investigations, legitimate and spurious claims for missing slaves would continue to be a force in Florida's tribulations.

Typical of the kind of pressures which Jay and Giddings found was a petition sent to Poinsett by a group of South Carolina citizens who had heard that Jesup had achieved a peace treaty. They were upset because they understood that there was no provision in it that the Indians should "make restitution of such stolen, and other property, to wit, negroes as they have now in possession or as has been allowed refuge there from its owners." They declared "that such a termination of the war (anxiously as we desire a return of peace) would be a sacrifice of the national dignity, and an absolute and clear triumph on the part of the Indians." Furthermore, they insisted that to let the Florida Indians leave without demanding such restitution was tantamount to "suing for peace on the part of the United States, and as evidence of a want of confidence in their ability to conclude the war, through the means of their belligerent and physical strength." [22]

Any solution in Florida that did not bring total victory— including deportation of the Indians and enslavement of the blacks was unacceptable to most citizens of Florida and bordering states.

Ironically, although the question of slaves harbored by Seminoles continued to perpetuate the war, it was now, for the most part, no longer relevant. With the emigration of most of the traditional chiefs and their black associates by 1839, Seminole leadership went largely to warriors determined not to leave Florida for any reason. On the other hand, citizens, certain that their lost slaves were being protected by the Indians, refused to believe assertions to the contrary. As in so many conflicts, the emotions lingered on after the problem ceased to exist.

By this time most battles over the fate of Seminole blacks were being fought in Arkansas.[23] Congress may have brought to light the importance of Negroes in the Florida wars but it could not hasten the end of the second one.

# 14

# General W. K. Armistead's
# Campaign, 1840–1841

*Neither the Sword Nor the Olive Branch Brings Peace*

"The white men are as thick as the leaves in the hammock;
they come upon us thicker every year."

CHIEF COACOOCHEE

THE SECRETARY OF WAR, in his annual report at the end of 1838,
announced that a large portion of the national troops had been employed in Florida during the year under the "indefatigable and zealous
officer," General Taylor. He commended the soldiers there for having
displayed a "spirit of enduring courage and perserverance" in the
face of impossible odds where the theater of war was a country of
dense forests, swamps, and morasses and the enemy active, subtle,
cruel, and invisible. However, he concluded, the government had no
alternative. Its obligation to the commerce of the country and to the
citizens of Florida demanded that "the utmost exertions be made to
drive these merciless savages from the country which they have so
cruelly afflicted." He insisted that no pains had been spared to achieve
this end but admitted that no method yet tried had succeeded in
achieving it.[1]

Each year the military units in Florida had swept through the major areas burning fields and villages and driving the Seminole allies before them. Each year they had drifted back, rebuilt their huts, and planted well-hidden fields. And each year, when the army was debilitated by fever and the heat of summer, they had come out to attack the settlements.

Of the more than two thousand Seminole allies now in the West, the majority had surrendered or been captured during negotiations rather than in battle. Those now remaining seemed unwilling to talk and too wary of being seized to come near the forts. Taylor's plan to cover the entire territory with a grid of garrisons in small forts was now abandoned although much of the territory had been cleared and made accessible by that effort. It had not, however, won the war. Even bloodhounds had failed to gather in the "intractables."

Yet Secretary Poinsett was not ready to throw in the towel; he had a plan. He suggested that one reason the Indians had managed to remain in control of so much territory was that after the attacks in 1835, the settlers had fled their plantations to hide in the few major towns and forts. He argued that if all had been forced to remain on their plantations and to protect them, the Indians would not have continued to raid, with impunity, those who stayed.[2]

In fact, many such refugees were still waiting near forts and towns for the war to be over, asking sustenance from the government meanwhile. Back in 1837, Poinsett had written Jesup that the object of Congress had been to, "succour the immediate wants of a people who had been suddenly driven from their homes and deprived of the means of supporting themselves, not to continue during the whole war to maintain them gratuitously, thereby withdrawing all motive for exertion on the part of those who might otherwise find means to maintain themselves." He had ordered that all rationing to Florida citizens cease—especially the use of army provisions to feed civilians who were contributing nothing to the war effort.[3] Now three years later, displaced citizens continued to drain military resources.

To encourage planters back to their lands as well as to win the war, Poinsett proposed a plan which Senator Thomas H. Benton introduced to Congress in 1839. It provided that every able-bodied man who promised to till the land and to defend it against the Indians would receive 320 acres in an area east of the Suwanee and south to Cape Sable. In return for this holding, the settler would be expected to help build a blockhouse and stockades within his district. Military protection would be available for all as well as rations of bread, meat, salt, and ammunition for those who ventured south of the With-

lacoochee. Each man must take land in the district he settled. He
would receive title to it as soon as he had fulfilled his obligations and
would pay no taxes until one year after his patent was granted.[4]

Congress debated the issue in 1840 but did not pass the bill. It
was opposed by those who feared a policy which encouraged planters
to bring slaves too close to the Seminole allies. One spokesman urged
that General Taylor or Clinch be given ten thousand troops to cover
the territory with a "military net" before the settlement project even
be considered.[5] In any event the government decided that the war
must go on.

On 1 May 1840, Brigadier General W. K. Armistead took over
the command in Florida. Walker Keith Armistead was born in Virginia around 1785; he graduated at the top of the second class at
West Point in 1803. He was an engineer who served in the War of
1812. In 1831 he was breveted a brigadier general after ten years as
a colonel in the Third Artillery. In Florida, he had under him 3,403
enlisted troops and 241 officers (of this force 564 were reported ill),
supported by a militia of 1,000 mounted and 500 foot soldiers under
Brigadier General Leigh Read of Tallahassee.[6] In retrospect this seems
an enormous number of troops to pursue an enemy now reduced to
less than a thousand, including women and children.

Throughout June, Armistead had units in the field. Lieutenant
Colonel Bennett Riley, Second Infantry, pushed into Big Hammock
where he found and destroyed a Seminole stronghold at Chacochatti.
Captain B. L. E. Bonneville, Seventh Infantry, interrupted nearly
one hundred Indians attempting to hold their Green Corn Dance in
Big Swamp just outside Fort King. Captain Beall, patrolling the
area between Forts Cross and Drane, destroyed a camp and took nine
prisoners at Annutiliga Hummock but insisted a large number had
been hiding there.[7] In spite of annual campaigns, the Seminole allies
were still in many of their old haunts.

Armistead, who had served under Jesup and Taylor earlier in
the war, knew how futile battles were and hoped to talk the allies
into emigrating. He had to succeed through bargaining because the
weather had made field campaigns impossible. After years of drought,
the rains had come; they had fallen through June, July, and August,
leaving the country "nearly covered with water." Swamps and hammocks were flooded and streams swollen. To mount a fall campaign
in such terrain seemed hopeless for it would prohibit movement of
men, horses, or supplies and bring sickness to the troops.

In spite of adverse conditions, Armistead kept small scouting parties in the field; they went in search of the enemy and occasionally found them. Usually the warriors escaped but they often lost their gear, rifles, and even horses in the process.

Early in October, General Armistead sent Major Greenleaf Dearborn out to Annutiliga Hummock to break up camps and capture any allies he could find. On the seventh, he met an old woman carrying sixteen sticks to signify that in so many days Halleck-Tustenuggee would come in for a talk. Dearborn relayed message to Armistead who ordered him to cease operations and await the chief.

On the twenty-third, Armistead met with Halleck-Tustenuggee and Thlocko-Tustenuggee (Tiger Tail). Although he could give them no alternative but to emigrate, he offered them and Arpeika each five thousand dollars if they agreed to go. The chiefs replied that they did not want to leave a country so well suited to their needs for an unknown one but they promised to gather their people and meet him at Fort King in fourteen days.

Armistead returned to the fort at once to plan for the meeting. He wrote Poinsett for permission to allow the Seminole allies to remain on the land ceded them by General Macomb and reported his offer of money to the chiefs. He suggested disbanding the militia which would not be needed if peace were achieved.[8]

In November, he received a reply from Poinsett which spelled out the policy he was to follow. The secretary denied the request to permit the Indians to remain on a small parcel of land south of Pease Creek. "After mature deliberation it appears to me that the President has no right to give any portion of the territory of Florida to the Indians. By a treaty made with them and ratified by the Senate, [in 1834] they ceded their lands for a valuable consideration to the Government, and this Department cannot sanction any arrangement which, in the contravention of the treaty, would retrocede any portion of that purchase." He admonished Armistead not to allow negotiations with two chiefs to interrupt hostilities against other bands. He suggested, in fact, that the probable success of the general's pacific policy would depend upon the vigor of his operations in the field. He approved indirectly of any money gifts Armistead might offer. "In negotiating with these Chiefs you will use your utmost endeavors to persuade them to emigrate, and you may offer what you may believe to be suitable inducements: for I do not entertain a doubt of the favorable action of Congress on an application to redeem a pledge given by the Executive under such circumstances."[9]

While Armistead waited for the chiefs to come in, he sent Major Dearborn on a scouting mission down the peninsula. He was to examine the territory between Pease Creek and Tampa Bay, breaking up any camps he found. He was to continue south as far as he could and return by boat, stopping at likely places to send search parties inland to look for signs of habitation.

That fall Captain John Page, who had escorted several parties of the southern tribes to the West, brought back a delegation of Seminole chiefs and warriors to urge their brothers to join them. The party arrived early in November. On 7 November, Armistead, with a retinue of aides, interpreters and troops met the Arkansas delegation at a spot outside Fort King. Here they awaited word from the hostiles. Almost immediately some Indians came in to say that the chiefs were ready to talk.

The warriors who arrived shortly thereafter were well dressed in deerskins or calico shirts and cloth leggings. The meetings took place in a beautiful wooded area with the negotiators seated on the ground or on fallen logs. Everyone ate, drank, and talked but the atmosphere was uneasy. Holartoochee, speaking for the emigrants, urged that all the Seminoles unite in the West. His reception was polite but cool. Remembering other white flag encounters, the hostiles kept their loaded guns nearby. Although the talks continued, everyone was wary and suspicious.

On the night of 14 November there was a state dinner. Halleck-Tustenuggee appeared in a headdress of long, black ostrich feathers. He was accompanied by a retinue who waited on him hand and foot. He was ready to talk about staying in Florida or leaving for a price but General Armistead, forbidden to give them land in Florida, offered the chief a treaty based on the government policy of immediate emigration to lands in Creek territory. Late that night the Indians disappeared into the wilderness leaving the general "subdued and broken-spirited." He sent troops after them but his men found not a single track.

Armistead's aide, Major Ethan Allen Hitchcock, had urged his superior to offer money, guns and ammunition, blankets, shirts, and cloth amounting to about twenty-one thousand dollars for each band that agreed to emigrate as it would be much cheaper than continuing the war. He asserted in his diary that the reason Halleck-Tustenuggee took his warriors and departed was that, even as Armistead was talking peace, he had Major Dearborn in the field and his refusal to offer the carrot instead of the stick brought about the defection of the Indians.[10]

John Page agreed with Hitchcock. He complained to the commissioner of Indian affairs that troops in the field—although not in the immediate area—had frightened the Indians. He was dismayed because Armistead had sworn to respect the white flag wherever he saw it but two days after Halleck-Tustenuggee and his warriors departed, the general issued orders to ignore all flags of truce and seize any Indian who appeared within reach.[11]

If Hitchcock and Page condemned the general for being too harsh, an officer under his command scored him for his credulity.

> One hundred and thirty warriors assembled in the neighborhood of Fort King and having feasted upon Uncle Sam's rations and amused our Governors with tales as smooth as those that fall from ladies' lips, they took to the hummocks one fair night without even so much as bidding the General farewell. You may cry peace! peace! but there is no peace; and so long as Government compels us to respect the delusive white flag (under whose folds the most shocking murders have been committed) and extend the usages of civilized warfare to these scoundrels, just so long will we continue to hear the cracks of the rifle and witness the bloody effects of the gleaming scalping knife.[12]

When he was convinced that the Indians were out of his reach, General Armistead called his chief interpreter, the Negro Primus, in for an explanation. Primus apparently "freed his mind, respectfully, but very plainly," on "the policy of sending troops into the swamps to kill the Indians while pretending to desire peace and trying to persuade them to emigrate." He noted the contradiction between the white man's words and deeds and insisted that the Indians would be perfectly satisfied with the country below Tampa.[13]

The general could do nothing about Poinsett's insistence that every Florida Indian must emigrate but he withdrew Major Dearborn. In disgust, Hitchcock wrote in his journal, "The General holds the olive branch in one hand and sword in the other and attempts to use both at the same time." He continued: "Our policy now is to ask the Indians in, assuring them that we are good friends (the evidence of which it is difficult to make them see), and finally to buy them with about ten times the money that would have purchased the whole tribe at the beginning of intercourse with them, before we had outraged them by injury, fraud, and oppression. We can do more with silver than with lead, and yet save silver in the end." [14]

The next day Armistead issued an angry edict sending the Second Dragoons to search the area around the Ocklawaha River, and destroy the enemy there, another detachment to scour the southern banks of the Withlacoochee and a third to cover Wacasassa country. He ordered that all wagon trains be escorted by at least thirty troops wherever they moved and that any enemy appearing with a white flag be taken prisoner at once.

In a few days reports began to come in from the field. The general learned that there were no Indians along the Ocklawaha, none in Wacasassa country, and none around Lake Tohopkoliga. Of all the commanders in the field, only Colonel Harney who had taken his troops into the Everglades had met the enemy. He had moved up the Miami River to Shark River and thence to Cape Sable. He reported that in "various skirmishes" he had killed four warriors and captured six others along with thirty women and children. One of his own men had been killed and six wounded, including his Negro guide. [15] The evidence was clear; the Seminole allies were now in the Everglades. To reach them, the army would have to go there too.

Meanwhile, the navy was working on a plan for winning the war. In 1837, Lieutenant Levin Powell had operated a fleet of small boats under General Jesup with the purpose of putting pressure on the allies from the south as the army pushed them from the north. Although their campaign had borne little fruit, the effort had given the Americans some knowledge of the Everglades where, they assumed, the enemy would finally congregate. [16]

In January 1840, Lieutenant John T. McLaughlin obtained permission to set up an operation similar to Powell's. He had three ships, the *Flirt*, the *Wave*, and the *Otsego* which operated out of Tea Table Key. Here he trained sailors in the use of small arms, boats, and canoes in preparation for an assault on the Everglades. He had a set of navy signal books in order to communicate with other naval forces but his was essentially an army operation under army control. For the first time, all the naval units in Florida were under one commander, Lieutenant McLaughlin, and his task force would be known as the Mosquito Fleet. [17]

By April McLaughlin was ready to draw his net around and over the lower peninsula. As the *Otsego* patrolled the west, the *Wave* cruised up and down the east coast. The *Flirt* covered the center position while a fleet of barges, under Passed Midshipman Montgomery Lewis, USN, crept in and out of the keys and islands between the reef and the mainland. On the tenth, his entire force rendezvoused at Cape Sable. While the large ships kept their watch along the coast, McLaughlin hoped to enter Florida by river from the west and be the first white man to cross the peninsula and emerge on the east coast.

The Seminole allies must have recognized McLaughlin's activity as a serious threat. When a party from the *Otsego* went ashore to examine the coast, they were attacked by fifty to eighty warriors. The sailors and marines returned fire until supported by reinforcements from nearby ships in a battle that lasted two and a half hours. Americans saw the Indians carry away two or three fallen comrades but sustained no losses themselves.

Though the Mosquito Fleet could cope with angry warriors, it was more vulnerable to tropical disease. A fever broke out among the men which so enfeebled them that McLaughlin had to abandon his plan to cross the peninsula. With those of his crew who were not ill, he kept exploring and charting the western portion of the Everglades. Since mangrove forests hid the true coastline, his men were forced to enter each break in order to map it. They covered much of Big Cypress which was thirty miles from north to south and fifty from east to west. Within that area the vegetation was so dense that the sun's rays rarely penetrated the earth's surface. Slime on the water and toxic vapors in the air made the men retch. But in spite of the difficulties, the crews of the Mosquito Fleet developed the skills necessary to travel in this inhospitable country. By the end of the summer they had mapped half of the western side of the swamp but had rarely encountered the enemy.

At this time John, Negro slave of Dr. Henry B. Crew, a customs officer slain by the Indians early in the second war, escaped from his captors and offered to lead the army to the Seminoles. Instead he was imprisoned and ignored. When McLaughlin heard about this, he requested that John be released and appointed a guide to help him seek out Chekaika's village. His request was denied.

McLaughlin continued his explorations, following the Miami River into some new territory but with temperatures as high as 120°F. in the daytime and his men forced to sleep on the thwarts of their boats at night, he could not sustain his drive for long. He returned to Cape Sable and began arrangements in August to enter the Everglades

from the west again. Short of men as always in the hot season, he sent
Lieutenant John Rodgers in the *Wave* to Camp Romano to pick up
all the able-bodies men in the hospital at Tea Table Key. Lieutenant
Edmund Shubrick followed in the *Otsego* a few days later, hoping to
spot some Indians along the shore. Rodgers assembled a crew from
the hospital, leaving only Midshipman Francis K. Murray and five
enlisted men to look after all the invalids in the hospital.

If the men in the Mosquito Fleet saw no Indians on their patrols,
they must have been closely watched by the enemy. No sooner had
the *Wave* departed than Chekaika attacked Indian Key, only a mile
from the hospital. He brought his warriors across thirty miles of
water in twenty-eight canoes. They beached them on the shore in
the dead of night and crept silently into the settlement. When the
alarm sounded, the citizens fled toward a schooner which lay at anchor
in the harbor. Thirteen never reached safety; among the dead was
Dr. Henry Perrine, a physician and botanist of high repute.

Midshipman Murray heard the news at daybreak. He took two
four-pounders, mounted them on carriages for six-pounders, and
placed them on barges. He mustered a crew of twelve able-bodied
sailors and seven volunteers from among the ambulatory patients.
Then, rigging his guns to the thwarts of his boats so that the muzzles
cleared the gunwales, he set out to the rescue. He hoped to destroy
Chekaika's canoes and thus his means of transportation. Before
Murray reached the key, Chekaika saw his little fleet approach and
turned the settlement's six-pounder, loaded with musket shot, on
the advancing naval force. Murray returned the fire from his makeshift guns but at the end of the third discharge, they recoiled and
fell overboard. He decided to return to Tea Table Key to protect
the hospital.

The Indians loaded all of their own boats and six taken from the
settlement and left with a large supply of provisions about two o'clock
in the afternoon. A helpless Murray counted 4 to 8 men in each
canoe—between 130 and 140 warriors—glide back to the mainland
with their booty.

McLaughlin received a message from Murray at Key Biscayne
the following day and hurried to the scene. He found only plundered
storehouses and a burned settlement. Rodgers, who was anchored
off Cape Romano, heard the attack but high seas kept him from
leaving until the next morning. They arrived too late to help.

Chekaika had led his warriors across thirty miles of open sea to
make a successful amphibious assault under cover of night. When

threatened by Murray's force, he had turned a piece of captured artillery on the approaching seamen. He had escaped laden with badly needed provisions. His raid was reminiscent of Osceola's brilliant attacks in 1835. This daring exploit might have been prevented had McLaughlin been given access to the knowledge possessed by the Negro, John, who was being kept in irons in Fort Dallas by Colonel David E. Twiggs for the crime of escaping from his Indian captors and offering to help the army find them.

McLaughlin was having other troubles with the government over Negroes, for many of his crews were free men of that race. While anchored at Key West in July, three blacks had gone ashore on ship's business. A local sheriff had arrested them under a territorial act passed in 1832 to prevent migration of free Negroes in Florida. McLaughlin was forced to go to court to obtain the release of his men but the Negroes were ordered to pay court costs although they had been arrested illegally! McLaughlin's repeated appeals to Washington for support in protecting his men yielded him nothing except warnings to be very cautious about letting blacks go ashore. Since all the sailors on the *Flirt* and several of the other crews as well were Negroes, this caused extreme hardship to his fleet.[18] In spite of such personnel difficulties, low complements due to illness, lack of equipment, and oppressive heat in steamy swamps, the Mosquito Fleet carried on.

What McLaughlin had failed to do, Colonel William Harney achieved. In December 1840, he prevailed on the commanding general to release John to act as his guide in an expedition against Chekaika. He borrowed sixteen canoes from the Mosquito Fleet in which to transport ninety men to the chief's hideout which was so deep in the Everglades the Indians felt no white man could ever penetrate it.

Harney violated General Armistead's ban on patrols dressing like Indians. His men, painted and garbed as Seminoles, now wise in the ways of the swamps, crept up on the camp and surrounded it before anyone realized what had happened. Four warriors were killed and six others seized along with thirty women and children. Harney, who meant to have revenge for his men killed on the Caloosahatchee, hanged the chief and four warriors from the tops of tall trees. Sprague reported, ". . . with sullen indifference they awaited their fate, asked for no mercy, but manifested, to the last moment, bitter contempt and malignity towards the white men."

A large amount of clothing, hardware, ammunition, and provisions identified as property taken from Indian Key in August was found in the camp. Colonel Harney left his victims swaying slowly in the wind but Arpeika found them a few days later and buried them.[19]

Impressed by his success against Chekaika, Harney arranged a joint effort with the Mosquito Fleet to go after Arpeika's camp. With the *Wave* cruising off Cape Romano, the *Otsego* near Cape Sable, and the *Flirt* patrolling along the reef to the east, he and McLaughlin left Fort Dallas on 31 December 1840 with ninety sailors, sixty marines, and twenty dragoons. Except for a few large boats which held ten men, most of the group traveled in small five-man canoes. They moved in single file about twenty paces apart, maintaining absolute silence so that whistled orders could be heard and acted upon. Each man carried rations for twenty days and ammunition with instructions to keep his musket by the thwarts, ready for action at a moment's notice. Moving only after dark to avoid detection, the force reached Chitto-Tustenuggee's camp after three nights of grueling labor only to find it deserted. The Indians had observed them in time to elude capture.

McLaughlin led a search party to a nearby island where he captured the wife of Chia and then, finally, the man himself. He now added to his staff one of the most renowned guides of the Everglades. It already contained John and Micco, a chief who had been captured in Chekaika's village. However, the search for Arepeika's village ended in failure.

McLaughlin and his men pressed on until they emerged on the west coast on 19 January 1841, thus achieving their aim to be the first white men ever to cross the Florida peninsula through the Everglades.

Later McLaughlin visited Washington to present a chart of the Everglades showing a route of nearly five thousand miles over which his canoes had pushed through the swamps and rivers. He insisted to the secretary of the navy that, with sufficient men and his own guides, he could bring the war to the Seminoles wherever they were.[20] The Mosquito Fleet had not yet come to grips with the enemy but they felt that they had the means by which to do so.

Meanwhile, on 28 December, the Indians attacked a party escorting an army officer's wife from Fort Micanopy to Watkahoota. They killed her and Lieutenant Sherwood, who was in charge of the party, and all but one of the soldiers. Halleck-Tustenuggee and Coosa-Tustenuggee were held responsible. Coosa surrendered himself and his band of thirty-two warriors and sixty women and children. He and his men accepted amnesty for their depredations and generous cash payments to leave. They embarked for Arkansas on 20 June of the following year but Halleck-Tustenuggee continued to resist.

As the year 1841 dawned, the American government was angry. Washington abandoned plans to achieve emigration by negotiation and ordered the army to "prosecute the war with vigor." Congress appropriated $100,000 in January to finance removal and $1,061,816 in March to "suppress hostilities."

As winter was the time to find Indian fields and destroy crops, the army set to work on this task. Some natives surrendered, a few were captured, but "the most zealous and intelligent, believing in the sacredness of the soil, as an inheritance from their forefathers, and reverencing with idolatrous fanaticism the graves of their men, women and children, whose spirits they believed hovered around them in their festivals," refused any contact with whites and threatened reprisals against any who dared even listen to proposals of peace and emigration.[21]

Although Captain Page's Arkansas delegation was in the field trying to persuade small bands to come in, they feared for their lives from two directions. The chiefs expected last-ditch warriors to attack them for urging emigration. They knew they were in danger from army units in the field who refused to withdraw while the delegation bargained. In January, Page wrote an angry letter to the Indian commissioner complaining that each time he and the Arkansas Seminoles convinced a band to come in, a scouting party would appear to capture or scatter them. In either case, all the hard work of bringing a group in peaceably had to be done over.[22]

If the American policy vacillated between armed confrontation and negotiation, so did that of the Seminole allies. After the attack on Indian Key and the resulting retaliation against Chekaika, the Indians decided to divert attention from the Everglades. Thlocko-Tustenuggee (Tiger Tail) hurried to Sarasota to talk peace. For twenty days he moved back and forth between the fort and his people. After collecting provisions for the women and children and arms and ammunition for his warriors, he and his people disappeared deep into the swamps. They hoped they were safe.

Operating in swamps as never before, the army still pursued the Seminole allies in vain. Sprague describes vividly the hide-and-seek game played between the United States Army and the Florida Indians.

Marches of weeks and months, through deep sand and muddy water, burdened with knapsacks and musket, exposed to a vertical sun and drenching rains, brought the troops no nearer the enemy, who with his rifle and few companions, watched their weary progress from day to day, intercepting detachments at every point, with a fleetness unexampled, eluding and misleading by their intimate knowledge of the country. . . . Disregarding the dictates of humanity, the Indian mother has been known to leave her infant by the wayside, lest the burden might impede her flight. If a sound was heard in the neighborhood of their secluded camps, to which they were not accustomed, the cracking of a bush, or the ill-omened croaking of an owl, a move was immediately made to a more retired spot.[23]

The weary soldier, plodding through deep sand and muddy water in pursuit of an elusive enemy arouses pity as does the even wearier mother who leaves her infant to be found by the army in order to stay and fight with her husband. Even then the American army had no doubt acquired a reputation for being kind to pets and babies in the midst of the most brutal wars. There are no statistics on illness and death among the Indians in the wild, although they quickly succumbed to disease and infection in prison or aboard their refugee ships or camps. The soldiers, on the other hand, were susceptible to the organisms in the stagnant pools from which they were forced to drink. Dysentary was the scourge of the Florida troops.

Sprague, the soldier, claimed that the men wanted to fight and win the war, but when they were in good health and had enough provisions and medical supplies on hand, word would come down that the unit must stay in camp for the movement of troops might scare the Indians and make them distrust peace offerings. Sprague was as upset as Hitchcock by the vacillation of the leadership between fits and starts of fighting and negotiation.

Hitchcock described the war in Florida as made up of periods of intense hardship and activity interspersed with long periods of waiting: ". . . the fact is that here, except when actually engaged in councils or conflicts with the Indians, we are sitting still in camp, waiting events, and every day is as quiet as the sabbath."[24]

Hitchcock managed to survive both the tribulations and the periods of inactivity very well. He always carried a small library with him and arrived in Tampa Bay in 1840 after weeks on board a ship with a notebook containing fifty pages of closely written comments on Kant's *Critique of Pure Reason*. Yet he confided to a correspondent, the Reverend W. C. Elliot, "This service is harder on me than on most others, for I know the cruel wrongs to which the enemy has been subjected, so I cannot help wishing that the right may prevail, which is, to use your own language, 'praying for the Indians.'" If many troops felt sympathy for the enemy, they also wanted to win the war and be done with it. They had moments of rage when a war party struck viciously at some innocent victim or a band slipped back to the wilderness after enjoying government rations on the pretext of agreeing to emigrate.

Sometimes the results were both tragic and comic. Coacoochee had attacked a theatrical party near St. Augustine and had killed some of the actors. After stealing the costumes and props, he had fled to Big Cypress Swamp to hide until the furor over his action had died down. In the meantime, his daughter had been captured in a skirmish near Fort Mellon. General Armistead determined to use the child to bring Coacoochee in to emigrate. A friend, Micco, was sent into the swamp with a white flag, a bottle of whisky, pipes, and tobacco. Micco came back a week later saying that Coacoochee would be in to talk peace. He carried eight sticks indicating the number of days until the chief should arrive.

Coacoochee had walked into the jaws of the tiger when he came to talk to General Jesup about his father; now he was going to do the same thing to secure the freedom of his little daughter. He had ridden a spirited horse through the streets of St. Augustine in September 1837, dressed in the colorful garb of a Seminole chief. On 5 March 1841, he approached Colonel W. J. Worth, one of Armistead's aides, in even more startling finery. Coacoochee wore the "nodding plumes, sock and busk" of Hamlet. The seven warriors who accompanied him were variously got up—one in the "simple garb" of Horatio, another in the royal purple and ermine of Richard III, others were decked out in spangles, crimson vests, and feathers. Coacoochee walked solemnly up to Colonel Worth and shook his hand. No one laughed. "His speech was modest. . . . His youth [He was about twenty-nine], his manly bearing, his intelligent face, the calm subdued intonations of his voice, his fluent speech and graceful gestures, won the sympathy of those around, and commanded the respect and attention of all."

Suddenly his little girl broke loose from the tent in which she was being held until the time to present her. She ran to her father with a handful of treasures she had gathered as a present—musket balls and powder with pieces of cartridges which she had picked up around camp and hid in anticipation of his arrival. When she proffered him her gifts, Coacoochee wept. So did some of the soldiers looking on. Sprague added that the scene was especially moving because "tears seldom give utterance to the impulse of an Indian's heart."

When Coacoochee had recovered from the emotion of seeing his daughter safe, he made one of the speeches that will stand with many others in the great literature of Indian oratory.

> The whites dealt unjustly by me. I came to them, they deceived me; the land I was upon I loved, my body is made of its sands; the Great Spirit gave me legs to walk over it; hands to aid myself; eyes to see its ponds, rivers, forests, and game; then a head with which to think. The sun, which is warm and bright as my feelings are now, shines to warm us and bring forth our crops, and the moon brings back the spirit of our warriors, our fathers, wives, and children. The white man comes; he grows pale and sick, why cannot we live here in peace? I have said I am the enemy of the white man. I could live in peace with him, but they first steal our cattle and horses, cheat us, and take our lands. The white men are as thick as the leaves in the hammock; they come up on us thicker every year. They may shoot us, drive our women and children all night and day; they may chain our hands and feet, but the red man's heart will always be free. I have come here in peace, and have taken you all by the hand; I will sleep in your camp though your soldiers stand around me like the pines. I am done; when we know each other better, I will say more.[25]

Coacoochee remained in camp four days before he was allowed to leave with his daughter and his companions. He returned ten days later to say that he would not be able to assemble his band until after the Green Corn Dance in June. On 22 March he again assured General Armistead that he was trying to gather his band. Military operations were suspended to help this effort.

Major Hitchcock was present during the encounter. Later he talked quietly with the chief who said that he had given up the war, knowing it could not last forever and that if it had to end some time, that time had now come. He was worried that his people would not accept the good faith of the army and he felt he needed time to convince them that the time had come to emigrate.

Then Colonel Worth came in and took over the interview. He

bullied Coacoochee, accusing him of deception. The chief answered the tirade with the remark that "The Colonel talks like an old woman." Worth, who was apparently nonplussed by the warm relationship he felt between Hitchcock and Coacoochee, said wryly, "I believe I shall have to hand him over to you. Major . . . you have completely won his heart!" Shortly after that Coacoochee came over, laid his hand on the major's shoulder and called him his brother.

After dinner Coacoochee and Hitchcock talked some more. The chief said that if he had half as many people as the whites he would "sweep the palefaces from the face of the earth!" and then apologized for his outburst. He went on in a sadder vein to ask why the white people would not be satisfied with coming into Florida and occupying "all the good places" and letting the Indians have all the "bad places." [26]

After the chief had returned to his people, General Armistead wrote to the adjutant general, "Coacoochee has ever proven himself an awful and designing enemy and my present determination would be to detain him as a prisoner," but such an act might prevent others from coming in.[27] Armistead knew his opponent and understood his influence over the Indians remaining in Florida.

Coacoochee did not lack courage nor was he a fool. It is difficult to determine why he appeared before the military powers dressed in Shakespearian costume. Was it an act of defiance, calling attention to a successful raid against the enemy or was it a bit of sly humor to appear decked out in white men's finery? Whatever the reason for the gay apparel, it masked a serious purpose.

During March 1841, 220 Tallahassee Indians and 6 Negroes were taken from Tampa Bay by way of New Orleans to Arkansas. Two hundred and five survived the trip. Another party of 200 left in May. This group was to be vaccinated and allowed to see the city of New Orleans before setting off up the Mississippi but the agent in charge discovered that "a sett of loafers from Georgia looking for negroes they pretend to claim" were lurking about the city. He reported "they have no more legal claim than I have" and kept the emigrants confined until he could get them out of the city.[28]

Meanwhile, Halleck-Tustenuggee and other chiefs were drawing supplies at Fort King while assuring the army that they were collecting their bands. When their demands increased, officials grew suspicious and refused any more provisions. That was the end of the peace talks. "Halleck returned to the hummocks, leaving in his trail sixty sticks, designating the number of his warriors, painted with blood; and cut upon the pine trees, rude characters representing the white man in conflict with the Indian in which the latter was victorious."

The overtaxed soldier watched such acts of defiance with despair. Coacoochee came often during the spring months with many warriors who collected provisions and whisky. He insisted he was trying to collect his people but they were frightened by the movement of troops and prone to disperse and hide. When he asked for large supplies to hold a council to induce Holatter Micco (Billy Bowlegs), Arpeika, and Hospetarke to bring their people in, he was given what he asked for but angry officers doubted his good faith. Armistead ordered him seized when next he appeared.[29]

In May 1841, Armistead's patience with Coacoochee was wearing thin. He sent word to bring him in. Major Thomas Childs sent Lieutenant William Tecumseh Sherman with eight or ten mounted men and a Negro interpreter to meet the chief. Coacoochee, with a dozen warriors, came to the fort to talk. Dressed in his best finery, he entered the citadel and assured the officers there that he was tired, wanted to give up, and would bring his people in if he could have a month to assemble them. The chief then proceeded to get "gloriously drunk." He left a few days later but kept sending for whisky and provisions. By the end of the month he was no nearer ready to leave. Either whisky dulled his perceptions or he over-estimated the patience of the Americans. The next time he came in, Sherman invited him to his private quarters for some special brandy and clapped him in irons as his troops rounded up the warriors and shipped them all to Arkansas.[30]

Discouraged because he had collected only 450 Indians (120 warriors) for emigration, Armistead again brought some chiefs from Arkansas to talk to their brothers in Florida. Alligator, Hotulke Emathla, and Waxi Emathla were in the second delegation. When they described the cold and dreary climate, the lack of game, the poor land, and the sickness besetting the emigrants in their new land, those still in Florida could not imagine exchanging what they had for what they would obtain if they moved. Here they had only one worry—to keep out of the hands of the whites. Sprague wrote bitterly, " . . . Had the enemy been kept totally ignorant of the country alloted them, better results might have been anticipated; but what they gathered from the honest confessions and silence of their brothers tended to make them venerate with more fidelity and increased love, the soil which they had defended with heroic fortitude for five consecutive years."

The Seminoles had fulfilled Osceola's prophecy that they would fight for five years. Sprague saw the Indians clinging to their institutions as an inheritance from their fathers, "... inculcated from youth and cherished with untiring assiduity in manhood." He deplored their fate but saw it before them and around them. "The plough-share and the pruning-hook follow closely upon their retiring steps; the busy hum of industry reveals their destiny, and drowns the discordant revels of the Indians camp.... " He looked into the future and predicted that "we cannot shake off the responsibility and remorse which will, in all future time, be identified with the fate of the red man."[31]

# 15

# Colonel W. J. Worth's
# Campaign, 1841

## *Coacoochee Meets Defeat with Dignity*

"They laid their manacled hands upon their knees and hung
their heads in silence."

LIEUTENANT JOHN T. SPRAGUE

IN MAY 1841, GENERAL ARMISTEAD was relieved of his duties in
Florida and Colonel W. J. Worth, who had been in charge of the
Eighth Infantry, was given command with the admonition "to
terminate as speedily as possible the protracted hostilities in Florida."
General Armistead left without claiming he had won the war. He
was not a man to imprint his personality on a given situation but his
successor was an entirely different sort of person. Worth's experience,
both in fighting and negotiating with the Seminole remnant, had
made him deeply aware of the problems he was inheriting. He was
decisive, aggressive, even ruthless in his methods. He would, indeed,
prosecute the war with vigor.

Williams Jenkins Worth was born in New York on 1 March
1794 of Quaker parents. He was in the mercantile business until the
War of 1812 when he applied for a commission and was made a
lieutenant in 1813. A protégé of Winfield Scott, he fought with him

at Chippewa, Lundy's Land, and Niagara. Although he was so seriously wounded at Lundy's Land that he was confined to bed for a year and permanently crippled, he remained in the army. He was breveted to captain after Chippewa, to major for Niagara, and to lieutenant colonel for ten years service. Breveted at last in Florida to brigadier general by President Tyler, he would fight valiantly in the Mexican War to earn the rank of brevet major general. Off the battlefield he was narrow, self-centered, acrimonious, and vindictive but in military action few surpassed him. His "proud, resolute, commanding mein under fire and promptness in decision on the field" gave those under him great confidence in his leadership. He died at the age of fifty-five of cholera in Texas amid bitter quarrels with old friends.[1]

In the summer of 1841, Colonel Worth assessed the situation. First there was the enemy. Chekaika and his lieutenants were dead, Coacoochee captured, and Arpeika senile. Who was left? Halleck-Tustenuggee, a savage, fearless Mikasuki and an indomitable leader, roamed from St. Augustine as far southwest as Fort King. Indians hiding in the Okefenokee and in other swamps along the Withlacoochee, Suwanee, Wacasassa, and other rivers, were coming out to prey on citizens. Waxi Hadjo had been waylaying the express from Fort Cross to Tampa Bay for months. Holatter Micco (Billy Bowlegs), Hotulke-Thlocko (the Prophet), and Hospetarke (Shiver and Shakes) headed an "active and vindictive" band which operated south of Pease Creek from Big Cypress to the Everglades.

Arpeika had a large number of women and children but only 17 warriors. Although the Prophet had only 38 fighting men, he wielded power way beyond military means by his incantations to harm those who chose to emigrate. Hospetarke, with a group of five other chiefs, called the Prophet a coward but followed him. He had a fighting force of 160 men who lived in the Everglades. Many of his warriors must have joined in Chekaika's raid.

Their families survived in the center of a swamp where they planted crops on a few ridges or islands. Everywhere else water, covered with slime and giving off noxious fumes, covered the land from six inches to two feet deep year-round. Although snakes and alligators abounded, the Seminole allies had perfected antidotes so effective that they had no problems with the former and were known to dine off both species. They had apparently come to terms with the fetid water as well for they navigated the Everglades from coast to coast without suffering as the Americans did.

Although most of the enemy had fled to the inaccessible swamps, it appeared that during the year the allies had returned again to many of their old haunts. Pascofa had forty warriors, some Creeks who had been brought down by the army to fight the Seminoles in 1836 and had defected to the enemy; they "infested" the country around Tallahassee for fifty miles. After a raid, they would retreat safely to their base on the Ocklockonee River. There was also a band of white men who robbed and murdered disguised as Indians. Thus the citizens felt threatened even in the shadow of the capital.

That summer there were 47,000 square miles in the hands of "an enemy revengeful, treacherous and subtle, striving for soil made sacred to them. . . . Every hummock and swamp was citadel to them; regardless of food or climate, they moved in groups of five or ten with ease, while the soldier dependent upon supplies, sinking under the tropical sun, could only hear of his foe by depredations committed in the section of the country over which he had scouted the day before." [2]

In accepting command of the Florida forces, Worth wrote to Adjutant General Robert Jones: "My first efforts will be directed, by negotiations or force to free the country between the Withlacoochee and frontier settlements from the small but desperate bands. . . . This once accomplished, a combined movement may be made, it is hoped successfully, on the southern Indians, who are meantime comparatively innoxious. . . ." [3]

Having assessed the enemy, Worth turned to his second problem —his own forces. On paper he had almost forty-eight hundred regulars but with over one thousand men and fifteen officers too ill to function, his army was reduced to about thirty-seven hundred. The militia, with their high-ranking generals, had been removed from the field, making it possible for a regular army colonel to take command. [4]

Worth's third problem was, as always, the climate. Past commanders had pulled their regular troops off the field during the hot summer months from May through August. Although the militia had operated during that time, the slower pace of action had inevitably given the Indians a respite in which to harvest their crops, rest, and regroup for the fall campaign. The colonel decided that no matter what the cost in illness and death to his own men, he would give the Indians no such reprieve that summer.

As Worth took command, he issued an order that all Indian passports were to be rescinded—no hostiles were to move back and forth through settled territory. Every area was to be patrolled constantly as long as there were troops able to stand on their feet. All Indians appearing at any fort or settlement were to be seized and held. There would be no restrictions on warfare, no parleying, no issuing of provisions, no chiefs moving to and fro across the land. Orders were to seek and destroy villages, fields, and supplies. Anything that might give sustenance to the Seminole allies was to be captured or destroyed.[5]

On 3 June Worth set out to implement the plan he had outlined to the adjutant general. He left Tampa with 140 men for Fort King because he believed Halleck-Tustenuggee was about to surrender. When he arrived on 7 June, he learned that the chief had abandoned his camp. Worth decided to make a "dash at him."

Lieutenant Colonel Bennett Riley and Major Joseph Plympton, with one hundred men of the Second Infantry, set off in pursuit. Their guide was a Negro who had lived with the band. After a hazardous march, they arrived at a village of twenty-five huts which had been Halleck's planting ground and the site of the Green Corn Dance. The place showed no sign of recent habitation for it was now the policy to leave a camp whenever one or more of their number was captured.[6]

On the day Worth left for Fort King, Major Thomas Childs and Lieutenant W. T. Sherman had captured Coacoochee. Against orders, Lieutenant Colonel William Gates had shipped him and his warriors forthwith to New Orleans. Worth, who wanted to use Coacoochee to bring others in, sent L. G. Capers, emigration officer, to bring the party back.[7]

Throughout the month of June, small forces fanned out to clear the area between the settlements and the Everglades. Captain Ker took a detachment of Second Dragoons on a boat expedition up the Ocklawaha. Colonels Riley, Clark, and Loomis scoured the left bank of the Withlacoochee. They captured a few prisoners whom they hoped to use for guides. Captain Hawkins of the Seventh Infantry saw some Indians driving away cattle they had stolen at Watkahootka. He recovered not only the cattle but thousands of pounds of dried beef. The expedition was not, however, an unqualified success for the Indians had eluded the captain and his men. Captain Sewall surprised Halleck's party on 30 June. The Indians escaped but had to leave twenty bushels of coonti and large quantities of beef behind. The army wiped out thirty acres of corn waiting to be harvested.[8]

As the season wore on, the army penetrated the heart of the Indian country. The troops found many islands highly cultivated with huts, palmetto sheds, and corncribs erected on them. They destroyed everything. Thlocko-Tustenuggee (Tiger Tail), watching from a treetop on one of the hummocks, saw his corn torn up by the roots and his house burned to the ground. The food uprooted that day would have fed his people through the coming year.

The army operations during June brought desolation to every part of the country inhabited by the Seminole allies. Too weak to resist, they fled, usually at night. As they slipped silently through the swamps, they leaped from log to log to avoid leaving footprints, they walked backwards, crawled on hands and knees, crossed and recrossed their tracks, scattered into groups of four or five going different ways to meet at a well-known campground. They had a system of patrolling with scouting parties to watch troop movements and warn the women and children.

The summer of 1841 was the first in which there was no Green Corn Dance. The dance at which the elders held court to judge infractions of tribal mores, when young men dropped their baby names for ones they had earned in war or at the hunt, when the fires of the old year were doused and new ones lit to signify the cleansing of the tribe,[9] the Green Corn Dance, with all its social significance, was not performed. The omission signaled, more than any other development, the destruction of Seminole society in the face of implacable pressure.

Since the men dared not shoot a rifle lest they give away their position and since their corn and vegetables had been razed, the people lived on coonti and went back to hunting with the bow and arrow.

As citizens kept a sharp watch for retaliatory attacks, soldiers struggled through the swamps for twenty-five days, destroying the Indians' means of subsistence. At the end of summer, thirty-two fields had been ravaged, 180 sheds or huts burned and five Indians captured. The price for this accomplishment was another thousand men ill, fifty dead or disabled.[10]

While his men were in the field, Worth attacked his fourth problem as the officer in charge of the war effort. He agreed with the president's critics that the war was costing too much and he thought he knew why. Since 1835, a huge civil service had grown up around the army in Florida. It seemed the military had become almost subservient to civilian officeholders. Clerks, mechanics, teamsters, laborers, Negro interpreters and guides, all flourished as a result of the war. "The planter, driven from his home without employment or means, reluctantly mingled with the avaracious multitudes thronging around the public crib." Most despicable of all to the soldier were the wealthy who, free from all danger, looked on from a distance, waiting for the end of the month to receive pay for the labor of their slaves.

The quartermaster paid out $65,470 every month of the war while the total cost per month reached $92,300. Over one thousand civilian employees drew salaries from $30 to $200 a month. The army supported 1,375 horses, 1,260 mules, 380 wagons, 5 steamboats, and 3 sailing vessels.[11] Worth planned to cut fat from the budget by eliminating freeloading bureaucrats and streamlining military operations.

As the soldiers pushed relentlessly against the enemy and the Seminole allies dodged and wove to keep out of their hands, Coacoochee languished in chains aboard a transport in Tampa Bay. Capers had fetched him from New Orleans to help Worth bring in the stragglers.[12]

In July, the colonel went aboard to have a conference with the chief. Coacoochee and his warriors shuffled slowly up to the quarter-deck, dragging their foot irons. They arranged themselves in order of rank and sat down. "They laid their manacled hands upon their knees and hung their heads in silence." Colonel Worth stood up to speak.

> Coacoochee, I take you by the hand as a warrior, a brave man; you have fought long and with a true and strong heart for your country.... Like the oak, you may bear up for many years against strong winds; the time must come when it will fall; this time has arrived. You have stood the blasts of five winters, and the storms of thunder, lightning and wind, five summers; the branches have fallen, and the tree, burnt at the roots, is prostrated. Coacoochee, I am your friend; so is your great father at Washington. What I say to you is true, my tongue is not forked like a snake, my word is for the happiness of the red man.
>
> You are a great warrior, the Indians throughout the country look to you as a leader, by your councils they have been governed. This war has lasted five years, much blood has been shed, much innocent blood; you have made your hands and the ground red

with the blood of women and children. This war must now end. You are the man to do it; you must and shall accomplish it. I sent for you that through the exertions of yourself and men, you might induce your entire band to emigrate.[13]

The speech delivered by Colonel Worth seemed so uncharacteristic that it must certainly have been written by the equivalent of a ghost writer—probably by an interpreter who had absorbed the Indian use of metaphor and parable to express ideas. The colonel sounded more like himself when, at the end of the address, he told Coacoochee bluntly that if he and his men could not convince the band to emigrate, he would hang them all from the yardarm.

As Worth finished his speech, there was complete silence on the quarter-deck. It was finally broken by the harsh grating of handcuffs and irons as Coacoochee slowly rose to speak. He said:

I was once a boy; then I saw the white man afar off. I hunted in these woods, first with a bow and arrow; then with a rifle. I saw the white man, and was told he was my enemy. I could not shoot him as I would a wolf or a bear; yet like these he came upon me; horses, cattle and fields he took from me. He said he was my friend; he abused our women and children, and told us to go from the land. Still he gave me his hand in friendship; we took it. Whilst taking it, he had a snake in the other; his tongue was forked; he lied and stung us. I asked but for a small piece of these lands, enough to plant and to live upon, for a spot where I could place the ashes of my kindred, a spot only sufficient upon which I could lay my wife and child. This was not granted me. I was put in prison. I escaped. I have been again taken; you have brought me back; I am here; I feel the irons in my heart. . . . We know but little; we have no books which tell us things; but we have the Great Spirit, moon, and stars; these told me last night, you would be our friend. I give you my word; it is the word of a warrior, a chief, a brave; it is the word of Coacoochee. It is true I have fought like a man, so have my warriors; but the whites were too strong for us. I wish now to have my band around me and go to Arkansas. You say I *must* end the war! Look at these irons! Can I go to my warriors? Coacoochee chained! No; do not ask me to see them. I never wish to tread upon my land unless I am free. If I can go to them *unchained* they will follow me in; but I fear they will not obey me when I walk to them in irons.

> They will say my heart is weak, I am afraid. Could I go free they
> will surrender and emigrate.[14]

Worth would not free the chief. He agreed that three to five of his
men could be unchained and given thirty to fifty days to bring in
the band. The ship was in deep water, the men in irons. They had
no choice.

That afternoon a nearby schooner fired a twenty-gun salute in
honor of a special occasion. It was the Fourth of July for 20,000,000
Americans. Lieutenant Sprague mused on the irony of fate that
caused a chief, "a man whose only offence was defending his home,
his fireside, the graves of his kindred, stipulating on the Fourth of
July for his freedom and his life." However, even that sensitive officer
did not spare a thought for the slaves who were certainly not celebrat-
ing Independence Day either!

Coacoochee chose five men to go to the people and urge them
to come in. Once more he used the opportunity to speak from his
heart.

> Has not Coacoochee sat with you by the council fire at midnight,
> when the wolf and white man were around us? Have I not led the
> war dance and sung the song of the Seminole? Did not the spirits
> of our mothers, our wives, and our children stand around us? Has
> not my scalping knife been red with blood, and the scalps of our
> enemy been drying in our camps? Have I not made the war path
> red with blood, and has not the Seminole always found a home
> in my camp? Then will the warriors of Coacoochee desert him? . . .
> The sun shines bright today, the day is clear; so let your heart be;
> the Great spirit will guide you. At night when you camp, take
> these pipes and tobacco, build a fire when the moon is up and
> bright, dance around it, then let the fire go out, and just before
> the break of day, when the deer sleeps, and the moon whispers to
> the dead, you will hear the voices of those who have gone to the
> Great Spirit; they will give you strong hearts and heads to carry
> the talk of Coacoochee.
>
> Say to my band that my feet are chained. I cannot walk, yet
> I send them my true word as true from the heart as if I was on the
> war path or in the deer hunt. I am not a boy; Coacoochee can
> die, not with shivering hand, but as when grasping the rifle with
> my warriors around me. My feet are chained but the head and

heart of Coacoochee reaches you. The Great White Chief will be kind to us. He says, when my band comes in I shall again walk my land free, with my band around me. He has given us forty days to do this business in; if you want more say so, I will ask for more; if not, be true to the time. Take these sticks; here are thirty-nine, one for each day; this much larger than the rest, with blood upon it, is the fortieth. When the others are thrown away, and this only remains, say to my people, that with the setting sun Coacoochee hangs like a dog, with none but white men to hear his last words. Come then, come by the stars, as I have led you to battle! Come, for the voice of Coacoochee speaks to you!

Even in chains, he could still speak as a chief but then came the time to send personal messages to his family, to his wife and to the daughter whom he had rescued from captivity only a short time ago. Coacoochee started to speak. He said, "Say this to my wife and child," and then he had to turn his head to hide his tears. Deep silence fell upon the company. The experienced soldier, the hardy sailor, the stoic savage—all accustomed to the brutality and carnage of war—stood in mute sympathy with the fallen chief.

"Without confusion, and without a word spoken, the irons were removed from the five messengers." When they were ready to go ashore, Coacoochee shook hands with each one as he passed over the side. To the last one, he gave a breast pin and handkerchief to give his wife and child.

The five messengers and Sole Micco, who had gone to seek Coacoochee when his daughter was a hostage, left next day. Micco returned in ten days with six warriors and some women and children. By the end of the month seventy-eight warriors, sixty-four women, and forty-seven children had drifted in a few at a time.

When all of his people had arrived, Coacoochee asked to have his irons removed so that he could meet his warriors like a man. This was done. Then he put on his crimson turban with three ostrich plumes, donned a many-colored frock and red leggings, and hung his glittering silver ornaments about his neck. Finally he thrust his scalping knife into the red sash around his waist and went to meet his band. As soon as his feet touched the soil of Florida, his haughty bearing returned. He waved his arms and stretched them high above his head. Then he let out a shrill whoop of triumph and freedom which was answered by a thunderous response from his people. As the crowd parted to make a path for him, he strode directly to the headquarters of the commander, walked up and saluted. Then he turned and spoke. "Warriors—Coacoochee speaks to you! You have listened to my word, and taken it, I thank you! The Great Spirit speaks in our councils. The rifle is hid, and the white and red man are friends. I have given my word for you. I am free; then let my word be true. I am done. By our council fire I will say more." [15] His official duty performed, he turned to his wife and child, greeting them with more affection "than generally belongs to the Indians character." What Coacoochee said to his people by their council fire has not been recorded but the chief kept his word to the Americans. From that moment on, he worked to effect the emigration of all Florida Indians. Yet even he could not perform a miracle. The remnants of the nation fought on.

Holatter Micco, Arpeika, Hotulke-Thlocko (The Prophet), Hospetarke, Fuse Hadjo, and Parsacke—chiefs who held out in the Everglades—met in council and decided to kill anyone who came bearing messages from whites. They hoped to assassinate Sole Micco who had brought in twenty women and children and two other chiefs. The Prophet remained the most adamant against emigrating, wielding tremendous power because the people feared his ability to punish by incantations.

Nevertheless, a messenger was shown the great Coacoochee and his comrades in chains and sent to tell the other chiefs that they would remain so until all came in. In ten days, the emissary returned with a number of subchiefs. No doubt, for some, their loyalty to Coacoochee was greater than their fear of the Prophet. Times hadn't changed completely, for Hospetarke remained in a camp outside Tampa collecting provisions and whisky for five days. He was so sullen and angry that no one dared approach him.

Coacoochee, who was in Tampa negotiating for his own release and that of his men, was finally allowed to go out. Dressed in his "official gaudy dress, and, rifle in hand, he mounted his horse." Man and steed seemed one as he rode slowly around to shake hands with the army officers around him; then he disappeared into the wilderness to seek the camp of Hospetarke. He was back before sunset with the old chief and eighteen warriors.

An astute army officer noted that the men were trading deerskins for powder rather than money; when they left they took food, liquor, and arms with them but left the women and children. Colonel Worth pursued and seized the chiefs; he brought them aboard a steamboat for a council which he convened at two o'clock. Worth sat at the head of the table in the wardroom while the chiefs assembled around it in order of their rank. On shore a company of soldiers deployed to intercept or kill any Indian who tried to leave.

Gopher John, the interpreter, stood by, "his tall person gaudily decked for the occasion with ribands and silver work." The officers, secretly armed with pistols, took their places. The colonel suggested that Hospetarke send for the women and children in the swamps; the chief replied that this could not be done until the next moon and no arguments could move him. Finally Worth stood up and shouted that the Indians had fooled the white men so many times, he could not believe them now. He ended by announcing, "Not one of you will again leave this boat."

At that moment a bugle call rang out, signaling each officer to his post. The doors of the cabin were closed by bayonets and officers drew their swords. The drum in camp beat to arms. A stunned silence followed. Slowly the Indians began to mutter and finally to protest loudly, brandishing knives and threatening the interpreter. When they saw that all was in vain, they begged to be allowed to go after their families but Colonel Worth was not beguiled by such an old ruse. He chose five warriors to go to camp with the message that if the women and children did not come in their chiefs would be hanged.

Coacoochee appeared when the coup was over, pretending he had been drunk and railing at the army for betraying his brothers. After a token protest, he took responsibility for the band of eighty-five year old Hospetarke: fifty-four warriors with seventy-three women and children. Irons were now removed from Coacoochee's men but Hospetarke and his were closely guarded aboard a prison ship although they were not chained.

Once the men realized they could not escape, they declared openly that they had never intended to surrender. They had come for powder, whisky, and bread. They told how they had always put everything they secured into a common stock which was deposited in a hummock about six miles away. There the women watched over the rifles and provisions. They had even agreed not to drink lest they become intoxicated and give themselves away in an unguarded moment. The chief was to signal the instant when they would all return to Cypress Swamp. Instead, Colonel Worth had given his sign first, making them all prisoners aboard a transport near Fort Brooke.[16]

That September and October the army took a "defensive posture," confining itself to protecting citizens while negotiations went forward. Many soldiers found the inactivity even harder to bear than the hardships of patrol and battle but they endured as best they could.

After Coacoochee had surrendered, he worked hard to bring in his fellow chiefs and their people. On 6 September, he set out with six warriors to interview Thlocko-Tustenuggee (Tiger Tail) and Nethlock Emathla. So opposed to emigration had they both been that Tiger Tail had cut his sister's throat when she began to weaken. Now they wanted to talk. Relentless pursuit during the sickly season, destruction of their crops, assistance to those who surrendered had all weakened the position of those who insisted on holding out.

Coacoochee and his men went into the wilderness on white men's horses but brought no whites with them. The chief rode boldly into the camp of his dangerous friends and called to them to come and talk like men. The three Indian leaders sat by the fire until dawn. At last Tiger Tail and Nethlock Emathla promised to send in their bands but refused to come themselves. Assured that their suffering women and children would be better off, they agreed to let them go but could not give up their own liberty.

Tiger Tail and Nethlock Emathla asked to talk to Alligator. That chief had been one of the most ardent opponents of emigration until King Philip and his men were captured during General Jesup's campaign. In a moment of despair, he had given up and turned himself and his people in. Regretting his hasty capitulation, he had later tried to take his band back to the wilderness under cover of a "White Feather" celebration. When his escape attempt failed, he had accepted the inevitable and begun to encourage his beleaguered friends to join him in Arkansas.

In the fall of 1841 Alligator, Hotulke Emathla, and Waxi Emathla came from Fort Gibson. Each brought with him one other warrior and an interpreter. After many discussions with the army and with their brothers in the swamps, they convinced seventy people from Hospetarke's band to give themselves up and meet the prison ship at Punta Rassa.[17] But even as the people waited in their camp for the necessary arrangements to be completed, they were uneasy. Night after night they sang and danced, offering sacrifices to the Great Spirit to avert the spells of the Prophet although he was two hundred miles away.

Those who refused to come in were gathered at Arpeika's

village in the center of a swamp in the Everglades. They had built
a comfortable refuge there. It included a council ground with a big
ring left by the feet of many dancers. Kegs of powder were stored
there from which a warrior took what he needed in battle but paid
if he were going hunting. There were still some small fields of corn,
pumpkins, beans, peas, and melons. If the planted food ran out or
was destroyed by the army, the people lived on coonti root, berries,
wild potatoes, and cabbage palmetto. Short of powder and afraid
the noise of guns would give away their position, the men often
hunted with bows and arrows. There were fish and oysters in abun-
dance on the coast but these nourishing sources of food could not be
procured without grave risk of being seen by patrolling enemy ships.
The chiefs still had a few cattle, hogs, chickens, and ponies although
the army had destroyed most of them. Whenever the chiefs came
into possession of any money, they converted it into silver orna-
mentation. Investment in stock or agriculture was much too risky
with the army always on the move. From this stronghold the Prophet
and a few other chiefs held the remaining Seminoles in fear of surrender.[18]

Coacoochee was anxious to depart for his new land. His people
were chafing under the restrictions of prison and longed to be free.
The army was obliged to keep two hundred men on duty daily to
prevent breakouts, and to illuminate the camp at night with beacon
lights that played on the surrounding area for a space of two square
miles to spot any individual who might attempt to leave.

The eleventh of October was the date set for departure for New
Orleans. The brig *Saratoga* had been chartered to take the people
as far as Fort Gibson. From there they would travel by wagon or
on foot for forty miles to reach the land assigned to the Seminoles.
As they waited for the day to arrive, the women and children were
everywhere cracking corn to eat on the journey. Old women and
little children went out into the woods to collect pine knots for fires
as the people had heard that their new country was destitute of such
fuel. In fact, they had no conception of the land to which they were
going; only when they saw that Coacoochee had been to New
Orleans and back did they give up their fear that they would be
thrown overboard as soon as they were out of sight of land.

Finally on the 20th, the bands of Coacoochee and Hospetarke,
comprising 290 emigrants, including 18 Negroes—some belonging
to Indians already in Arkansas—went aboard the vessel. There were

also 14 Mikasukis—like all other Florida tribes, they were treated as Seminoles and, indeed, the two groups had been constant allies against the whites.[19]

As the ship was made ready for departure, the emigrants assembled on deck. They gazed mutely at the vast expanse of water before them. The chiefs stood silently on the quarterdeck; then Hospetarke put his head between his hands in a gesture of submission or despair. The warriors stood stony-faced and motionless. Coacoochee, from his position above the others, looked forbidding. Then someone—no doubt a newspaper man—asked him what he was thinking. He replied, "I am looking at the last pine trees on my land." Neither Hospetarke nor the warriors moved or spoke but Coacoochee seemed to exude a determined cheerfulness to counteract the silent tears of the women and children.

He thanked the officials for their kindness to his people since he had brought them in and asserted that although he was leaving his country forever against his will, he could go, knowing in his heart that he had never done anything to disgrace it. His manner was calm and subdued. Without a sign of the grief he felt, he stood before his captors and told them how he felt. "It was my home, I love it; and to leave it now is like burying my wife and child. I have thrown away my rifle; have taken the hand of the white man, and now say to him, take care of me."

"Thus," wrote Sprague, "was Florida relieved of the most formidable chieftan and the most desperate band that ever sought shelter in her hammocks and swamps... these emigrants set sail, upon what to them was a boundless sea, for a country they knew not where, trusting in the guardianship of the Great Spirit, and the intelligence of the white man."[20]

Both the Great Spirit and the white man were to disappoint the young chief. His party reached Fort Gibson on 10 November where, under the influence of Micanopy, they agreed to go to a spot on the Deep Fork River.[21] They had barely crossed the Arkansas when they were overtaken by a blizzard. Here they huddled, in their light clothing unused to the cold weather, by their campfires. They refused to go farther—perhaps fearing that even worse things were in store for them if they went on.[22]

At this time Coacoochee was about thirty years old. He was to continue, for years to come, to fight for his people. But he had, in truth, given up the rifle and the scalping knife. He would learn to use the weapons of diplomacy with equal skill. His oratory was a reflection of his intelligence and character as well as of his talent with words.

While Coacoochee and Alligator had reasoned with their unwilling friends about the need to emigrate, Colonel Worth had arranged to cooperate with the Navy and marines to go after the last remnants who were holding out.

# 16

## Colonel Worth's

## Navy Campaign, 1841–1842

### The American Army and Navy Unite
### against Five Hundred Indians

"We are not inaptly compared to ... men harpooning minnows and shooting sandpipers with artillery."

M. M. COHEN

IN SEPTEMBER 1841, while Colonel Worth negotiated with Coacoochee and lured Hospetarke's band onto his prison ship, he planned
his military campaign. He ordered Lieutenant McLaughlin's Mosquito Fleet, at anchor near Indian Key, to cooperate with the marines
stationed at Fort Dallas and with the army in an all-out effort to
penetrate the Everglades. He was determined to seek out Arpeika
who remained adamant in the face of both force and blandishments.
The ancient chief was supposed to be entrenched near Cape Sable.
(More likely he was at Locha-Hatchee near Fort Jupiter.) Worth
ordered Army Captain Martin Burke, with a few men, to enter the
Everglades by way of the Miami and Navy Lieutenant John Rodgers,
with a crew, to approach them by the Shark River. They were to
use any means at their disposal to secure the Indians or to drive them

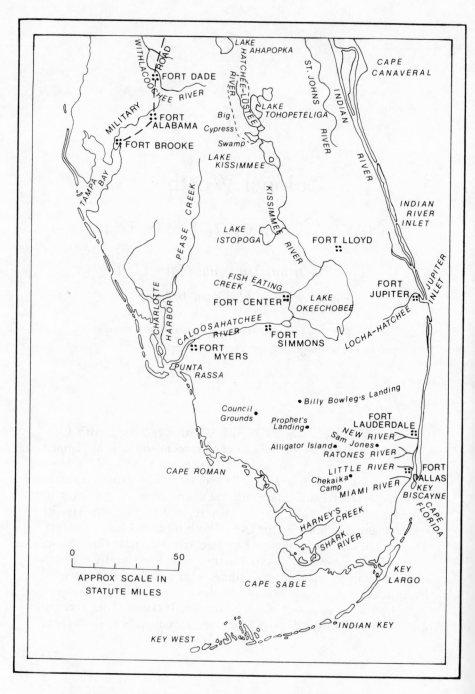

5. *Seat of the Florida Wars, the Peninsula. By E. Glendon Moore, based on maps in the National Archives collection.*

toward the Caloosahatchee. They were to "get" Sam Jones or his "fortune-teller," Hotulke-Thlocko, a Creek with vast influence over the people. They were given carte blanche as to method. Worth wrote, "If the opportunity occurs & you find that the Indians may be operated on by money, you are authorized to indulge in great liberality, to be paid when objects are accomplished. I will see all your promises fulfilled." [1]

By October, McLaughlin's Mosquito Fleet was double its original size. He had at his disposal three Treasury cutters, the *Madison*, the *Jefferson*, and the *Van Buren*, besides a new schooner, the *Phoenix*, built to his specifications. For transportation through the Everglades there were one hundred canoes. Most of these were thirty feet long and four feet wide; they were hollowed out of huge cypress logs. His men were armed with Colt's repeating carbines for added fire-power. He assigned the *Flirt* and the *Otsego* to patrol the east coast while the new crews of the Treasury cutters and the *Phoenix* went through intensive training along the Florida reef before being given their cruising stations. [2]

On 10 October, he set out with a force of two hundred sailors and marines to ascend the Shark River with Rodgers. His troops searched all nearby islands as they proceeded. On the fourteenth, they reached the site of Chekaika's village where they met Captain Burke who had arrived from Fort Dallas. From there they joined forces and moved on to Prophet's Landing on the edge of Big Cypress. Finding no Indians, they turned southwest and followed a stream through mangroves into a "grassy lake studded with islands." They saw two Indians in a canoe some distance away, pursued them to fields they were cultivating and took their cooking utensils, pro-visions and canoes. They followed the trail of ten or twelve people (probably Prophet's band) for two days before losing it. Along the way, they destroyed fifty or sixty acres of pumpkins, beans, peas, and other food. They continued to the sea, emerging from the Ever-glades about fifteen miles north of Cape Romano. Lieutenant Rodgers took his detachment on north to the Caloosahatchee. [3]

In September, Major Thomas Childs had taken a force of 180 men on an expedition down the east coast to Jupiter Inlet. Half the group traveled south by land while the others, in thirteen canoes, followed the sea. They came across a six-mile coastal area covered with fields of pumpkins, potatoes, peas, melons, tobacco, rice, and sugar cane "in the highest state of cultivation, many of them would have been creditable to an approved farmer." The gardens were separated by small patches of brushwood or swamplands. At intervals, camps—apparently occupied by one person within the past three days—occurred. Each had a trail leading to the coast and an elevated position where a lookout had a good view of the north and south. Although the guards had escaped to warn their people, Child's troops destroyed the fields completely.[4]

The "approved farmers" who had managed to produce such lavish crops under conditions of war on land generally considered unfit for cultivation were, no doubt, the women and children of the remnants of the Seminole allies. The industry and ingenuity needed to perform this miracle under the very noses of the American military defy description. The anguish at seeing all of their efforts go for nought must have been intense. Yet they refused to despair— dodging, hiding, and resisting to the end. The armed forces pursued as relentlessly and more efficiently than ever. Unable to catch the people, they had to content themselves with laying waste their crops in the hope of starving them out of their retreats.

Throughout the winter, in a well-coordinated effort between different branches of the armed forces, small groups of marines and navy men in boats worked with dragoons of the army. Supplies were transported to three depots within the Everglades and not more than thirty miles from Fort Simmons. When a patrol went out, officers and men packed on their backs seven days' rations and a blanket. Each group took one mule to carry cooking utensils and other gear. Then they fanned out in all directions, guided by experienced trackers. They carried with them Alligator's speech begging the hostiles to join their brothers in Arkansas.[5]

Men of every service branch worked together. They waded in water three to four feet deep, struggled over soggy hummocks and climbed through cypress knees and tangled vines. They slept in their canoes or on the damp ground; the only hot meals they ate were cooked over small fires built on a pile of sand in the prow of a boat or kindled around a cypress stump. They were wet, hungry, tired, and sick but although "subjected to privations, fatigue, and disappointment; subordination, cheerfulness and resolution marked the conduct of all engaged in the expedition."

Once when Lieutenant McLaughlin's men were scouting the shores of Lake Okeechobee, they were under strict orders to maintain complete silence and, to avoid detection, were allowed no fires. Suddenly the weather grew cold and a high wind blew up, causing rough waters. Men fell ill in great numbers. At last McLaughlin authorized the doctor to light a fire inside a camp kettle to prepare medicine for the men. In spite of their precautions and for all their suffering, these scouts never caught the enemy.[6]

Colonel Worth sent Major Thomas Childs to the Locha-Hatchee River near Fort Jupiter to find Arpeika, who was reported to be hiding there. Then he dispatched Major W. G. Belknap to track the Prophet in the mangrove swamp near Key Biscayne. Since Belknap's men were forced to travel light in order to follow the wily Prophet, they were sometimes reduced to eating cabbage trees to stay alive. Although the Indians eluded both scouting expeditions, the armed forces acquired useful knowledge of the country and showed the enemy that they could penetrate their most "secret recesses."

After the negative report from Major Childs, McLaughlin volunteered to make another search for Arpeika along the Locha-Hatchee. Since it was a ten-day march there and he had food for only nine days, he put his men on half-rations in order to make the scouting expedition. His troops "accepted all hardships with good grace and showed eagerness to find the enemy at any cost." On 12 December they sent back their sick and disabled and entered the swamp. Once there, it was one continual portage with men carrying their canoes between spots of open water. After a week of searching, they found a few canoes but no Seminoles.[7]

The Eighth Regiment had 450 men searching Big Cypress Swamp. One unit found Arpeika's deserted town. They came upon the council ground with its ceremonial ring, large and much worn, now empty and desolate. Perhaps, never again would Seminoles celebrate in Florida the Green Corn Dance after a good harvest or a Scalp Dance after a victory.

On 18 December, the Eighth Regiment was still pushing their column through pine and cabbage trees over the spongy ground. They came upon the trail of a six-year old which they followed for a whole day. Later they saw evidence of four or five men, a woman, and two children—one of which was occasionally carried. They never found their quarry.

The heat was intolerable and, suddenly, on the twentieth, they were attacked by twenty warriors of Bowlegs' and the Prophet's bands. Two members of the patrol were killed. With no solid ground available, the survivors buried their casualties by sinking them in the "second flag pond." Then they returned to headquarters.

The men observed Christmas Eve by eating the first real hot meal they had enjoyed in weeks. On Christmas Day, they gathered in a tent and celebrated with two bottles of whisky. On the thirtieth, they returned to the swamp and on New Year's Eve they came upon the bodies of their two dead comrades, now savaged by alligators and floating in the swamp. Around ten the next morning they reached a newly deserted Indian camp but having seen the victims of the last engagement, the Indian guide suddenly became ill and refused to lead the way any farther. The rest of the party (not feeling too well either!) returned to camp.

A last reconnaissance ordered almost never took place because the boots of the men chosen were not fit for marching. Finally, a canvass of every man in the unit produced enough serviceable shoes for one patrol! This one was no more successful than its predecessors.

The campaign of Big Cypress was over. The armed forces of the government had driven the Indians out and broken them up, destroyed their food supply, and shown them that the American fighting man could go wherever the Indian warrior retreated. The soldiers returned to the coast, exhausted, weak, and ill but satisfied that they had done their best. One of them wrote in his diary, "The only reward we ask is the end of the Florida War."[8]

While neither Lieutenant McLaughlin with his boat crews around the Locha-Hatchee nor the Eighth Regiment in Big Cypress had captured any Indians, a detachment of sixty men in twelve canoes under Captain R. D. A. Wade had better luck. They had come upon an Indian fishing and had forced him to take them to his village. Here they captured twenty persons; eight warriors who tried to escape were killed. Leaving the prisoners with the unit surgeon, they compelled an old Indian to lead them to another village which they surrounded. Here they surprised and seized twenty-seven more. When he brought his patrol back on 11 November, Wade could report he had killed eight men, taken fifty-six prisoners, destroyed twenty canoes and seized thirteen rifles, twelve well-filled powder horns, a quantity of balls, and buck-shot with other munitions for defensive operations.[9]

In November, McLaughlin had reported eighty men seriously ill and fifteen dead. At the end of December, he sent fifty north with medical surveys; one hundred others were sick. Five more had died of disease or accidents which occurred when the new Colt rifles exploded during practice.[10] While navy casualties from sickness seemed exorbitant, the army surgeons had made some progress in the treatment of yellow fever. Out of 2,428 ill in July, they had managed to return 806 to duty. Twenty-one had died and 13 had been discharged because of illness.[11] In other words, they had achieved a cure in one-third of the cases and kept death and disability to less than 2 percent. This was a real improvement.

Describing conditions in 1836, John Bemrose, a hospital steward, wrote that it became so natural to be surrounded by the dead and dying that when he heard of a new casualty, his only thought was where "to lay him out" and how to obtain another coffin. He felt his callousness grew out of an excess of misery. Had their senses not been blunted, the hospital staff would have gone mad under the strain.[12]

Bemrose gives a vivid description of the illness suffered by American troops in Florida. As the hospital steward in charge of the wounded and ill brought back from the first Battle of Withlacoochee, he had much experience of it. Before he left the service to return to his native England, he almost died of the fever himself.

Dysentary, apparently caused by drinking stagnant water, was a scourge of the troops throughout the war. When on the march, Bemrose had the task of riding ahead to find clear water for the sick and wounded before the horses waded in and muddied the pools. Often when there was no clear or running water, the men drank the scum-covered, slimy liquid that abounded everywhere. They were too thirsty to think of the consequences.

Victims of the fever sometimes went about their business until they fell unconscious before anyone knew they were ill. They ran a high fever which seemed to peak at noon in wild delirium. Just before death, the men often bled from the nose. Bemrose believed that he saved his own life by bleeding himself when his doctor refused. The hospital steward had observed another physician use the method efficaciously on many patients.

If a man fell ill in the field, he was placed on a rude litter. On the march he might be carried between two horses or by four of his fellow soldiers. Sometimes there was a tent or a rough lean-to of branches thrown up for the sick. Often the men lay on the ground unprotected from rain and sun. Bemrose could not decide which was better—or worse! Inside the shelters, the sweltering humidity added to the heat of fevered bodies created a steam bath. Men cried for the relief which he could not give them. Outside, they might be subject to a broiling sun or a downpour in spite of his best efforts to protect them.

There wasn't an army building in Florida that could keep out the sand flies, mosquitoes, immense spiders, chiggers, black fleas, and other pests. Just outside every camp lay the wilderness. There wolves howled, owls hooted, and bullfrogs added their croaks to the night cacophony. To the fear of death (with which every soldier battled) were added other nameless ones brought on by the strange sounds of the dark unknown which surrounded them.

Nurses might feed, offer a drink to, or turn a helpless man but Bemrose never had time to visit a patient more than once a day. His medications were simple: quinine for the fever, "Barton's Mixture for Catarrh" to ease respiratory ailments, and a diet of thin gruel for dysentary. The latter was also administered for other ailments and to all the wounded.

No matter how severely injured a man was, the treatment was the same. Bullets were removed, the wounds washed and "poulticed" daily, and the patient fed a diet of gruel. Around the camp "hospital" this was known as the "Battle of Water Gruel." Back in 1836, it seemed to be the only victorious one for the army in Florida. Only one man wounded at the Withlacoochee died under the procedure.[13]

If a navy man were wounded or became ill on patrol, he lay in a boat or was left in a temporary camp while his unit performed its duties. Conditions may have been worse for sailors and marines than for soldiers because they constantly operated in the most unhealthy climate and terrain.

In spite of his heavy casualties, Lieutenant McLaughlin determined to continue his campaign to rout the enemy from the Everglades. The *Phoenix* and the *Otsego* maintained surveillance of the passes on the west coast; the *Madison* and the *Wave* cruised along the reef; the *Jefferson* and the *Van Buren* patrolled the east coast. The *Flirt*, serving as a depot for the expedition, remained at Key Biscayne.

On 13 January 1842, McLaughlin sent Lieutenant John B. Marchand, with 120 men from the *Van Buren* and the *Wave*, to explore Cocoanut Island. This unit tried to enter the Everglades by three different rivers from the west coast but the water was too low even for canoes. They found no recent signs of Indians.

A month later, McLaughlin sent one unit to enter the glades from the west and one from the east. Lieutenant Marchand led the western pincer. He left on 11 February, traveling along the southwest edge of the glades and searching among the seaward islands. He could not penetrate too far inland because of low water. On one remote island his men found a cache of prepared coonti, clothing, and cooking utensils which they destroyed. They entered the glades at Harney's River and proceeded to Cocoanut Island. As they could no longer use their canoes, they made camp and sent out a scouting party.

The patrol came upon two camps—one with fires still burning and food cooking. The men destroyed both. Since the trails led east, Chia assumed that the people were moving to coonti ground on the east coast. Marchand decided not to go on to Lake Okeechobee but to follow the trail. All through March, his patrols found canoes and equipment abandoned; they destroyed large quantities of cultivated crops. Although the Indians managed to keep ahead of the troops and out of sight, they must have suffered terrible privation as they fled, often leaving most of their possessions behind them. The sailors suffered also; they were "broken down and barefooted."

Lieutenant John Rodgers took the east pincer. In two months, he and his men explored Lake Okeechobee, a cypress swamp east of it, the Kissimmee River, and Lake Tohopekagliga.[14]

Passed Midshipman George Henry Preble, in command of the men from the *Jefferson*, kept a diary of his experiences on the Rodgers mission. On Monday, Valentines Day 1842, Preble and his men got under way at daylight. They were part of a long line of canoes moving silently in single file through rivers, lakes, and swamps in search of Arpeika or any of his cohorts. They entered New River at its source and followed it to abandoned Fort Lauderdale. Here they picked up an Indian guide. That afternoon they came to on the left bank and pitched their tents in an open pine barren with palmetto undergrowth. Each day, as they pushed through the wilderness, they were up and away at dawn and each afternoon they stopped between four and five o'clock at a spot where they could beach their canoes for the night.

Preble's unit came to Lake Okeechobee, The Big Water, on Washington's Birthday. Several patrols were sent out to look for evidence of the enemy in the surrounding country. The next day the *Madison* and *Jefferson* crews began to march inland. They waded about two hundred yards through cypress and willows, up to their waists in mud and water, until they came to a belt of saw grass "at least fifteen feet high." They pushed through fifty yards of this before they reached dry land and found themselves on a wide plain of palmetto scrub dotted with cabbage trees and pine hummocks. Dense woods surrounded the plain. No one found anything but long-abandoned camps which the guides thought might have been forsaken when the Indians entered the Everglades in 1837. They returned at noon and followed a river along the coast of the lake. That night, as they camped in their canoes, the coast was low, the night rainy, and the mosquitoes plentiful!

On the second of March, after a grueling search, a unit under Lieutenant William Lewis Herndon found Fish-Eating Creek. The next day Preble took his boats up it to Fort Center. On 5 March, all but the "sick, lame and lazy" proceeded up the creek, pushing their canoes through weeds until the stream became a wide swamp. As he lay in his canoe that night, Preble remembered it was Saturday and thought wistfully of his friends at home. The next day he wrote a vivid description of his surroundings which illustrates why the Seminoles fought so hard to remain in the area:

> Sunday, M'ch 6.—After hauling the canoes over two troublesome places re-entered ... a beautiful stream, clear, with a beautiful sandy bottom ... Saw immense flocks of cranes, pink spoonbills, curlew, and wild turkeys. ... Also, a large number of alligators; killed two small ones and cut off their tails for eating; caught a soft-shelled turtle and a hard-shelled turtle and had them cooked for supper, with a fry of some little fish that foolishly jumped into one of the canoes. ... Two veteran cypress stretched their scraggy arms over our camp, draped in moss to the very ground.[15]

On Monday Preble's unit followed the creek through its narrow bounds until it became a broad river and then trickled to a narrow stream again. On 9 March, the expedition entered the Kissimmee River. In the afternoon they passed a pine-log stockade, "one of the numerous posts held by the army in times gone by. The enclosure was choked with weeds, logs had fallen out, and those yet standing were partially burnt down."

For several days the men dragged their canoes over "grass roots that choked the river in places where the canoe's sprit (a fifteen-foot pole) failed to touch bottom. On the fifteenth, they came upon a live oak hummock where Indians had dressed deerskins about two weeks before. In the afternoon they found an Indian burial mound. Preble offered his men money for anything they dug up. Using their paddles, they set to with a will but found only a few bones and some blue glass beads.

On the nineteenth Preble and his men discovered they were lost. They marched four miles over pine barrens and through swamps up to their waists in water in a vain search for a stream that would lead them back to the Kissimmee. That night Preble read Ezra, Nehemiah, and Job!

The next day they reached the outlet of Lake Tohopeteliga.

Here they found fresh moccasin tracks, roots newly dug, and ground freshly turned. Orange peel lay scattered about and a youngster had played in the sand. An examination of the tracks suggested the flight of one small family. On finding this evidence of human habitation, everyone stopped and kept perfect silence. About half-past four flames rose up across the lake. As soon as dark fell, the Americans took off in their boats to examine the fire. Preble put a contingent of marines ashore to explore while he and the sailors waited to support them if they heard guns fired. At midnight they took the marines back aboard their canoes and continued to search until three in the morning before returning to camp without finding a sign of the Indians.

On Monday they rested at an Indian camp where corn, melons, and tobacco grew and filled their boats with fruit from "sour orange-trees." As they explored the shore, they found a saddle—probably belonging to an express rider—and the remains of two oxen.

On the twenty-fourth, they left the lake and reentered the Kissimmee where they were soon carried along on a swift current. They captured over thirty young cranes but ate only the livers. On Sunday they were back at Fort Gardner. The next day they entered Okeechobee, "made sail to a stiff breeze," and reached Fort Center before sundown. That night they ate venison and salmon.[16]

On 1 April, they left the lake and proceeded toward the Everglades again. Now they could no longer skim along with full sails; instead they dragged their canoes through saw grass or mud; again they slept in their boats. They continued to kill snakes daily and to rob cranes' nests of eggs and of young birds.

Each day Preble and his men alternately pulled and dragged their canoes along the edge of the swamp. The water was extremely low. At last the going became so difficult that it took all hands to pull one canoe through the saw grass but they finally entered the creek which led into New River. Again they spent the night at Fort Lauderdale. On the morning of 11 April 1842, they passed the bar at the entrance of New River without damage and sailed down the coast about twenty-five miles. Here they boarded their brig, picked up their mail, and enjoyed the amenities of civilization for the first time in fifty-eight days.

The eastern pincer of McLaughlin's force returned to Key Biscayne without having made contact with the enemy but they had burned some deserted Indian camps and cultivated fields. They had lived in their canoes or in tents for two months, wrote their commander John Rodgers, "with less rest, fewer luxuries, and harder work," than slaves.[17]

A few days after their return to their ship, Preble was on the sick list. He suffered from a "badly inflamed" foot and ulcerated legs caused when cuts from the saw grass became infected by the mud through which they had marched. On the twentieth, he was sent to the officers' quarters at Indian Key for medical attention. Although the doctors thought they might have to amputate both legs, they finally managed to save them. However, it was more than two years before all the sores healed and many more before Preble no longer felt the effects of his days spent in a dugout in Florida.

Colonel Worth wrote the adjutant general on 20 June to commend McLaughlin and his "gallant and accomplished officers" for their zeal and devotion during the expedition. He praised the "cordiality and confidence" which had prevailed between "both branches of the common service, whether united on land or on water."[18]

As McLaughlin's fleet started north to rest and recuperate at Norfolk, a heavy squall struck the *Jefferson* as it stood off Cape Canaveral. Lieutenant Herndon on the *Madison* thought they had been struck by lightning and came to the rescue. Unaware that the *Jefferson* had anchored while the men cleared the wreckage he misjudged the distance and ran into its starboard waist. Through a stygian night, the crews worked to repair the damage and get both ships under way. On 18 July, the squadron—including the two battered ships—finally anchored in Hampton Roads.[19]

Although they had seldom engaged the enemy, by the end of the war the men of McLaughlin's Mosquito Fleet had brought fighting naval units to the very heart of the Everglades. This service also provided training for naval operations in the Mexican War of 1846–1848. Many of McLaughlin's officers reached the peak of their careers during the Civil War.[20] Some sacrificed their lives or health. Passed Midshipman Preble was one of the lucky ones; he did not lose his legs as a result of his injuries in the Florida war and he achieved a distinguished career in the United States Navy, retiring as a rear admiral.

Lieutenant John T. McLaughlin, who seemed willing to risk the health and lives of many men to prove his theory of riverine warfare, probably sacrificed his own. He died at his home in Washington, D. C. on 6 July 1847—just five years after he had shown that his canoe sorties were a legitimate offensive military strategy designed to seek out and destroy the enemy.[21]

Major William G. Belknap, whose troops had actually encountered the enemy in the battle with Bowlegs and the Prophet in December 1841, spoke for all who had pushed through the southern peninsula, "If we have not succeeded in capturing the Enemy, we have so harrassed them, driving them from one secret hiding place to another, penetrating where the foot of the white man has never before trod and pushing them finally to the Mangrove Islands, that they must be induced eventually to surrender, or at all events, to remain in this remote region of retreat where nothing need be apprehended from their hostile incursions."[22]

Indeed, the Navy had driven the hostiles from their "secret recesses," had destroyed the crops they had planted and tended under such adverse conditions, had caused them untold suffering and hardship *but* they had not caught them! Boatloads of sailors and marines had chased a mother, father, and child in vain. They had put out the fires, perhaps eaten the cooking food, destroyed personal possessions of fleeing Indians *but* the victims had escaped. What the Mosquito Fleet campaigns in the Everglades cost in money may never be ascertained; their cost in the health and lives of sailors was immense. Yet they brought in a mere handful of hostiles. Even though the navy conquered the environment, they never humbled the foe!

The army did no better. One day in the fall of 1841, a lame Indian had come in to Fort Fanning and reported that ninety-five Seminoles under four chiefs were nearby. To secure less than a hundred people, including women and children, the following efforts were set in motion. Colonels John Garland, Gustav Loomis, and William Whistler moved their units from Forts Fanning and Micanopy while others from Fort King continued to seek Halleck-Tustenuggee along the St. Johns. Guards from the Second Dragoons patrolled the highways. Detachments from the Fourth Infantry left Fort Cross to scout the Annutiliga and Chacochatti hammocks and the swamps around them. No one found a single Indian. A detachment which had operated from Big Cypress Swamp was finally withdrawn with like results.[23]

It would appear that Colonel Worth, in his determination to end the war, was pouring troops into the field against scattered remnants. There were no longer any large groups of warriors seeking to attack, only sporadic depredations and families dodging and hiding before relentless pursuit. The American troops were "not inaptly compared to . . . men harpooning minnows and shooting sand pipers with artillery."[24]

   As the military scurried to and fro across the land in search of
the enemy, Alligator went into the Everglades with some friendly
Indians, made contact with some subchiefs, and secured one of
Arpeika's lesser chiefs with sixty-seven followers. Thirty-two of
these warriors![25] Words seemed more effective than force, yet no
commander of the Florida forces had dared hold his fire long enough
to let negotiation work. One after the other, sincerely determined
to negotiate a peace, grew trigger-happy when the hostiles walked
out of a council well supplied with necessities provided by the government as an inducement to talk or emigrate. Others were forced by
indignant citizens to return to the field if a depredation occurred
against settlers while talks were in progress.

# 17

## Colonel Worth's
## Final Thrust, 1842

### *Halleck-Tustenuggee Makes a Last Desperate Stand*

"Give me a jug of whisky for I have lost sight of the last
hummock on my land."

*A Chief on his way to Arkansas*

As ELEMENTS OF THE ARMY worked with the Mosquito Fleet to corner
the hostiles presumed to be hiding in the Everglades, Worth determined to corral the Mikasukis still operating along the St. Johns and
some Creeks entrenched along the Suwanee. At the end of 1841,
Colonel John Garland wrote from Fort Fanning to Colonel Worth
that the only Indians left in Middle Florida were Mikasukis under
Chiefs Chitto-Hadjo and Halpatter-Tustenuggee. (This was not
Alligator, who was now working with the Americans to induce his
brothers to join him in Arkansas, but a Creek chief. From now on
the name Halpatter-Tustenuggee will refer to the Creek.) Garland
planned to approach the hostiles with 125 men to fight or talk as the
situation warranted. He had brought in under guard two Creek
chiefs, Hotulke and Cholotchy, and he expressed the conviction that
Octiarche, operating again in his old territory between the Suwanee
and the Withlacoochee, would come in with forty warriors.[1]

235

A meeting with Octiarche was finally arranged, in January 1842, near the mouth of the Withlacoochee. Nethlock Emathla, held at Fort Brooke with his cousin, Tiger Tail, 52 warriors and 110 women and children, was dispatched by ship to talk emigration with the Creek chief. From the ingenious excuses and evasive language of Octiarche, it soon became clear that he did not intend to do more than acquire provisions and ammunition to continue his resistance. The Americans called a meeting for the twelfth on Nethlock's ship but Octiarche absolutely refused to step aboard. He remembered too well what had happened to Hospetarke and others who went to a council held on a seagoing vessel! Had he entered the transport, he would never have set foot on Florida soil again.[2]

Although Octiarche slipped from their net, the army had more success in another direction. Pressed by land and water, Indians in the south were forced to leave their hiding places. Waxi Hadjo, one of the youngest and most intelligent chiefs in the Big Cypress, was intercepted as he tried to retreat from Lake Okechobee. He had with him seventeen warriors and thirty women and children. When pressed for information on Billy Bowlegs and the Prophet, he could only reply that when he saw them last, they were fleeing from the Everglades with only their families.[3]

Worth was still trying to bring the Middle Florida Indians in to emigrate by negotiation when Halleck-Tustenuggee made a mistake. With seventeen men, he attacked the settlement of Mandarin, burned the village, and killed two women and a child. This cruel act caused panic in the region for it was a thickly settled area. While the citizens and the army debated the question of whose negligence had permitted the sortie, Worth sent his troops into the field again. He ordered Major Thomas Childs to scour the country north to Palatka; then he sent Colonel Bennett Riley to examine Tomoka, Spring Gardens, and all streams entering Dunn's Lake. He was to concentrate on Haw Creek. Worth forced Halleck's brother, Emathla Chee, to act as a guide.[4]

Everyone knew approximately where Halleck's hiding place was for he had been emerging at intervals for seven months to attack travelers on their way to St. Augustine or those going to Picolata on the St. Johns River. He had with him thirty-five warriors, a few Creeks and Seminoles but mostly Mikasukis who considered Florida soil theirs by right. Short Grass (Powis-Fixico), with five men "known as crafty and vindictive Indians," was his ally.[5]

While fifty men of the Second Infantry plied the St. Johns in boats to cut off Halleck's retreat, Major Joseph Plympton, with sixty men, followed the trail from Mandarin. His party was led by scouts who knew both the terrain and the enemy well. They marched for days through water that ranged from ankle to waist deep. Finally they came upon the chief's main camp where they counted the remains of sixteen fires that did not appear to be older than thirty-six hours. Here they picked up a fresh trail which led them to the spot near the head of Dunn's Lake where Halleck and his men were prepared to make a stand. Plymton's men smelled then saw smoke from the hummock on which the Indians were ensconsed. When the major heard the whistle signaling the hostiles to their positions, he quickly drew his own troops forward. As usual the Indians were entrenched on a mound surrounded by water. They had thrown up a log breastwork behind which they felt secure.

As the Americans pushed forward through the "moat" in front of them, the enemy whooped and screamed to frighten them. However, the soldiers were no longer intimidated by their opponents' psychological warfare. They continued to advance until they were hit by a sharp volley from the right. This was returned with such vigor that the Indians shifted position and attacked from the center and left. The Americans diverged into a V formation and fired from either side of the barricade while a company of dragoons crept around to the rear. Realizing that they were surrounded, the warriors held their ground for less than half an hour before slipping through the ranks of the Americans. The Indians left two wounded on the field and a trail of blood which testified to other injured as they disappeared into a trackless waste which even Plympton's men could not penetrate. The Americans had one killed and three wounded. After the battle, they returned to Halleck's camp where they destroyed or captured much of the band's gear and possessions.[6]

Plympton's troops found a camp on the Tomoka River near King's Road which Halleck's women and children had occupied. The major reported it was so well disguised that without the help of Indians and blacks who had lived with the group, they would never have noticed it. Apparently Halleck would not have stayed to fight if he had not had to cover the retreat of his civilians who were only a day in advance of the warriors. During the skirmish, the women and children fled across the St. Johns somewhere between one army patrolboat and another. Plympton had also placed units in ambush at every ford of the Ocklawaha to intercept the chief and his warriors but they moved on to a spot ten miles below any known ford through land considered impassable even by Indians and there escaped the net.[7]

As Halleck eluded the army on the eastern side of Florida, other Indians were proving as intractable in the west. Octiarche appeared to be collecting arms and provisions under false pretenses. It was even rumored that he planned to kill Nethlock Emathla for his efforts to negotiate. Tiger Tail was secretly trying to induce some of the Indians awaiting transport at Fort Brooke to fight again. When Nethlock's messengers to Octiarche didn't return as expected, he decided that the Creek leader really meant to harm him or his men. He asked the army to let him take a group of thirty armed warriors into the woods to seek revenge on the Creeks. Although this entailed a great risk, he was supplied with horses and ammunition and allowed to go. Tiger Tail would not accompany the party.

Two nights later, the guards at Fort Brooke noticed that the women were moving out of camp with small packages. When they reported this to their superior, the officer-in-charge hurried to Tiger Tail's tent. He found it empty. A party sent in hot pursuit recaptured the chief's wife and son as well as five other women, including two wives of the chief's younger brother who was with Nethlock's war party. Colonel Loomis then seized and disarmed every Indian at Fort Brooke.[8]

When the unsuccessful expedition against Octiarche returned, every man had to come to the commanding officer's tent to lay down his arms. Each warrior was immediately placed aboard a transport in Tampa Bay and never permitted to step on Florida soil again. Their women and children were allowed to join them along with a few other Indians ready to emigrate. Only Nethlock Emathla and his sisters remained at Fort Brooke. On 5 February, 230 Indians embarked on the ship *Rosalind*. Included in the group were 68 warriors—Seminoles, Creeks, Tallahassees, Mikasukis, and Uchees. There were many braves but no major chiefs.[9]

With at least half the Indians in Florida safely on their way to Arkansas, the army again turned its attention to the remaining Creeks and Octiarche. The chief was thought to be hiding in Cook's Hummock on the Esteen Hatchee River west of Tallahassee. Colonel Josiah H. Vose marched directly toward the area from the west while Colonel William Whistler approached it from the Suwanee. They might never have found Octiarche if he had not set upon a family of settlers, killing the mother and one child and leaving four others for dead.[10] With angry citizens in pursuit, the chief fled to the Suwanee, leaving behind the corn and bacon he had taken from the farm.

Captain B. Thornton, Negro Jim, and an Uchee Indian followed Octiarche's trail all day. By nightfall it had led to the swamp where the Creek camp was located. Thornton secured his horses and crept into the swamp with twenty men. Having learned to move without a sound, they reached undetected the spot where the palmetto sheds of the enemy stood. The time was an hour before dawn. The troops surrounded the camp and waited for daybreak. Captain Thornton and Jim stood only ten feet from the sleeping warriors. The women and children lay around them. "An Indian arose, stretched himself and looked at the stars . . . evidently nervous and with a troubled mind. He stirred the fire, rubbed his sleepy eyes, and as though overcome with constant watching, sat down again, when his head drooping upon his chest, he was asleep. A woman sat down by his side, while her child played listlessly with his hand. . . . Gray dawn was just approaching, when the men . . . become impatient. The noise increasing, alarmed the sleepers who, with one bound, and a shrill whoop . . . cleared the entire command. The soldiers desisted from firing as the women and children would have been victims. The warriors escaped." [11]

Thornton reported four women and three children (one a Negro girl of twelve) taken prisoner.[12] Sprague commented that the human feeling had prevailed again and recounted how often a soldier had shared tobacco or rations with Indian prisoners after pursuing them for days and nights through hummock and swamp. Perhaps angered by the fierce attack by Octiarche on an innocent woman and children, he speculated that had every captive been hung on the spot, the war might have been quickly ended.[13]

According to the official report and Sprague's account, all the wounds in Mrs. Richard Tilles and her children were made with arrows, indicating that the Indians were either short of ammunition or anxious to do their damage quietly. The facts suggest the possibility of three lives lost (one of the children died later of her wounds) over a few pounds of corn and bacon and some gun powder.

It was, indeed, a frustrating situation for Colonel Worth and the citizens. Five hundred times as many troops as warriors were in the field; friendly Indians were trying to assist by persuasion. Yet the natives held possession of the country in that, although few in number, they could commit murders which no forecast, precaution, or military might could prevent or punish! No one could predict how long it would take to assure the safety of every settler.

In spite of past failures, Worth ordered another sweep of the countryside. The results were all negative. Colonel Whistler found no sign of the Creeks in the Wacasassa country. Colonel Loomis wrote from the Withlacoochee, "all our labour so far has proved of no avail. No recent traces of the Enemy can be found." Major Childs reported from Fort Lauderdale, "It is not necessary for me to say how much I regret that these successive efforts to find the hiding places of Jones and his band have been in vain."[14]

On 14 February, Colonel Worth reported to Adjutant General Winfield Scott that there were now no more than 301 Indians in Florida—112 warriors and 189 women and children. Among them were 120 Creeks—including 45 warriors—who had not been in Florida when the war began.

Worth asked permission to cut his troops in Florida by as much as five-sixths and to allow friendly Indians from Arkansas to move among those still in the swamps, urging them to emigrate. The troops would be used only to protect white settlements and the Indians would be allowed to plant and settle as long as they remained south of Pease Creek. They would be permitted to trade freely at all military posts. Worth reminded Scott that in no other case of Indian removal had there been an instance where a few had not remained. He wrote, "... the operation since June conclusively demonstrates ... the utter impracticability of securing them by main force. ... Every exertion of force, while it tends to make the enemy more wild in his habits and savage in his nature, places the object in view, his total expulsion, more remote."[15] Worth had seen unmistakable evidence that massive armies would never catch the handful of Indians that remained in Florida. He asked permission to end the war, leaving a few remaining natives in the lower peninsula.

Colonel Worth, whose toughness in battle had never been questioned, now found himself in the center of a storm. When this letter was made public, some declared his proposal was a compromise of honor for the nation and the army. "The contest ... had been commenced, and should be preserved in, so as to vindicate the potency and efficiency of our arms and illustrate the blessings of a bountiful treasury," quoted Sprague. He personally felt that the Treasury had "already lavished millions without obtaining either glory for the military or satisfying the expectations of the people."[16]

According to Sprague, the men in the field were suffering every kind of privation and difficulty, including disappointment at not being able to find the enemy. He noted bitterly that the public called for vigorous prosecution of the war, retrenchment of the military force, and expulsion of the Indians all at once. Citizens must be protected at all cost but the drain upon the national treasury must cease. Everyone else knew exactly what ought to be done but it was left to the commander in Florida to devise some means to capture the remnants and then to suffer disgrace if he failed.

It is easy to understand Sprague's resentment but his evaluation was only partially true. For, though every man who took command in Florida suffered various forms of criticism and dismay over his failure, nearly every one of them left the field as a newly promoted general. When victories came, they did so, not from miracles, but from hard-won knowledge of the terrain and the enemy.

As usual, Colonel Worth went on with his plans, impervious to press or public. In the spring of 1842, he turned his attention to the swollen ranks of civilians working for the army. Outposts were abandoned and troops concentrated so that means of transportation could be reduced. The number of horses, mules, and wagons, and the amount of forage was cut to the bone. Clerks, teamsters, wagon masters, stable keepers, mechanics, and day laborers were discharged; steamboats and sailing vessels dispensed with. From now on, Worth intended to confine operations entirely to the military in quantities "adequate to the numbers and dispersed condition of the enemy." [17]

On 10 April 1842, another hundred Indians left Fort Brooke for New Orleans under Major L. G. Capers, disbursing agent of Indian Affairs. Twenty-five warriors remained behind to act as trackers and guides for the army. They were allowed to keep their families with them. [18]

Among the chiefs who left on this convoy was Nethlock Emathla. The Tallahassee had fought hard for his land until he had to surrender; then he had worked to bring others in. Now old, he was dignified, distinguished, calm, and intelligent.

One who remained to work for the army was Holartooche, another Tallahassee of about fifty years of age. He stood over six feet two inches tall and was described as "well-proportioned and erect, with a heavy, rough countenance, small dark eyes, heavy eyebrows, large mouth and lips compressed, indicative of firmness and resolution." Holartooche usually spoke in a subdued manner except when he referred to his childhood home.

His father's village was on the site of the present Tallahassee which was taken over by the citizens to be the capital of the territory. As a young man, Holartooche had fought against General Jackson at the battle of Suwanee Old Town in 1818. He was at the councils that resulted in the Treaty of Payne's Landing in 1832. He had not wanted war but had lived with it during most of his adult life. He told his captors: "I was opposed to open hostilities and, to avoid collision, moved with my band from one secluded place to another. My last town was in the Annuttiliga Hummock; I thought it secure, but the troops closed in upon us from year to year, depriving us of crops and subjecting our women and children to sickness and want. [Even] to hunt, fish, or plant led to discovery of our hiding places."

Finally in 1841, he and his band surrendered. Sprague declared that Holartooche was distinguished for "wise and deliberate counsels." Coacoochee for "daring and savage acts of the warrior;" and he predicted the former would be more effective in the new land. He did not foresee that the daring, savage warrior, Coacoochee, would be able to transform himself into a skilled and persistent negotiator when the time came. In fact, no Indian chief in Florida ever appeared braver than did Coacoochee on two occasions when he bargained first for his father and then for his daughter from positions of great military weakness.

Although Colonel Worth had the armed might, he may have felt in the spring of 1842 that he was operating from a position of weakness. His intelligence sources indicated that the numbers and dispersed condition of the enemy were as follows: Arpeika was hovering around the headwaters of the Locha-Hatchee River with less than fifty people—mostly Mikasukis with a few Seminoles; the Prophet and Bowlegs were near Mangrove Lake at Key Biscayne with less than forty people; there were sixty Seminoles and some stragglers of other tribes on or about the Kissimmee; Halleck-Tustenuggee, still near Haw Creek, was thought to have only ten men left (an erroneous estimate); the two Octiarches ranged between the Suwanee and the Withlacoochee with forty-seven Creeks; Halpatter-Tustenuggee, with three or four other chiefs, led a band of forty-nine—including Creeks, Tallahassees, and Mikasukis—and ranged the hummocks of the Esteen Hatchee River; and there were about twenty Creeks in the hummocks of the Ocklockonee.

The colonel's task was to devise a scheme to find and capture these Indians even though the hiding places in Florida were as good as they were numerous. The Indians had their problems too. As their numbers decreased, they had been forced to reorganize. Those on the southern tip of the peninsula had finally broken the spell of the Prophet (Hotulke-Thlocko) and had cast aside the octogenarian Arpeika in favor of Holatter Micco (Billy Bowlegs). Fuse Hadjo had been chosen sense-bearer to the new chief. The strategy of the three hundred hostiles left in Florida was to move in parties of five or ten persons and to disperse even more when pursued.[19]

Unable to gain support for his plan to declare the second Florida war over even though only a few hundred Indians remained in the area, Worth had to take to the field again. He selected the capture of Halleck-Tustenuggee as his next objective.

Word had come into army headquarters that Halleck had retreated with his party across the Ocklawaha toward the Withlacoochee. Scouts reported that he had crossed the Tampa road fourteen miles south of Fort King and gone into Long Swamp. On 10 April, Worth sent a small detachment to sweep the country southeast of Fort King to the Wacasassa and areas south of there. He dispatched another unit to watch the Ocklawaha to prevent Halleck from returning to his old haunts east of the St. Johns.[20]

In a larger sweep, he sent out the troops which had been guarding the emigrés at Fort Brooke against a series of targets: the Wahoo Swamp, the Withlacoochee River, the cove of that river, and Lakes Panee Sufekee and Charlo Popka. Companies under Colonel Garland and Majors Belknap, Plympton, Graham, and McCall penetrated the swamps in every direction. Although they scoured both land and water without seeing a single Indian, they destroyed many camps and abandoned cornfields. On 16 April they rendezvoused at Jumper Creek. No one had any success to report. The officers were mortified; Chief Holartooche and five companions who had acted as guides and trackers were humiliated and baffled.

The following day, Holartooche found a single track which led toward Lake Ahapopka.[21] When he had determined that it might also lead to Halleck's new camp, he went to Colonel Worth's tent. He asked that if he led the army to the place, that the women and children be spared and the warriors treated with respect. He must have received some assurance for when Colonel Worth himself took four hundred men against the band, Holartooche led the way.

The next morning was beautiful. The column moved out with the Negro interpreters and friendly Indians in advance of the troops. The guides were inspecting every blade of grass and every twig, looking for footsteps. Suddenly the chief became very excited. He explained to the officers: "This blade of grass was trod upon this morning; you see it is crushed; the sun, nor the light of day has not shone upon it; had either it would have wilted. You see it is green but not crushed. Here are more. . . . There is the print of a foot."

By the great distance between the footprints, the chief decided that a messenger was running to spread the alarm that the army was coming. After following the track for about three miles, Worth came to the hummock where Halleck and forty warriors were preparing to make a stand. As the soldiers waded through mud and rotten vegetation to reach the battleground, some of them vomited from the stench. For a time, the Indians stood firm; they were protected by a partial breastwork of fallen timber and by a thick undergrowth which hid them from the approaching army. The soldiers could see the "manly frame" and hear the voice of Halleck-Tustenuggee as he urged his men on. He and his warriors were naked, their bodies painted scarlet and decorated with the scalps and other trophies of white victims. They concentrated their fire on the Indian guides and Negro interpreters whom they must have felt were traitors. As the balls flew thick around Gopher John, he pulled from his pocket a well-filled flask and said to the officer beside him, "I feel all over, mighty queer, de injen fight so strong! I must take a big un," and drained his bottle, reprimed his rifle, whooped, and was lost amid the foliage and smoke.

Holartooche, mounted on a fleet pony, his breast bare, his sleeves rolled up to the shoulder, his long black hair, streaked with grey, streaming in the wind, raised up in his stirrups. With his rifle waving in the air, he gave his piercing cry which had once cheered the Seminole to victory and charged fearlessly. It was as if, in the heat of battle, he had forgotten that the enemy were now of his own race. The warriors whooped and yelled as they defended their hummock but the army advanced steadily and returned yell for yell. Unable to retreat in a body, the Indians dispersed into parties of four and five and disappeared. Again the hostiles escaped capture but at what a price!

They were forced to leave behind "large quantities of dried deer meat, dressed deer skins, half-finished moccasins, axes, hoes, kettles and articles of clothing." The well-made huts indicated that this was a permanent camp. The women and children had fled in such haste that they had abandoned their thimbles, needles, thread, and beautifully ornamented dresses.

The guides set off to follow the trails but lost them in the water about two miles beyond the camp. The fleeing Indians carried two badly wounded comrades but, in spite of this burden, they escaped from the detachments sent to pursue them. Only one old man, Halleck's father-in-law, was taken. Of the warriors active in the engagement, two were killed, two badly wounded, and one taken prisoner. The army lost two dead and three severely wounded.

Private Wandell gave his life in that colorful little skirmish. To bury him, his friends got down on their knees and dug a grave with their hands and their tin cups. Then they wrapped his body in his blanket and placed it in its lonely resting place. They disguised the spot so that the Indians would not disinter and scalp him. "His requiem was the distant yell of the savage, the discharge of musketry, and the shout of the victors."[22]

Osone Micco (King of the Lakes), the old man taken prisoner, went out to seek his son-in-law and found him only six miles away. Halleck sent word that he wanted to talk but first someone must send him a shirt as he had lost his in the battle. The next day he sent two messengers to ask for tobacco and whisky. There was no doubt he intended to stock up on supplies and then flee. Worth decided to play along until the chief put himself in a position to be seized.

On 29 April, the chief surprised everyone by coming boldly into camp, accompanied by two wives and two children about ten or twelve years old. He saluted the sentinels gracefully as he passed by, looked carefully about him, and dismounted before the commander's tent. The two leaders greeted each other cordially. The officers assembled to meet him—ostensibly to give evidence of kindly feelings but actually to meet a man who had eluded them so successfully for nine months! Colonel Worth, who questioned Halleck for some time, found him interested in peace but not in emigration. Halleck went back to his own camp before dark, accompanied by Holartooche and the Negro Primus, obviously pleased by his reception. He returned the next morning with five messengers whom he promised to send to the Creek Chief Octiarche. He delivered his message in the presence of the officers and sent his emissaries on their way.

As Halleck-Tustenuggee and the army waited to hear from Octiarche, an old pattern began to develop. The chief grew more and more arrogant in his demands for fresh beef, flour, and whisky. Colonel Worth sent Major Garland, Captain McCall, and Lieutenant Sprague out to his camp one day to pay their respects to the old men and women of the band. While there, they observed that the camp could not be taken by surprise. Worth then invited the chief to go with him to Fort King. Halleck accepted eagerly for he planned to buy powder and lead to take back to the wilderness when he returned. However, Worth had left orders that as soon as he and the chief had left, Major Garland was to "seize the entire band, tie them hand and foot, and send them to Fort King."

With the chief gone, Major Garland ordered games and dances for the people and plied them with food and drink. As they expected their leader back on the third day, they prepared a special feast. At the appointed time all the people gathered at the camp. As they rejoiced over the arrangements, Garland asked a subchief to make sure that everyone was present. Then at twelve noon he announced to them in a quiet, calm manner that they were all prisoners. At first the Indians thought he was joking but when the bugle sounded and armed men surrounded the party, they realized they were captives. Five women were sent out to bring the luggage into camp.

That night twenty-five men were bound and guarded by fifty soldiers. As each man told where his weapon was hid, soldiers gathered up twenty-five excellent rifles. Some were in hollow trees, some under logs, some wrapped in moss and buried, and others hidden among the palmettoes. Many of the provisions distributed in the recent past were found wrapped in palmetto leaves. That night the women were not allowed to communicate with their men-folk.

A messenger was sent to Colonel Worth to tell him that the coup had succeeded. When an excited soldier dashed up to his commander on a lathered horse and handed him a message, the chief realized that something was amiss. He soon learned that he and his people were captives; he would never be permitted to return to his beloved woods again. "He stood erect, quivering with excitement, brushing his fingers through his long, black hair, his eyes sparkling with fire, his breast heaving in agony as though about to grasp and tear in pieces the perpetrators [of this act]." Then he saw the guard of soldiers around him and mastered his anger. "Silently he sank unconscious upon the ground, trembling with exhaustion, his head drooping upon his bosom, his arms hanging listlessly by his side; at length, the intensity of feeling gave way to sobs and tears."[23] Halleck was taken under guard to Horse Key—an island from which there was no escape—at the mouth of the Suwanee River. Here his band would meet him. Colonel Worth reported to the adjutant general that the entire band, except for two warriors, were in his possession.[24]

Why Halleck fell into the same trap as so many chiefs had before him is hard to understand. In fact, when the messengers came back from Octiarche and heard what had happened to him, they thought he had contrived his own capture. When they said as much one night, the chief leaped up and knocked down two of his accusers. He seized a third, "a stout, athletic man," whom he struck in the breast with both feet. Then, grasping his victim by the throat, he thrashed his body to the ground and, seizing his ear in his mouth, severed it close to the head! "Dilating his sinewy frame, extending both hands to heaven, with his eyes and nostrils distended with rage, he ground the ear in his teeth, like a mastiff, then, spitting it upon the ground and clearing his mouth of coagulated blood, screamed with savage delight and vengeance: 'Tustenuggee . . . Halleck-Tustenuggee!!'"[25] Tustenuggee! Warrior! Halleck—the Warrior! Alas, Halleck, the Warrior, would fight no more in Florida. His shouts of "Warrior" rang through the night. He was incensed that anyone would think he could surrender. The furious, trembling figure of the magnificent chief, swaying in the flickering light of half-extinguished brands, sent a thrill of horror and pity through the assembled crowd. For a moment, everyone present must have felt the agony of that free spirit now caged, emasculated. At last when the guards moved to subdue him, he was almost helpless from over-exertion and excitement. His two wives "watched with the quiet submission of the Indian female," and wept silently as he was led away.

Sprague had been a party to the perfidy that led to Halleck's downfall but he felt the same compassion and respect for him as he had for the other great Indian leaders. He wrote: "Whatever sins may be laid to the charge of this Indian chieftan, or however diabolical the instinct of his nature, his land was dearer to him than life. For it he had fought boldly and unceasingly; and had adopted the alternative of the feeble, treachery, against the strong, to maintain his inheritance. . . . If this trait in the savage be patriotism, Halleck-Tustenuggee's name should stand eternally side by side with the most distinguished of mankind."[26]

As Halleck-Tustenuggee and his band languished in confinement on Horse Key, they were very unhappy. Benumbed by drinking, they wrangled and quarreled, accusing each other of responsibility for their plight. Their faces were scarred by scratches and blows received during these altercations. One subchief tried to strangle himself by placing a noose around his neck and fastening it to the end of his foot. He was wrapped in a blanket with his little daughter and when he began to extend his foot to draw the cord tight, she screamed and brought others to prevent him from carrying out his plan. Another chief, on his way to Arkansas, cried: "Give me a jug of whisky for I have lost sight of the last hammock on my land." Now Halleck and his people had little else to console them. They were in a stockade from which neither guile nor brute strength could release them. Convinced there was no way to escape from Horse Key, he decided to emigrate.[27]

Runners were sent out to bring in five men who were elsewhere on the day of the coup and five who had been wounded. Three men went to Haw Island and brought back plunder, including cloth, blankets, calico, and five cannisters of powder, which the band had collected over the years. By July, the people were begging to leave the prison island. On the fourteenth, a company of forty warriors and eighty women and children embarked for New Orleans. "They were sullen and morose; nothing but the presence of a company of Seventh Infantry on board the boat, caused them to refrain from giving vent to their savage and revengeful passions."

The chief was especially angry because he felt that Colonel Worth had not acknowledged him as a brave warrior who had fought for his land to the last moment. He shouted that he had been hunted like a wolf and was now to be sent away like a dog. His expression was so ferocious and his manner so threatening that soldiers seized him, afraid that he might draw his knife and lash out at those about him. Perhaps Colonel Worth eyed this chief with some trepidation too for, instead of addressing a farewell speech in person, he sent a written message. When the paper was read to him and Halleck realized he had been mistaken, "he wept like a child."[28]

How different was Halleck-Tustenuggee from Osceola and Coacoochee who accepted their fate with calm stoicism! Yet there is something truly heroic in the wild passion of this untamed savage as he stands defeated in the midst of a crowd of curious white men who watch his suffering and despair.

Halleck was about thirty-five when he was captured—tall, sinewy, well-formed and erect. In conference he was so mild and bland it seemed impossible that he could be capable of violent passions or the perpetrator of cruel and reckless murders. As a Mikasuki, he felt that the land really belonged to him and his people. He considered himself a warrior but in 1839 he had been asked to speak when

General Macomb came to work out a peace. He had acquitted himself well, "evading with tact and shrewdness all inquiry as to the number and locations of the principal chiefs." From then on, his people had regarded him as a leader. Many Floridians would sigh with relief when his ship set its course toward New Orleans and they were certain he could trouble them no more.[29]

Just before he left the area, Halleck spoke to a council at the Wacasassa River. He was authorized to promise the remaining natives that if they moved south of Pease Creek and ceased their attacks on settlers, they could, for the present, hunt and plant and live in peace. If they rejected the offer, the pursuit would begin again. The Indians chose to believe the chief; they accepted the conditions. Seven years had passed since the Seminoles decided to repudiate the Treaty of Payne's Landing and fight for their homes.[30]

In 1836, when Osceola sent his message to General Clinch, predicting that the Seminoles could hold out against American might for five years, [31] no one believed him. Even after the attacks on Wiley Thompson, Dade's unit, and the St. Johns plantations, most experts thought the Seminole allies had won with an element of surprise and a great deal of luck.

In 1835, no one paid heed to Lieutenant George A. McCall who, in a letter to his father from the battlefield, described how the Indians had outmaneuvered General Clinch and held their own against many times their own number. He predicted that the war might last as long as seven years.[32] No doubt even he was surprised when his forecast came true!

# 18

# Colonel Josiah H. Vose's
# Non-Campaign, 1842

*Octiarche and Tiger Tail Are Brought Down*

"I see the sun for the last time."

THLOCKO-TUSTENUGGEE (Tiger Tail)

IN MAY 1842, PRESIDENT TYLER approved Colonel Worth's plan to allow the few remaining Indians some land deep in the peninsula where they could set up their villages and plant their crops.[1] On the eleventh, Adjutant General Winfield Scott wrote Worth that he could declare the war at an end whenever he felt the time was right. On the twenty-second, Worth, in turn, informed McLaughlin that he should disband his forces and dismiss his ships as fast as he thought practicable.[2] This process was completed by 31 August.[3]

All through June and July, Worth continued to assess the situation. He reported to the adjutant general that he had cut expenses for the war by $15,000.00 a month for a total of $174,923.90 during the fiscal year 1841–1842.[4] Since he had been in charge of the war, he had shipped west 662 Indians and Negroes. He assured his superiors in Washington that there were no more than three hundred Seminole allies left in all of Florida.[5]

Although the enemy had dwindled to a mere handful, there

were still some formidable chiefs at large. Unconquered in August 1842 were the ancient and senile Arpeika, the Prophet (now shorn of his power), Holatter-Micco (Billy Bowlegs), Halpatter-Tustenuggee (the Creek), Chitto-Hadjo, Cotsa Fixico Chopca, Pascofa, Octiarche, and Tiger Tail (who had just escaped for the fourth time!).[6]

Arpeika and the Prophet, with their people, were already established on Lake Okeechobee within the reservation. Billy Bowlegs and two of his subchiefs had made arrangements with the army to move their people down there. The others were still studying their options. Most of them seemed unwilling to emigrate, except Tiger Tail, who had committed himself to go with his people but was too ill to be moved.[7] Octiarche was in the vicinity of the Suwanee gathering his people to move south of Pease Creek.

Feeling that the situation was under control, Worth issued Order Number Twenty-Eight, formally concluding hostilities, and turned over the details of withdrawing the army to Colonel J. H. Vose. President Tyler promoted Worth to brevet brigadier general and announced to a relieved nation that the Florida war had truly come to an end.[8] But even as the president was speaking, trouble occurred. Chief Pascofa, who headed a band of Creeks usually called Ocklocknee because they lived on the river of that name, was accused of raiding in the Apalachicola valley.

Harassed and threatened by "lower class" whites, some reckless young warriors, waiting to move south, attacked a party at San Petro, killing two. A posse of twenty, under militia Colonel Bailey, pursued the band of ten, killing two and wounding five.[9] It was later discovered that the braves knew nothing of the "peace." Another party attacked a carriage near Chocochatti, wounded a man and killed his granddaughter.

One of Vose's major problems appeared to be that of reaching the scattered remnants of the Seminole allies to give them the message that if they traveled peaceably to the area south of Pease Creek, they could live there unmolested. He believed the chiefs were fulfilling their pledges surely, if slowly. The Seminoles and Mikasukis were settled on the land assigned them; only the Creek chiefs were still at Cedar Key working out arrangements for their people to move south. Vose sent runners into the field to spread the word to the stragglers unaware of the armistice that they would be safe if they moved south.[10]

The citizens refused to consider extenuating circumstances and demanded that armed forces capture and punish the Creeks. A man of sound judgment and of thirty years experience in the army,[11] Vose prevailed on the militia to wait a few days while his troops sought the specific Indians who had committed the depredations.

Even when ordered by the secretary of war to reopen the war, he resisted. Vose explained that if he could get the message of the armistice to the most isolated bands, he could move them to an area where they could no longer harass the citizens. He claimed that the settlers now so determined to exterminate every Indian in Florida were the very ones who had refused to fight—even for their homes—when the enemy were more numerous. He ordered the commanding officers of every fort to name an emissary to go abroad among the people, warning them of the "inevitable disaster which must attend their hostile demonstrations."[12]

While Vose waited for his runners to find the Creeks, he did some sleuthing on his own. He found that whites had pillaged a canoe and stripped Indian fields of corn and peas before the attack on Chocochatti. The guilty citizens offered to return the plunder but convinced Vose that at least some of his problems stemmed from behavior of the whites.

The colonel now had Indians coming by land and sea from the Everglades to trade (as per agreement) at Tampa while others were converging on the city in order to move south toward the reservation. He worried that they would be attacked by angry settlers.[13]

During the year, Congress had finally passed the Armed Occupation Act entitling a family to obtain 160 acres of land if the head of the household promised to defend his holdings.[14] Among the families thus settled, the fear of Indians seemed almost paranoiac even though official investigations found their fears groundless.[15] Many others who had left their plantations during the war seemed to prefer to wait for their provisions as "suffering inhabitants." If these were late or not forthcoming, the hungry whites (in a reversal of roles) stole from the Indians rather than plant their own crops, thus inviting retaliation. Vose hoped to control "the vagabond class" in the territory who tended to gather in large bodies and threaten to make war upon the Indians. Adjutant General Jones ordered the colonel to furnish armed guards for all Indians traveling through the territory.[16] This would have been an excellent plan if Vose could have predicted when or where small bands of Indians would be traveling.

When Vose received another message from the secretary of war ordering him to take the field to catch and punish the Creeks, he replied that to do so would be to "forfeit every pledge" he had made to them. He was sure that to resort to force would not only scatter those Indians already assembled but would incite others to more acts of retaliation. He replied to the secretary that he was delaying implementation of the order.[17]

The Creeks were gathered on Cedar Key, drinking themselves into a stupor and begging for more whisky. Unscrupulous whites plundered their camps and harassed them constantly. Yet the Indians were slow to move south. On 5 October, Nature solved the problem. A storm destroyed everything on the key and the Indians had to leave.[18] By the end of October, Colonel Vose was able to report to General Worth that he had ascertained the numbers and location of all the Indians left in Florida. He had pacified them and was ready to act either offensively or defensively as required.

Vose had devoted his entire campaign to separating Indians and whites without bloodshed. The result was that both groups were suspicious of him and even Washington questioned his will to "win" a war declared ended! After his regiment left Florida on 30 September, he asked permission to follow it. Furthermore, he wrote Worth that "since affairs did not seem to be as well settled as had been anticipated," he hoped the general would resume command. On 1 November, Worth returned, after three months leave.[19]

Worth found that times hadn't changed much in Florida. On 10 November, Octiarche came to Fort Brooke to complain that Holatter Micco (Billy Bowlegs) was trying to assert his authority over all the Indians left in the state. Old enmities between the Seminoles and Creeks were reasserting themselves. Captain Seawell, commander of Fort Brooke, was told to seize Octiarche since his constant assertions that he meant to die upon the soil indicated that he had no intention of emigrating. The chief and his men continued to come warily to the fort as they used every opportunity to buy lead and powder.

Thlocko-Tustenuggee (Tiger Tail) was in a camp near Cedar Key.[20] He had apparently forgotten his promise to move south and was idling away his time in "the most brutal intoxication." Lieutenant Sprague, with a sergeant, went to his camp and found him "in the midst of a scrub, stretched on a bear skin before a small fire." There were six men and eight women and children with him. The warrior's face was scratched, bitten and beaten in drunken brawls until it was so swollen that he could not see.[21] He was quite unable to travel. This time Sprague decided that the camp could be surrounded and the small band seized. Shortly thereafter a detachment of the Third

Infantry picked up the enfeebled Tiger Tail with his little company and carried them off to Horse Key from which there was no escape.[22] Because of his knowledge and pleasing manners he had been treated with consideration by army leaders throughout the war. Back in his wilderness camp, he would laugh at those who had given him presents and had fed and clothed his women and children. He had boasted that he never intended to keep his promises to Coacoochee and Nethlock Emathla. But no one had ever escaped from the stockade at Horse Key and Tiger Tail would be no exception.

Thlocko-Tustenuggee was secured in November.[23] In late December, Octiarche was still loitering about the garrison, arguing and complaining but making no plans to move south. Usually a reserved man, his uncharacteristic grumbling was to have disastrous results. On the twentieth, he was invited to the commanding officer's quarters to talk. As the chief was explaining that he was, himself, satisfied to emigrate but found it difficult to control his young warriors, a cordon was drawn about his party and all were taken into custody. His band of fifty-one people, including twenty-nine warriors, was brought to Horse Key and interned with Tiger Tail. Middle Florida was now cleared of any Indian menace.

From Horse Key the two bands were sent to New Orleans. The 250 souls gathered there were a motley crowd of Seminoles, Creeks, Tallahassees, Mikasukis, Uchees, and Hitchitees. Most of them were remnants of defunct bands with neither kinfolk to support them nor chiefs to lead them. As long as they were fighting a common enemy, they had worked in harmony to protect their land but now old feuds were renewed, old passions rekindled, and vicious crimes committed. Only army troops managed to keep them in control until they reached Arkansas.[24]

Thlocko-Tustenuggee was gloomy and reserved; he spoke to no one but a sister who watched over him and waited on him with complete devotion. From the time the chief left Florida his health failed rapidly. While he was still in the barracks at New Orleans awaiting transportation up the river, he became very ill. In his delirium he muttered a "talk" in which he repeated the names of friends and familiar places in Florida. He sang an Indian song to which he kept time by clapping his hands. On the day of his death, he asked to see the sun set. He lay gazing at it intently for some time, then he shook hands with everyone around him and said, "I see the sun for the last time." As the last rays lingered on the horizon, he closed his eyes and folded his arms. Thlocko-Tustenuggee, known as Tiger-Tail, was dead.[25]

Here was an Indian who had lived with and learned to love a white family, had observed the Sabbath even after he returned to life in the wilderness, had dressed as an Indian but spoken the language and observed the manners of the whites. When he chose to cast his lot with his red brothers, he had only partly turned his back on his white friends. It is possible that the point of no return came as he watched from a treetop members of the race that had once befriended him burn his house and tear up his fields. At any rate, as the struggle to preserve his culture and his land grew fiercer, he had used the very qualities he had learned from whites and his knowledge of them to outwit and deceive them for years. Coacoochee would adapt to a new land and continue to fight for his people. Thlocko-Tustenuggee, whose knowledge of whites might have made him equally effective, saw his last sunset in a refugee camp while barely half-way to a new life.

When Octiarche was secured and forcefully removed from Florida, he was forty-four years old. He was over six feet tall with a frame "remarkable for symmetry and strength," a rugged face and and a manner that was stern, calm, courteous, and dignified. He seldom drank and never to excess, never gave advice or expressed an opinion without mature reflection. He avoided collisions with whites if possible but, when pushed to the limit, he fought hard for his land, his life, and his liberty.

Octiarche was a Creek who had been driven out of Georgia in 1836 at the end of the Creek War. With sixty men and thirty women and children, he had fled across the Chattahoochee River into Florida. He came at last to the Okefenoke Swamp and from there he took his people to Cook's Hummock near the Esteen Hatchee River about eighty miles from Tallahassee. He had sent messengers with the pipe of peace to the Seminoles and Mikasukis, urging that they all co-operate against the whites. His plan was to remain quietly in a remote area but to fight vigorously if molested.

In battle his tall figure and loud voice, urging his comrades to fight was a common sight. He customarily painted one side of his face red, the other side black, and his breast a variety of colors. Sprague wrote of him; "In action, he was bold and dauntless; in council reflective and dispassionate. Among his companions, enterprising and resolute, commanding within the band perfect obedience;

exercising a salutary influence by his integrity, consistency and
sobriety."[26] Sprague felt that if allowed to remain in Florida he
would have been a friend to the citizens but he had been seized to
prevent bloodshed between himself and Billy Bowlegs as the old
grievances between Seminoles and Creeks rose again to the surface.
The chief who stayed hidden in the swamps was still in Florida; the
one who took his complaints to the army and hung around the fort
was shipped off to Arkansas.

Octiarche may have known exactly what he was doing for the
perfect obedience he was once accorded no longer prevailed as his
restless warriors chafed under the restraints of the reservation. Perhaps
their chief thought they would have more scope for their energies
in the West while Octiarche, himself, would be spared a power
struggle over chiefly prerogatives that loomed over the horizon in
Florida.

With the departure of the large band of Creeks, the territory
was almost rid of the tribe that was considered an intruder by both
Seminoles and whites. There remained only Pascofa's band. They
had sought peace with Colonel Vose in the summer of 1842 but the
commander had been too busy with Octiarche and Tiger Tail to
respond positively. Now he hoped they could be contacted and
brought in without coercion.[27]

# 19

## The Final "End"
## of the Second Florida War

*Colonel Hitchcock and Chief Pascofa*
*Make and Keep Some Promises*

"The Indians have been talked out of Florida."
ETHAN ALLEN HITCHCOCK

AS A LAST RESORT IN NOVEMBER 1842, Worth decided to buy the remaining Seminole allies out of Florida. He offered a reward of three hundred dollars for each chief and one hundred dollars for every warrior to the troops who could bring in those who were holding out. He sent Colonel Ethan Allen Hitchcock a confidential memorandum which gave him authority to pay from five hundred to a thousand dollars to two civilians who claimed they could contact Pascofa.[1]

On 28 November, Worth directed Hitchcock to reopen the war which had been declared over so often. Colonel Hitchcock was at Fort Stansbury when he received his orders.[2] While he awaited transportation, he wrote twenty pages in his diary on the ideas of such "organizers of human thoughts" as Plotinus, Saint Paul, Mahomet and Josiah Smith.[3]

Hitchcock's philosophical bent was not the only characteristic

257

which set him apart from his fellow officers. He was born in 1798 in Vermont and named after his grandfather on his mother's side, Ethan Allen. He graduated from West Point in 1817 because it was in the tradition of the family to be in the military. Although his inclination was always toward a life of contemplation, he earned an excellent reputation as an efficient officer whose men liked and respected him. He was a popular instructor at West Point when he got into trouble by defending the men against certain punishments which he said interfered with their civil rights. He refused to give in, even to pressure from Washington. To remove an embarrassment, the army posted him to a pioneer outpost, Fort Snelling (now St. Paul, Minnesota, but then a garrison against the Sioux Indians). This frontier station was so remote it was assumed the brash young officer would never be heard from again.

While spending a long winter in the north, Hitchcock wrote the president of the United States a complete resumé of his conflict with authority. It documented clearly that the trouble at West Point had come about because the secretary of war had been uninformed about army regulations and ashamed to admit it. Not long after the president received his letter, Hitchcock had orders reinstating him as commandant of cadets at the academy.[4]

It wasn't long before he was in hot water again—this time because others interfered when he tried to enforce discipline. More than once, cadets appointed by friends of President Andrew Jackson were punished or sent home for infractions of the rules. Each time this happened the president intervened and ordered the boys reinstated. Hitchcock refused to take them back and resigned from the academy rather than knuckle under to pressure from the White House. After that he had several assignments in remote areas before he arrived in Florida with General Gaines in 1836.[5]

It was during another Florida tour under Colonel Worth in 1840 that Hitchcock met and befriended Chief Coacoochee. At that time he decided that the only way to bring about removal of the Florida Indians was to offer them advantages for going.[6] Now that he had been given authority to bring an end to the hostilities, he hoped to use the methods he had urged on his superior two years earlier.

He "felt deeply the delicacy of his position." He was a military man in command of a military force, yet he hoped to accomplish this military mission without the use of military might. Should his plan fail, his career could be jeopardized. However, he had never before let his concern for his career affect his actions.

Although his orders from General Worth were to "pursue, capture and destroy" the remaining Indians, Hitchcock resolved to "remove them without the shedding of blood." He wrote in his diary: "I have been much with Indians and look upon them as a part of the great human family, capable of being reasoned with and susceptible of passions and affections which, rightly touched, will secure moral results with almost mechanical certainty. I repeatedly urged Mr. Poinsett, when he was Secretary of War, to voluntarily assign to the Indians some small part of Florida, and they would soon be willing to go West.... Even if the war was originally unavoidable, which I do not believe, there have been many lives and at least ten million dollars wasted to pay for a ridiculous pride in warring against a handful of savages."[7]

Hitchcock left Fort Stansbury on 9 December 1842, to end the second Seminole war once more. As soon as he arrived to take up his duties, he was approached by two companies of volunteers who put themselves at his service. Determined to try peaceful means rather than force, he dismissed them saying he would call on them if needed.[8] He then chose two companies (eighty men and two officers) out of his own regiment and marched with them to the Chattahoochee River where they all boarded a steamer and set off down the Apalachicola in search of the hostiles.[9] Thus it was that the war which had *almost* started on that beautiful river was to *almost* end there as well.

The band that Hitchcock was after was a party of Creeks that had escaped when their people emigrated from the Apalachicola in 1838. The remnants had retreated to the Ocklocknee River, established a new home there and come to be known as the Ocklocknee Indians. Their chief, Pascofa, had eluded capture when the war was last "ended" by Colonel Worth in 1841. From time to time they had taken revenge over the loss of their lands by burning buildings and killing inhabitants up and down the Apalachicola Valley.

Hitchcock anchored his steamer at a place called Fort Preston.[10] He had brought with him two "friendlies," Ocklese and Necose Hadjo, whom he sent out to look for any Indian who could be induced to come in for a talk and who would take a message back to his people.[11] After two days, his emissaries came back bringing with them a shy, young man of twenty. Hitchcock greeted the youth with gentle courtesy, fed him, and asked him to take a message to Pascofa that a conference was requested. After being fed a second time, the boy went away and came back a couple of days later with the message that his chief was on the way. Three men came in the next day.[12]

A few days later, Pascofa arrived and walked boldly into the camp.[13] Hitchcock took the chief outside where the two men sat on a log in the forest and talked alone except for an interpreter. The chief admitted that he and his people were so isolated that they could not long exist where they were. They were also in danger because of their attacks on whites. Hitchcock made plain that the government had never meant the offer of land in Florida to be permanent and that the only hope for him and his people was to emigrate peacefully. Pascofa finally agreed to come in the next day with his warriors provided the event would be marked by proper ceremonies. After sharing a meal, the two men shook hands and Pascofa returned to his swamp.

The next day the chief approached the camp with ten warriors. The men were "wretchedly" dressed in deerskins and "dirty tattered" shirts but they had feathers in their scalp locks in honor of the occasion. They fired their rifles into the air to signify that they came in peace.

Hitchcock met the party flanked by all of his officers. Everyone shook hands all around and talked briefly about their pleasure at the prospect of peace. They drank a toast in some "abominable stuff" from a tin cup. Then the colonel took the Indian leaders into the woods for more talk and a ceremonial smoking of the pipe of peace. The Creeks appeared satisfied at the manner of treatment they were receiving and agreed to return in three days with their people.

Before he departed for the wilderness, Pascofa told Hitchcock that his band was destitute and that he was very happy at the prospect of peace. "Been rained on for years, but the sun is now shining," he had said. He took with him a blanket for his wife whom he said was almost naked.[14]

It was Christmas Day of 1842 and the men in camp had nothing to do but wonder if the chief would keep his word. Pascofa had sent in a doeskin which held five gallons which Hitchcock had filled with liquor and returned. Would the Indians have a big celebration at his expense and disappear? On the twenty-ninth, several warriors came in to report that their people were slowly gathering. Hitchcock invited them aboard his ship but they firmly declined. They said that they were frightened to come out along the Apalachicola because of the depredations they had committed but that if Hitchcock would give them some provisions and take his boat to a certain spot on

Ocklocknee Bay, they would meet him there. Hitchcock agreed very reluctantly because he was afraid of being duped as many officers before him had been. In the end, he decided to trust the Indians. He sent his two companies back to Fort Stansbury and continued by boat with only twenty men to the designated meeting place.

Hitchcock was determined to use his peaceful methods without compromise but he was far from sanguine. He wrote in his diary: "Much anxiety as to whether the Indians will keep their contract. Pascofa has received the consideration in liquor. . . . If he fails to perform his part of the agreement I shall feel at liberty to take possession of him, if he gives me a chance, and compel him to send a runner for his people. The camp is full of speculation. If I am compelled to seize Pascofa he shall never touch ground again short of Arkansas." [15] Even the mild and friendly Hitchcock was ready to use the much abhorred method of his former commander, newly-promoted General Worth, if success in securing this band and ending hostilities in Florida required it! He stopped at Apalachicola and bought "some calico, ribbons, needles and thread, and a few knick-knacks" before proceeding into the Gulf of Mexico and on to the mouth of the Ocklocknee.

When Hitchcock arrived at his destination on New Year's Day, there was not an Indian in sight. When no one had arrived by the eighth of January, he ordered the ship to start up the Ocklocknee although this river had never been explored by white men and no one knew if they were sailing into an ambush. Several more anxious days passed. At last the colonel sent a party in a rowboat up the river to explore. They returned with Pascofa, who came aboard apologizing for the delay. He said his people were nearby and asked if they might have a dance to commemorate their last hours in Florida.

Lieutenant Henry, supply officer, issued a shirt and turban to each man and a calico dress and kerchief to each woman. He also gave them blankets and food. There were only about fifty people in all. That night fires flared up in the thick woods and the Indians danced for the last time on their beloved native soil. The officers joined in the festivities.

The next day all the Indians boarded the ship. As they approached the dock, they appeared suddenly to realize their plight. The men became serious and silent. The women wept. Hitchcock spoke to them, telling them they would be taken care of and treated well. Pascofa's lips trembled and he could not reply. Hitchcock turned to a woman standing nearby with a child in her arms and told her that she would no longer have to live like a wild animal pursued through the forest, that she could now bring up her children in peace and safety. But she merely hung her head and burst into tears. Whether she preferred her wild existence or was merely frightened by a strange future, Hitchcock did not say and, perhaps, did not know.

The colonel noticed that among the people who came aboard there were no children between the ages of four and fourteen. He believed that gave credence to the rumor that this band had put to death their children to prevent their cries from giving away their hiding places and to make flight easier. If so, the people had paid a terrible price for a few more years of freedom in the wilderness. Now they were sent on their way to Cedar Key and from there to Arkansas under the command of junior officers.[16]

Hitchcock was elated. He wrote, "But now the Indian War is finished—ended—closed for the last time. The Indians have been talked out of Florida."[17]

The citizens had much to celebrate in the new year, 1843. On January thirteenth, Governor Call addressed the Senate and House of Representatives to announce that Lieutenant Colonel Hitchcock's expedition had successfully secured the last Creek band. He exulted, "All apprehension of danger is now removed—not an Indian remains. The last war whoop has been heard on our southwestern border and peace and security are permanently restored in that quarter."[18]

Pascofa and his band departed Cedar Key for New Orleans on 21 January; they left New Orleans on the steamer *William Gaston* and after several mishaps arrived in Arkansas in April 1843. However, all the Seminoles had not left Florida. General Worth, "making a virtue of necessity," agreed that the remnant should be allowed to remain. The lives of fifteen hundred white soldiers and at least thirty million dollars had been sacrificed to remove less than six thousand Indians and a handful of Negroes.[19] There is no way to measure the loss of black and Indian life and property, the misery and heartache they endured in defense of their liberty. If one counts at least two men severely wounded, maimed, or chronically ill for every one who died on the battlefield, Americans paid one of their own for every two of the Seminole allies removed!

Even at such a price, the people of Florida were not entirely quit of the Seminoles. Colonel Hitchcock and Governor Call might declare the war over but all the Indians were not removed from

Florida and the United States government had still a few more follies to commit and more money to squander in pursuit of their final removal to the West.

*Part Four*

# THE THIRD FLORIDA WAR

*Bribery and Bullying for Emigration*

*1848–1858*

# 20

# The Final Indignity,
# 1848–1858

*Private Enterprise Is Enlisted to Buy the Seminoles*
*out of Florida But only Tracking Them*
*like Hunted Animals Succeeds*

"In this last hour of tribulation and sorrow we can, whilst
remembering their sufferings and extenuating their cruelties,
shed a tear over their departed hopes, and point our children
to the example of what a united people can do in defense of
their homes."

*Editorial in the* Boston Herald, 1858

In 1842, General Worth had made an agreement with the few
remaining Seminole allies in Florida that they could stay in their
Everglade retreat if they did not bother the white settlers. For seven
years the Indians kept their promise and, unmolested by whites,
grew in numbers to between four and five hundred.

By 1845 there were 120 warriors capable of taking the field
(70 Seminoles, 30 Mikasukis, 4 Uchees, and 4 Choctaws). Seventy
of those had grown from boys into manhood since the second
Seminole war began. Others were no more than forty years old

except for Arpeika (in his nineties) and his second-in-command, Assinwar (sixty). Holatter Micco (Billy Bowlegs), son-in-law of Assinwar, was thirty-three years old. As a direct descendant (nephew) of Micanopy and of his brother, the Alachua Bowlegs, he ruled the Seminoles who lived along the Caloosahatchee River and Pease Creek. Assinwar spoke for the Mikasukis whose villages clustered around the southwest shores of Lake Okeechobee.

The land they inhabited was nearly inundated most of the year but it abounded in game and seafood. The people obtained food, clothing, and shelter from the deer. They raised some horses, cattle, hogs, and poultry; they grew corn and vegetables on the higher hummocks.[1] With a staple like coonti, as well as such fruits as oranges and bananas which grew in the area, the allies prospered in their secluded reservation.

In 1848, Indian Affairs were turned over to the secretary of the interior who appointed S. Spencer to be subagent for the Florida Indians.[2] The following year, Captain John C. Casey was made their agent. When he arrived, he found the Indians imbued with distrust of the United States government and set out to restore their confidence. On 25 June, he wrote to Adjutant General Jones that he was leaving for the Caloosahatchee and Charlotte Harbor to determine the feelings of the Seminoles regarding emigration.[3] For although the Indians had remained quiet, the citizens had carried on a relentless campaign for total removal.

In July, the agent reported that he had visited Sarasota, Charlotte Harbor, Pease Creek, and the Caloosahatchee. He had penetrated each as far as a ship could go but had found only one group of Seminoles. These had been so wary that they had refused all gifts except whisky and tobacco. Although they finally accepted some calico, they would give no information about the whereabouts of their chief, Holatter Micco. They did reveal that the Mikasukis, Tallahassees, and Creeks were with Arpeika and Assinwar on Lake Istokhoga.[4] Undaunted, Casey continued to haunt the Gulf Coast with the hope of contacting the Seminole chief.

Suddenly, Indians attacked a plantation on New River, killing one man. All the settlers immediately abandoned their plantations. Lieutenant Commander B. W. Couch, who had taken a crew of twenty men in a Coast Guard cutter to investigate the incident, found the frightened citizens huddled on Cape Florida. On 31 July, he took them aboard his ship and made a sweep up both the New and Miami rivers but he found no sign of Indians.[5]

In the meantime, Casey had been waiting near the ranch of his guide, Felipe, a Spaniard who farmed near Sarasota. He hoped that Holatter Micco would come to see him there. Instead he received word that a store near Pease Creek had been attacked. Hurrying there to assess the facts, he found two persons dead and the entire complex burned and looted.[6]

Terrified Florida citizens demanded that an expedition go against the Indians but Brevet Major–General D. E. Twiggs, in charge of Florida troops, allowed Captain Casey to go in search of the chiefs to request a conference. The agent sailed down the coast toward Sarasota Bay, leaving "packages and signs of friendship" to encourage the Indians to meet him. Finally, late in August, Felipe reported that he had found a small white flag made by fastening heron feathers to a stick. Atop the staff was a string of white beads and a twist of tobacco. The flag had been attached to a tall pole and left in a conspicuous place. Casey felt sure it meant the Indians wished to talk with him and to smoke the pipe of peace.[7]

On 31 August, he anchored his small sloop in Sarasota Bay and waited. A few days later, three Indians appeared at the edge of the forest. Leaving Sampson in the boat, Casey approached them. When he extended his hand to shake that of the foremost one, the warrior took both his arms above the elbow and shook him heartily. The other two men did the same to signify special friendship. They explained that they were messengers from Holatter Micco who wanted Casey to know that all should be made straight. Since it was late in the evening, a meeting was set for the next day. In the meantime, one man would go aboard the sloop to explain everything while the other two remained on shore.

The following day, the spokesmen asserted that the Indians unanimously disavowed violence and would punish the men responsible. When Casey asked why Bowlegs had refused to meet him, they explained that the chief had been on his way to greet the agent when word was brought to him of the attack at New River. As soon as he heard the news, the chief had hurried home to call in all his men who were out hunting and had sent a runner to Casey to ask him to wait. The runner had returned a few days later carrying a flag which Casey had left. It appeared the agent had departed just one day before the messenger arrived.

In the meantime, before Holatter Micco could take action, news reached him of the burning of the store at Pease Creek. Chitto-Hadjo, a subchief, had taken a few warriors and hurried after the culprits, overtaking them as they were on their way to attack other nearby settlements. The men responsible for both outrages were five outlaws who refused to abide by the laws of the tribe; they were being watched in their village on the Kissimmee River and would be turned over to white authorities if a meeting could be arranged. The flag had, indeed, been the Seminole chief's request for a conference.

Casey arranged for a meeting with General Twiggs to take place on 18 September. Two of the emissaries returned to camp to bring their chief with them while the other accompanied Casey back to his headquarters as a sign of the Indians' good faith.[8]

True to his word, Holatter Micco arrived with thirty-seven subchiefs and warriors to meet with Twiggs and Casey. The Mikasukis were still on the road but they had authorized Bowlegs to act for both groups. The chief agreed to surrender the five men in custody. Two of them were sons of Chitto-Tustenuggee who had dealt with General Macomb in 1839.

The next day the Mikasukis arrived to support Bowleg's assurances; both Assinwar and Holatter Micco went aboard the sloop to talk with General Twiggs. They asked for a month in which to bring in the culprits because the area over which they must travel was flooded, they had few ponies, and the prisoners were armed and desperate. Twiggs believed the chiefs were sincere for they had boarded the ship without hostages although Casey had offered to provide some. It was agreed that the chiefs would deliver up the renegades to General Twiggs on 19 October.[9]

On the appointed day, Holatter Micco brought in three of them. He carried the hand of one man who had been killed in the attempt to apprehend him; another had escaped. The chief said that he had done all he could to make reparations and that he had insisted that all his warriors be present to see what happened to anyone who attacked white people. General Twiggs accepted these efforts as satisfactory. In reporting the conference to his superiors, he asserted that although he had not been able to find evidence of any personal assaults on the Indians to account for the outrages, he had learned that many warriors bitterly resented a recent Florida law which forbade them to go unescorted beyond their boundary for any reason.[10]

While Casey had been working to resolve the immediate problem of vindication for the Indian depredations, the secretary of war was considering means to achieve total removal. Unwilling to risk another armed conflict, he authorized the agent to offer $100 to every man, woman, and child who would agree to go West. He followed this with a proposal that the entire group be offered $215,000 to depart. The secretary was simultaneously arranging to bring a delegation from Arkansas to urge their relatives to remove. If both these measures failed, Twiggs was informed, the army would receive orders to take other measures.[11]

Under such pressure, the general abandoned his resolve to forego mention of emigration and brought the matter up as soon as he had taken custody of the prisoners. Holatter Micco was stunned. He had done all in his power to conform to the white man's law and bring the criminals to justice, why then should the whole Indian community be held responsible for the acts of a few? Surely white men did not follow this practice in their own society?

Like every military commander in Florida before him, Twiggs was caught between Scylla and Charybdis. If he steered in one direction, he ran into the rock of implacable government policy, if he veered the other way he sank into the whirlpool of the perplexities of dealing with Seminole customs and attitudes. He and Casey had to find some way to cope with the Indians who had no intention of leaving Florida and with the federal and state governments who were determined they must go.

Difficulties developed over what to do with the Indian prisoners. Twiggs wanted to use them to force their relatives to move to Arkansas. T. Hartley Crawford ordered them turned over to the Florida courts for trial. Twiggs warned the War Department that an outbreak of hostilities could be disastrous and asked that Captain Casey be recognized for having reestablished contact with the Indians and for having almost certainly averted another war.[12]

The general reminded Commissioner Crawford that there had not been a single violation of Worth's treaty along a frontier of nearly three hundred miles during the past seven years. He insisted that if removal must occur, time would be much more important than money in achieving success. He warned his superiors against force as his predecessors had done. "To remove these people with the least delay, we must take time enough to avert war, whether weeks, months, or years be required. . . . Proclaim war and in a week 10,000 men would not secure the planter and his family from Cape Sable to Georgia."[13]

To Lieutenant Colonel W. G. Freeman at Army Headquarters, West Point, he recounted the old, weary tale of trials besetting a military commander in the Florida Everglades. He recommended that a row of forts be built between the settlers and the Indians if forced emigration were attempted but he warned:

> Here if the enemy runs and escapes, you are defeated; your strength, your stores are exhausted. He is uninjured; his munitions are on his back, his food in every stream, in every bush, his bread on every acre he passes by; he flies and leaves no trace behind; his person, the object of your pursuit, driven from one fastness, finds shelter in a still more impenetrable swamp in your front or rear, to the right or left; he sees your camp fire, and hears the sound of your receding forces as they pass in fancied pursuit. Your numbers, then, must make up for his intelligence and fleetness. Every hammock and swamp must be frequently swept, that he may find rest in none; life must become a burden, and for rest he must seek another land.[14]

At one point, General Twiggs tried to pass the job on to the navy by suggesting that the only way to find and remove the remaining Indians was through the use of a task force of small boats.[15] It was obvious that this experienced army officer would do anything to avoid a land war in the Florida Everglades.

In September 1849, Marcellus Duval, agent to the Creeks in Arkansas, began to collect a group of Seminoles who would go to Florida to urge those who remained to emigrate. On 3 November, he arrived in New Orleans with a delegation led by Halleck-Tustenuggee who was carrying a message from Coacoochee. In the group were four Mikasukis besides the chief, three Hitchitis and Alachua, three Tallahassees and an interpreter. The terms laid down to them were that they would be liberally paid if successful, paid according to their performance and sincerity if not.[16]

Before he left Arkansas, Duval had expressed doubt over the advisability of reading Coacoochee's speech to his compatriots in Florida for it was couched in language that might do more harm than good. Coacoochee was fighting desperately in the West and in Washington for the right to move his people and their annuity out of control of the Creeks. Consequently Duval suggested to the commissioner of Indian Affairs that the subject of where the new emigrants must settle should be tabled during discussions in Florida![17]

If the Americans were somewhat less than honest in their motives

regarding the forthcoming negotiations, the Indian delegation may
have been dissembling too. One wonders how they could urge their
friends to emigrate when they, themselves, had suffered so much in
the process. Perhaps they were lured by an opportunity to travel, to
visit old friends and habitats, to receive money and presents.

On 12 November, the delegation arrived at Fort Brooke. The
members were given ten days in which to hunt and collect root
medicines before starting for Pease Creek. There they would pick
up provisions supplied by the government and wait for the runners
sent out to arrange meetings. It was thought by some that the lives
of those urging emigration might be in danger if safe passage were
not arranged in advance.

Duval reported to Washington, "The impression appears to be
universal here with the army, that it is impossible to effect a peaceable
removal . . . such however is not my opinion can the delegates bring
about a council." He, too, urged that his party be given time to
establish the proper mood and to work in their own way without
army or government interference. He expressed complete confidence
in Halleck-Tustenuggee. "The leader is a daring chief & one whom
I have never known to violate his word, and until he does, I shall
place as much reliance in him as any I have known." [18]

Duval delivered his party at Pease Creek on the nineteenth. On
the twenty-second, they departed for the Indian settlements with the
understanding that they would try to return by the middle of
December bringing Bowlegs for a conference with General Twiggs.
Duval repeated Twiggs' opinion that the depredations had occurred
from resentment over being prohibited from crossing the boundary
for any reason and he expressed doubt over the wisdom of offering
the Indians money to remove as this would only give them false
notions of the value of the land they were leaving. [19]

Duval, who had urged patience in November, was upset by
December. On the tenth, he wrote an angry letter to the commissioner of Indian Affairs asking why he had not received authorization
in Florida for the policies he hoped to pursue. He complained that
General Twiggs was taking over the conference and expressed doubt
that the Indians would consent to remove if the army was allowed
to enter the proceedings. He also urged that talks take place on a
private one-to-one basis as he had never known the Indians to authorize delegates to speak for an entire group. Duval wanted to go
to Charlotte Harbor where he could deal with any Indians who came

in without interference from the military but he needed money for trade goods and support from the Bureau of Indian Affairs to deal with Twiggs.[20]

Indeed, one can sympathize with Duval for he had received his orders to form the delegation from the secretary of war and been told he must work with existing authorities in Florida, yet, as Indian agent he operated under the commissioner of Indian Affairs in the Department of the Interior. Nor could it have been easy for General Twiggs and Captain Casey who, having built a fragile relationship with the Indians, must now stand by and let someone else interfere.

Meanwhile the settlers, sensing that the Indians might soon have some money if they agreed to move, pressed their claims for losses and depredations. Attorney E. B. Gould requested five thousand dollars for his clients who had suffered in the "outburst at Indian River." Duval passed the claim on to the commissioner with an estimate that others would ask at least ten thousand more.[21]

During this period, the commissioner's mail was sprinkled with offers from private citizens who claimed they could bring the Indians out of Florida—for a price! The citizens of Florida sent him a long memorial detailing the atrocities of recent attacks and insisting that whites were completely innocent of any mistreatment of the Indians. They urged immediate removal by any means.[22]

Although Twiggs and Casey had worked hard to establish rapport with the Indians, everyone knew that the general had over seventeen hundred troops at his command. The chiefs were well aware that Florida citizens were urging military action to effect a hasty and complete removal.

No one knows what occurred between Holatter Micco, Assinwar, Arpeika, and the delegation but Halleck-Tustenuggee must have given them some indication of the difficulties which the Seminoles were enduring as they tried to build new homes in the midst of their enemies, the Creeks. He must have told them of the unscrupulous merchants who raised the price of wagons, horses, and mules whenever a load of emigrants appeared, of contractors who made money by selling poor rations at high cost, of the barren land, the rivers that flooded every spring destroying crops and even homes, of the cold climate, and of strange illnesses which had beset nearly every party of emigrants who moved West.

Halleck must have told his friends in Florida about Coacoochee's desperate struggle to protect Seminole blacks who were under constant threat from both Creeks and whites. In fact, Duval was said to have obtained his position as Indian agent for the Seminoles with the hope of making money on the side by picking up slaves for the eastern market. In any event, his two brothers—William J. and Gabriel—were active in such trade.[23] While the Florida Indians now had few blacks to worry about, they could scarcely fail to realize that life in the West held little for them. They declined to come out and talk. Since neither Duval nor Twiggs could reach them, the year 1849 ended on a note of indecision and confusion.

On 19 January 1850, Twiggs held one last meeting with the delegates. He presented a proposal which promised each warrior who emigrated five hundred dollars when he reached Arkansas, each woman and each child one hundred dollars. He offered Holatter Micco ten thousand dollars if he would use his influence to bring out the entire group. The government would pay all transportation costs plus subsistence for a year in the West. It would reimburse each family for livestock left in Florida, would provide blankets and clothes as well as a doctor to protect them on their journey.

Halleck-Tustenuggee and his party returned to the swamps with Twiggs' offer. They came back shortly with sixty persons who accompanied the delegation aboard the *Fashion* bound for New Orleans. They all arrived at Fort Smith on the first of April.[24]

Twiggs was replaced by Brevet Brigadier General Thomas Childs; Duval went back to Arkansas with his delegation, leaving Captain Casey to pick up the pieces and restore his lines of communication with the Florida Indians.

In charge again, the agent moved down to Fort Myers on 21 May and remained there until 2 June 1850 but neither Holatter Micco nor Assinwar appeared. A few subchiefs and warriors emerged to declare they preferred war to emigration. When one very old man came out to express a desire to remove, Casey sent him back to bring in his sons. He didn't return.[25]

In July a settler reported that his nephew, whom he had sent on an errand to a neighbor's farm, had been captured by Indians. He said the boy's horse had returned riderless late that night with part of the lad's suspenders braided into its mane. The man asserted that he had heard Indians discharging their guns during the day. Soon other settlers began to report evidence that some Indians were outside their boundary.[26]

Although the people of Burton and Marion counties were upset over the incident, they allowed Casey to attempt to negotiate for the boy. The chiefs identified the culprits but expressed fear of trying to catch them as they might retaliate by attacking the settlements. They were part of a group of twenty warriors who refused to acknowledge the authority of either Arpeika and Assinwar or Holatter Micco.[17]

Since the American authorities now knew who the criminals were, Casey hoped the army could apprehend them and hold them hostage for the boy. But before any action had been taken, the Indians appeared with three men whom they said were guilty of kidnapping and killing the lad. They turned the men over to the whites' courts as a token of their determination to live in peace. Before the Indians could be tried, they hanged themselves in their cells.[28] In his report to Washington, the agent stated that the incident occurred because the Indians had been denied the right to buy powder for hunting since the incidents of 1849. This, he declared, was tantamount to denying them food and clothing and the cause of deep resentment among some of the warriors.[29]

In his annual report for 1850, the secretary of war asserted that there was peace in Florida since Captain Casey had assured him that the people of the state need fear no harm as long as they left the Indians alone. However, the citizens were so determined to be rid of the native peoples in their midst that they passed an act providing for the raising of a regiment of mounted volunteers to aid the regular army. If the federal government refused to declare war, Florida would remove the Indians single-handed. Having set aside two million dollars for that purpose, they asked the War Department to provide the transportation for the emigrants. The secretary replied that two million was entirely too much money for the task at hand and that, while the national policy was to remove all Indians from Florida as speedily and finally as possible, it did not appear that war was the most effective method of implementing it.[30]

By the spring of 1851 another delegation from Arkansas was in Florida visiting relatives. Although Holatter Micco came out to meet them, he would not talk emigration. One Uchee family expressed a desire to go West but General Childs insisted in his report to Adjutant General Jones that this meant nothing for it consisted of seven people who had been "barely tolerated by the Seminoles for their worthless habits."[31]

In desperation, the United States government decided to give private enterprise a go at solving the problem. In 1852, General Luther Blake of Alabama was given a contract to effect removal. He was authorized to draw $10,000 for expenses plus $5 per day for himself. Furthermore, he was allowed $800 for each warrior and $425 for each woman or child brought in.[32] The government's idea was that the money was to be paid to each Indian as an inducement to emigrate but the contract was so vague that there was no direct obligation on Blake's part to give any of the money to any Indian.[33]

Blake arrived at Fort Myers on the Caloosahatchee in March and set up an office there. Although he reported to the secretary of war that he felt the citizens of Florida had exaggerated the danger posed by the remaining Indians, he could not agree with Casey either on how to deal with them. In fact, he finally succeeded in having the agent recalled—temporarily.[34]

Blake had barely arrived when an incident occurred which ruined all chance of success he might have had. In March, Captain Aaron Jernigan of the militia trailed a small group of Indians until he caught them, attacked them, and captured one old woman and a small child. Why the captives were imprisoned is a mystery as they had committed no crime unless they were outside the reservation without cause. While awaiting her fate, the woman hanged herself while authorities sought in vain for information on the identity of the child's parents. Jernigan had driven the Indians deep into the swamps where no one could find them, much less negotiate with them.[35]

There was worse to come. In April, apparently with Blake's approval, Militia Major General B. Hopkins captured eleven Indians and wounded one woman. When the prisoners were brought in, they turned out to be harmless captives of which ten were ill. General Childs was dismayed because he felt it would interfere with negotiations. Afraid of retaliation, he was obliged to send escorts with all supply trains in the vicinity. He wrote Blake asking for instructions on what to do with the prisoners and expressing concern over developments, "The Indians certainly cannot have much confidence in any promises or professions that you may be making them if their women are captured and shot at, neither can I command the troops understandingly if I am not fully acquainted with your views and wishes."[36]

Blake felt confident because the Arkansas delegation was enjoying good relations with the Florida Indians. He should have known that this had nothing to do with whether or not the Indians would emigrate. He apparently looked to the militia, the organization in which he held his rank, to continue to bring in groups by force. He did not realize that by undercutting the Indian agent and the regular army, he had lost two necessary allies and that by using force on harmless Indians, he had stiffened the resistance of those who remained in the swamps.

In July, he finally succeeded in contacting Holatter Micco and invited him to take a small delegation to Washington and New York for conferences. The chief decided to use the occasion for his benefit and asked for fourteen hundred dollars as compensation for lost cattle in addition to another sum for stolen slaves. Blake agreed. Without authorization from Washington, the general, the chief, and three subchiefs set off about 11 September. When they arrived, the secretary of war not only arranged for their entertainment but approved a chit for six hundred dollars to provide clothing and presents for the chiefs while they were in New York.[37]

In Washington, Holatter Micco, having seen the might and authority of the government with which he was dealing, put his mark on a paper which obligated him to move West. But as soon as they returned from their trip, Bowlegs and his subchiefs took their new clothes and their presents back to their villages where they remained incommunicado. Blake accused Casey of subverting his plans and complained to Washington until the agent was removed from office.

By December 1852, Blake was so discouraged with his efforts that he suggested the only way to dislodge the Indians was to survey the entire area. He recommended that the crews be accompanied by three hundred Creek warriors who could operate much less expensively than the army.[38]

As the spring of 1853 approached, the Indians remained friendly—coming daily to trade and talk—but Holatter Micco remained in seclusion. No one would talk emigration.

The Alabaman became so desperate that he offered from six to eight hundred dollars for each Indian brought to him. Certain of retaliation should citizens begin kidnapping Indians, General Childs took pains to verify that Blake was actually offering such rewards. Incensed, he wrote the adjutant general that a citizen agent was within his command and, without advising him or consulting him, had taken measures which could bring on a war for which the people and the United States government were wholly unprepared. He asked for instructions.[39]

In December, Assinwar and Holatter Micco sent word to General Childs, through a member of the Arkansas delegation, that they would never emigrate but they promised to remain peaceful so long as they were not molested.[40]

Although Blake continued to exert every effort to bring in more Indians, he had no success. In May 1853, he was ordered to turn over all public records, property, and funds to Captain Casey. He had managed to secure thirty-six Indians of which seven died before they reached Arkansas.[41]

Although he was never reprimanded for his unauthorized trip to Washington with the four chiefs nor for his other expenses, Blake had trouble collecting the money. The bill he presented to the secretary of war must have seemed a bit excessive. It read as follows:

| | |
|---|---:|
| Visit to Washington of four chiefs . . . . . . | $ 2,430.90 |
| Preliminary arrangements . . . . . . . . . . . . . | 10,000.00 |
| Total expenses of Western Delegation . . . | 12,075.00 |
| Removal of thirty-six Indians . . . . . . . . . . | 20,270.00 |
| Per diem at five dollars per day . . . . . . . . . | 4,230.00 |
| | $48,905.90 |

The above bill did not include another five thousand dollars for transporting emigrants.[42]

Having established testimony as to the effectiveness of private business when it elects to do government work, Blake went back to Alabama. General Childs wrote the adjutant general that it had been a mistake to remove Captain Casey, whom the Indians trusted, with a new man. Casey was no doubt reappointed on Childs' recommendation.

For two years there was almost no contact between the citizens of Florida and the Indians who stayed deep in their swamps. Then, in December 1855, Lieutenant Hartsuff, with a United States civil engineer crew, was surveying an area on the borders of the Everglades and Big Cypress when he came upon a garden where Holatter Micco had some magnificent banana plants of which he was immensely proud. Hartsuff's men amused themselves by shooting down pumpkins whose vines had grown up the trees and then hacking down the banana plants. When the chief took them to task, they laughed at him. They had deliberately destroyed something that took years to create just "to see how old Billy would cut up."[43]

"Old Billy" cut up! The next morning Holatter Micco and his

warriors attacked the surveying crew, wounding several.[44] War was declared immediately in spite of the fact that the Indians had been deeply provoked. Secretary of War Jefferson Davis authorized Colonel John Munroe, in charge of military affairs in Florida, to call out five companies of volunteers to serve six months unless discharged.

Munroe renewed efforts to rid Florida of all Indians. In February 1856, he sent a message to Colonel H. Brown, commanding at Fort Brooke, saying that any honest proposal to bring in friends or families to emigrate should be met with an invitation for them to do so openly under a pledge of kind treatment and fair terms. But, said Munroe, "Should any leading Indians present themselves and make propositions for a treaty to remain in the country . . . " they were to be placed in irons and forced to serve as guides. Any man or boy who refused to act as a guide would be flogged first; if he still resisted, he would be hanged. He justified his order by saying, "This painful resource is almost the only one we can adopt for shortening the work and will therefore be sternly enforced."[45]

In the mini-Florida war which followed this announcement, three skirmishes took place between January and April 1856. There were some killed and wounded in each but the results of all were inconclusive.

A delegation of western Seminoles was in Washington to sign a treaty finally separating them from the Creeks.[46] They were disturbed because of bad weather, crop failure, lack of equipment promised them, and trouble over their blacks. When asked to urge their Florida brothers to join them there, they told the secretary of war frankly that to try to force emigration to a place as bad as Arkansas was manifestly ridiculous.

Captain John Sprague, now stationed in New Mexico, asked to be allowed to talk to the Florida Indians because they would remember and trust him from his contact with them almost a decade earlier but he was turned down. The government chose instead to send scouting parties to pursue the Seminole allies, destroy their camps, and capture the people.

A series of ignominious actions took place in 1857. In July, Captain Jacob E. Mickler followed a trail, found a camp, and captured nine women and six children. One woman put up such a fight that it took four soldiers to carry her from her home. In August, Captain William H. Kendrick pursued about six Seminoles, killed one man, and captured a child. In November, Captain W. H. Cone, with 115 men, surprised a party of Indians, killed one warrior, and captured eighteen women and children along with large quantities of provisions. No Americans were killed in this encounter but many of the men came out of the swamps ill and exhausted.

Although the number of Seminoles brought in for emigration by these methods was pitifully small, the Indians were badly hurt when the army razed their villages. In November, Captain J. Parkhill found a village of about thirty lodges with forty acres of cleared land around it. "... Large quantities of pumpkins, potatoes, peas, corn, and rice were found—the corn, peas and rice hid away carefully in houses built off in the swamp." A trail leading to the storage bins had been carefully concealed but the soldiers found it. The ground was literally covered by pumpkins of all sizes; vines had grown into the trees until they looked as if they too sprouted pumpkins. The ground was full of potatoes. The soldiers were ordered to destroy everything.

The next day another thirty lodges and many fields were found. Although the Indians fled, abandoning their homes, they were pursued and caught. This time they turned and fought, killing an army captain and wounding five men.

Toward the end of December, Captain W. Stephens, with ninety mounted volunteers, found a village in the Big Cypress with "fifty neatly built palmetto houses," and many cultivated fields. Again the Indians fled but were soon overtaken by the army and decoyed into an ambush where five warriors were slain and two mortally wounded. The Indians managed to kill one soldier.[47] This shabby little encounter ended the fighting in the third Seminole war.

According to Kit Carson, who knew Indians well, the red man never killed a white man in times of peace "without he deserved it." Yet, for Holatter Micco's retaliation upon those who destroyed his garden, a third expensive war was fought to little purpose.

In January 1858, a party of forty Seminoles and six Creeks came from Arkansas under John Jumper, chief of the Western tribe. Polly, niece of Holatter Micco, went into the Everglades and brought her uncle out. Agent Samuel Rutherford was waiting for him with generous terms if he would emigrate.

When the Seminole chief looked back over the chain of events that began when Hartsuff and his crew wantonly destroyed his cherished banana trees, which led to his own attack for revenge, which brought about almost total destruction of his peoples' homes and crops, he must have decided there was no safe place in Florida for him or his clan. Even the presence of the surveying crew, symbol of the end of Indian territory and harbinger of individual white farms, must have warned him that the end was near. He decided to take the money.

He accepted $6,500 for himself, $1,000 apiece for each of four subchiefs, $500 for each warrior, and $100 for every woman and child. The total thus expended was $44,600. One hundred and sixty-four people left, of which 123 came in voluntarily and 41 were captured.[48] The ship which carried them to New Orleans was called the *Grey Cloud*.

A soldier who watched the departure wrote to the *Boston Herald* that "at the hour set, the troops of the post, under Captain Brannan, were judiciously posted, without the knowledge of the Indians, at points selected to meet and prevent any treachery that might be contemplated. As the appointed hour drew nigh the excitement on the part of the whites was intense. But soon all fears were at an end." The procession emerged from the hummock and wound its way slowly to the wharf. "Silently they took leave of their much-loved Florida. Warriors, who had defended their country to the last, shed tears and with aching hearts passed on to the deck steamer. The scene was one to be remembered and calculated to excite the sympathies of the most inveterate Indian-hater."[49]

Holatter Micco (Billy Bowlegs), sometimes called "King" or "General," was the last prominent chief to leave Florida. He was, at the time of his departure, about forty years old. "He had a fine countenance, expressive of intellect and great firmness." Although he was highly respected for his character and because he spoke English well, he had nevertheless been elected chief of the Indian remnant in 1842 because of his royal antecedents. Among those who emigrated with him were ten Mikasuki warriors from Arpeika's band, including Assinwar. Twelve warriors remained with the redoubtable old Sam Jones—now over one hundred years old—promising to emigrate after his death. Soon after the party arrived in Arkanasas, on 26 May, an epidemic of fever struck, killing a number of emigrants before they could begin to settle in their new land.[50]

In his annual report for 1858, the secretary of interior admitted that the Seminoles had completely "baffled the energetic efforts of our army to effect their subjugation and removal."[51]

As the Florida war came to an end one last and final time in April 1858, another war loomed on the horizon of the American experience. Only three years would pass before shots fired on an army fort in South Carolina would start a conflagration that would obliterate the little Florida wars from the American mind. An editorial in the *Boston Herald*, taking note of those wars, seemed strangely prophetic:

> The agonizing struggle, extending through a period of twenty-three years,[52] has at last terminated in the ruin and destruction of the gallant Seminole. . . . It is idle to seek to correct the errors and injustice of a past generation . . . [but] in this, their last hour of tribulation and sorrow, we can, whilst remembering their sufferings and extenuating their cruelties, shed a tear over their departed hopes, and point our children to the example of what a united people can do in defense of their homes.
>
> Patience, heroism, and fidelity, such as the world may admire have been exhibited to us, inculcating a lesson not to be lost upon us now that our national councils are torn by intestine strife. The Seminoles as a nation [in Florida] have been destroyed, but what an array of glory, faith, horrors, and anguish does this retrospect present![53]

# Abbreviations

| | |
|---|---|
| AGOLR | Adjutant General's Office, Letters Received |
| A&NC | *Army & Navy Chronicle* |
| ASPFR | *American State Papers, Foreign Relations* |
| ASPIA | *American State Papers, Indian Affairs* |
| ASPMA | *American State Papers, Military Affairs* |
| FHQ | *Florida Historical Quarterly* |
| JNH | *Journal of Negro History* |
| OIALR | Office of Indian Affairs, Letters Received |
| OIALS | Office of Indian Affairs, Letters Sent |
| USACC | United States Army Continental Commands |
| SWLR | Secretary of War, Letters Received |
| TP, Florida | *Territorial Papers of the United States, Florida* |
| USED | *United States Executive Document* |
| USHD | *United States House Document* |
| USHED | *United States House Executive Document* |
| USMD | *United States Miscellaneous Document* |
| USSD | *United States Senate Document* |
| USSED | *United States Senate Executive Document* |

# Notes

*Part One:* THE FIRST FLORIDA WAR, 1810–1818

*1. The Battle at Prospect Bluff*

1. Loomis to Patterson, 13 August 1816, *United States House Document 119* (*USHD 119*), 15th Cong., 2d Sess., 15.

2. Herbert Aptheker, "Maroons within the Present Limits of the United States," *Journal of Negro History* (*JNH*), 24, no. 2, (April 1939): 167–184.

3. Kenneth W. Porter, "Negroes and the Seminole War, 1817–1818," *JNH* 36, no. 3, (July 1951): 259–264.

4. *United States House Document 122* (*USHD 122*), 15th Cong., 2d Sess., 10.

5. *USHD 119*, 15–17.

6. *Army & Navy Chronicle* (*A&NC*), 2, no. 8, (1836): 114–117.

7. *USHD 119*, 17–21.

8. *A&NC*, 2, no. 8, (1836): 116.

9. Ibid.

10. Porter, 249–280.

11. John W. Monette, *History of . . . the Valley of the Mississippi*, 1: 90.

## 2. The East Florida Annexation Plot

1. Ray A. Billington, *American History before 1877*, 109.

2. Charlton W. Tebeau, *A History of Florida*, 104.

3. Caroline Mays Brevard, *A History of Florida: From the Treaty of 1763 to Our Own Times*, 1: 29.

4. Billington, *American History before 1877*, 92.

5. Edwin C. McReynolds, *The Seminoles*, 43.

6. Michael Paul Duffner, "The Seminole-Black Alliance in Florida: An Example of Minority Cooperation," 11. One source says the word comes from the Muskogean *este* (men) and *Semole* (free); Marjory Stonemen Douglas in *The Everglades* translates it as "people of distant fires," while Swanton interprets Seminole as "one who Camped out from regular towns."

7. Most historians credit Secoffee with founding the Seminole nation.

8. John R. Swanton, *The Indians of the Southeastern United States*, 181.

9. McReynolds, 5; John K. Mahon., *History of the Second Seminole War, 1835–1842, (History)* 2.

10. Mahon, *History*, 2; Duffner, 11.

11. The Creeks signed a series of treaties with the Americans acknowledging responsibility for slaves who disappeared during the American Revolution, Creek wars, and the War of 1812. They agreed to let whites enter their villages to search for missing slaves. Some bands moved rather than comply with those treaties.

12. Mahon, *History*, 4–5; Swanton, 181.

13. Duffner, 2, 12–13, 24; Porter, "Negroes and the East Florida Annexation Plot, 1811–1813," *JNH*, 30, no. 1 (January 1945): 11–13.

14. I. A. Wright, ed., "Dispatches of Spanish Officials Bearing on the Free Negro Settlement of Gracia Real de Santa Teresa de Mosè," *JNH*, 9, no. 2, (April 1924): 145–149. Spaniards protected blacks who embraced the Catholic religion.

15. Porter, "Negroes and the East Florida Annexation Plot, 1811–1813," 12.

16. Billington, *American History before 1877*, 92; Michael Kraus, *The United States to 1865*, 158.

17. Kraus, 236.

18. Joshua R. Giddings, *The Exiles of Florida . . .*, 29. In his book, Giddings refers to the blacks and Creeks in Florida as exiles forced to leave their rightful country to escape persecution.

19. Porter, "Negroes and the East Florida Annexation Plot, 1811–1813," 15–16.

20. Jacob Rhett Motte, *Journey into Wilderness . . . 1836–1838*, 214–215.

21. John Lee Williams, *The Territory of Florida . . .*, 240.

22. Francois A. Chateaubriand, *Travels in America*, 164; Duffner, 66, 104.

23. Wiley Thompson to Lewis Cass, *American State Papers, Military Affairs*, (*ASPMA*), 6: 533.

24. Carl Degler, *Neither Black nor White*, 78; James Africanus Horton, *West African Countries and Peoples*, 8; Duffner, 48, 32–36.

25. Newhell Miles Puckett, *The Magic and Folk Beliefs of the Southern Negro*, 43–44.

26. William C. Sturtevant, "The Medicine Bundles and Busks of the Florida Seminoles," *Florida Anthropologist*, 7, (May 1954): 31–70; Mahon, *History*, 13; Francis Harper, ed., *The Travels of William Bartram*, 323.

27. Williams, 249.

28. Thomas Lorraine McKenney and James Hall, *History of the Indian Tribes of North America . . .* , 82–83.

29. Sturtevant, "Seminole Myths of the Origins of Races," *Ethnohistory*, 10 (1963): 80–81; Washington Irving, *A&NC*, 11, no. 19 (1840): 294–295.

30. Duffner, 44, 45–46.

31. *Encyclopaedia Britannica*, 1959, 2: 505.

32. George P. Rawick, *The American Slave: A Composite Autobiography*, 17: 27–28; Duffner, 69.

33. Porter, "Negroes and the East Florida Annexation Plot, 1811–1813," 16.

34. Porter, Ibid., 14; Duffner, 64.

35. Billington, *American History before 1877*, 107.

36. Tebeau, 102.

37. Duffner, 21–22.

38. *American State Papers, Foreign Relations (ASPFR)*, 3: 571; *United States Miscellaneous Document 55, (USMD 55)*, 36th Cong., 1st Sess., 36.

39. *USMD 55*, 36; *United States Statutes at Large*, 3: 471–472.

40. *USMD 55*, 25–27.

41. Ibid., 22–24.

42. *ASPFR*, 3: 573; Rembert W. Patrick, *Florida Fiasco*, 114–127. Patrick documents thoroughly the fact that President Madison and his secretary of state, James Monroe, secretly encouraged Mathews until public opinion forced them to repudiate him, leaving their agent to take the blame rather than embarrass the administration.

43. Porter, "Negroes and the East Florida Annexation Plot, 1811–1813," 9–10.

44. *Niles National Register*, 3, no. 20, (16 January 1813): 311; Porter, 17.

45. Porter, "Negroes and the East Florida Annexation Plot, 1811–1813," 19.

46. *State Papers & Publick Documents of the United States, 1789–1818*, Thomas B. Wait, ed. Series 1, 9: 175–177; Porter, "Negroes and the East Florida Annexation Plot, 1811–1813" 21; Patrick, 201–206.

47. Porter, Ibid., 23; Patrick, 207. Patrick claims that King Payne was only wounded and lived for several months after the battle.

48. *Niles Register*, 3 (14 November 1812): 171; Ibid., 3 (12 December 1812): 235–237; Porter, "Negroes and the East Florida Annexation Plot, 1811–1813," 21–24; Williams, 198.

49. *Nashville Clarion* (13 July 1813) in Patrick, 231; McReynolds, 49–50.

50. Porter, "Negroes and the East Florida Annexation Plot, 1811–1813," 27–28; Rufus Kay Wyllys, "The East Florida Revolution of 1812–1814," *The Hispanic American Historical Review*, 9 (November 1929): 415–445.

51. *USMD 55*, 40; *American State Papers, Indian Affairs* (*ASPIA*) 1: 844–845.

52. *USMD 55*, 38.

53. Patrick, 194. Patrick says that Kindelan, by using Indians and blacks, had forced the Americans to give up the siege of St. Augustine without firing a shot or using a Spanish soldier.

### 3. A Third Invasion of Florida
### for the "Great and Sacred Right of Self-Defence"

1. K. W. Porter, "Negroes and the Seminole Indian War, 1817–1818," *JNH*, 36, no. 3, (July 1951): 265–272.

2. *ASPMA*, 1: 682, 722–723.

3. Ibid., 748–749.

4. Ibid., 723–724.

5. Ibid., 686.

6. Ibid., 6: 749.

7. *United States House Executive Document 14* (*USHED 14*), 15th Cong., 2d Sess., 7–9.

8. *ASPMA*, 1: 697–698.

9. *USED 14*, 46–49.

10. *ASPIA*, 2: 563–584. William McIntosh was a half-blood Creek chief of Coweta Town, capital of a Lower Creek tribe that sided with the Georgia whites. They and their chief had assisted Colonel Clinch in the attack on the Negro fort. In fact, McIntosh is quoted as saying that his mission in that engagement was to capture Negroes and return them to their masters. In 1825, he would be put to death by his own people for signing the Treaty of Indian Springs without consent of the council of his tribe.

11. *ASPMA*, 1: 700.

12. Ibid., 722.

13. Porter, "Negroes and the Seminole Indian War, 1817–1818," 273–275.

14. *USED 14*, 52–54; *ASPFR*, 4: 599–600; *ASPMA*, 1: 701.

15. *ASPMA*, 1: 721–734.

16. Ibid., 680.

17. Every tribe or remnant of a tribe in Florida came to be part of a category known as "Seminoles."

18. Henry Steele Commager, *Documents of American History*, 169. The Treaty of San Lorenzo, negotiated by Thomas Pinckney, stated: "The two high contracting parties shall, by all means in their power, maintain peace and harmony among the several Indian Nations who inhabit the country adjacent to the lines and rivers, which, by the preceding articles, form the boundaries of the two Floridas. . . . And whereas several treaties of friendship exist between the two contracting parties and the said nation of Indians, it is hereby agreed that in the future no treaty of

alliance, or other whatever (except treaties of peace), shall be made by either party with the Indians living within the boundaries of the other, but both parties will endeavor to make the advantages of the Indians' trade common and mutually beneficial to their respective subjects and citizens, observing in all things the most complete reciprocity."

19. *ASPMA*, 1: 680–681.

20. Ibid., 735–739.

21. *ASPFR*, 4: 624.

22. Billington, 139.

23. *ASPMA*, 1: 708.

24. Ibid., 749.

25. Porter, "Negroes and the Seminole Indian War, 1817–1818," 277.

26. *ASPMA*, 1: 723.


### Part Two: THE COLD WAR, 1818–1835

#### 4. The Troublesome Presence

1. Tebeau, *A History of Florida*, 117.

2. John T. Sprague, *The Origin, Progress, and Conclusion of the Florida War*, 19.

3. Giddings, *The Exiles of Florida*, 72.

4. *ASPIA*, 2: 248–252.

5. Presumably the Creek nation was defined as including even the Seminoles who had not considered themselves Creeks for almost half a century!

6. Charles J. Kappler, *Indian Affairs: Laws and Treaties*, 2: 26.

7. Ibid.

8. Giddings, 67.

9. The fact that the Seminoles had hated and feared the Creeks for years and had seceded from the parent tribe half a century earlier was never acknowledged by the Americans. Such a policy may have been a deliberate tactic to justify obtaining Seminole Negroes under terms of Creek treaties even though no Seminole chief had signed any such agreement.

10. *ASPIA*, 2: 253.

11. The use of the pronoun "our" indicates how completely elements of the American church had accepted slavery as an institution compatible with Christian principles.

12. Jedidiah Morse, *Report to the Secretary of War on Indian Affairs*, 282; McReynolds, 88.

13. Morse, 283; McReynolds, 89.

14. Williams, *The Territory of Florida*, 279–285; Kappler, 2: 203–204.

15. *ASPIA*, 2: 431.

16. Ibid., 441.

17. Ibid., 638.

18. Brevard, 87–88; *ASPIA*, 2: 89–90.

19. *The Territorial Papers of the United States, Florida Territory* (*TP, Florida*), Clarence E. Carter, ed., 23: 22. Neamathla had settled his people in Florida after his Georgia town was destroyed by Gaines in 1817.

20. *ASPIA*, 2: 638.

21. Ibid.

22. Ibid., 686.

23. Ibid., 690.

24. Ibid., 694.

## 5. Colonel Gad Humphrey's Campaign

1. Kappler, 2: 205–207, "Whereas Neamathla, John Blunt, Tuske Hadjo, Mulatto King, Emathlochee and Econchatimicco, six of the principal chiefs of the Florida Indians and parties to the treaty, to which this article has been annexed, have warmly appealed to the commissioners for permission to remain in the district of the country, now inhabited by them, and in consideration of their friendly disposition and past services to the United States, it is therefore stipulated, between the United States and the aforesaid chiefs that the following reservations shall be surveyed and marked by the commissioner." Because of this additional article, six chiefs were allowed to remain on the Apalachicola River in return for their signatures on the treaty.

2. J. T. Sprague, *The Florida War*, 33–34.

3. Humphreys to James Gadsden, 8 July 1825 in Sprague, 30.

4. *United States Senate Document 512* (*USSD 512*), 23rd Cong., 1st Sess., 2: 235; "Sec. 15. *And be it further enacted*, that no Indian, or descendant of any Indian, residing within the Creek or Cherokee nations of Indians, shall be deemed a competent witness in any court of this state to which a white person may be a party, except such white person reside within the said nation."

5. *The Statutes at Large*, William Waller Hening, 6: 128.

6. Duval to Humphreys, Sprague, 35.

7. Duval to McKenney, *United States House Executive Document 17* (*USHED 17*), 19th Cong., 2d Sess., 26–27.

8. Humphreys to Duval in Sprague, 39

9. *USHED 17*, 15.

10. Signed by chiefs who had been bribed with plantations on the Apalachicola River.

11. Duval to Humphreys in Sprague, 42.

12. Ibid., 43.

13. Humphreys to McKenney, Ibid., 46–47.

14. Brooke to Humphreys, Ibid., 52–53.

15. Smith to Humphreys, Ibid., 53–54.

16. Ibid., 62–64.

17. Minutes of a talk held at the Seminole agency on 14 January 1829, Ibid., 65–66.

18. Ibid., 68–69.

19. Ibid., 71.

20. *USSD 512*. This document, containing four thousand pages in five volumes of correspondence in the War Department relating to Indian removal from 30 November 1831 to 27 December 1833, tells a sad tale. A government that keeps records as carefully as the United States, leaves for posterity documentary evidence that does not make good material for a Fourth of July speech. In the past, not many Americans have availed themselves of these documents—certainly not those who wrote elementary and secondary school history books.

21. Ibid., 3: 361.

## 6. The Treaty of Payne's Landing

1. Office of Indian Affairs, Letters Sent, M21, Roll 6, 48–51.

2. Documents Relating to the Negotiation of Ratified and Unratified Treaties with Various Indian Tribes, RG 75, T-494, Roll 2, Gadsden to Cass, 25 May 1832.

3. Kappler, 2: 345.

4. Office of Indian Affairs Documents, RG 75, T494, Roll 2, Gadsden to Cass, 25 May 1832. Since Gadsden never submitted minutes or a report of his meetings, there is no record of how he obtained the chiefs' signatures on the treaty; Mahon, *History*, 75.

5. Kappler, 2: 352.

6. *TP, Florida*, 24: 728, 740; Records of the United States Senate, RG 46, Document 23B–C1.

7. K. W. Porter, "Abraham," *Phylon*, 2, no. 2 (1941): 105–116; idem, "The Negro Abraham," *FHQ*, 25, no. 1 (July 1946): 38; *A&NC*, 4, no. 24 (1837): 378. Abraham signed at least some papers by making his mark, indicating he could not read or write.

8. W. A. Crofutt, ed., *Fifty Years in Camp and Field: Diary of Ethan Allen Hitchcock, U.S.A. (Hitchcock Diary)*, 80–81.

9. C. M. Brevard, *History of Florida*, 1: 121.

10. E. C. McReynolds, *The Seminoles*, 144; *ASPMA*, 6: 493. Governor Eaton wrote to Secretary of War Lewis Cass, "Our Indian compacts must be construed and be controlled by the rules which civilized people practice because in all our actions with them we have put the treaty-making machinery in operation precisely in the same way and to the same extent that it is employed with the civilized powers

of Europe. The rule practiced upon by us has been, and is, that the ratification shall take place within either an agreed time or a reasonable time." However, both the courts and the executive branch chose to ignore Governor Eaton's argument that the delay in ratifying the treaty could nullify it.

11. *TP, Florida*, 25: 129; *ASPMA* 6: 539.

12. Mark F. Boyd, "Asi-Yaholo, or Osceola," *FHQ*, 33, (January to April 1955): 273; *ASPMA*, 6: 539.

13. J. L. Williams, *The Territory of Florida*, 217.

14. Myer M. Cohen, *Notices of Florida and the Campaigns 1836*, (*Notices*), 239; J. L. Williams, *The Territory of Florida*, 272; William and Ellen Hartley, *Osceola: The Unconquered Indian*, 16.

15. *ASPMA*, 6: 67–68.

16. J. L. Williams *The Territory of Florida*, 272.

17. *ASPMA*, 6: 65.

18. Sprague, 81.

19. Hartley, 129–130, McKenney and Hall, *History of the Indian Tribes of North America*, 2: 208.

20. *ASPMA*, 6: 76.

21. Thompson to General George Gibson, Ibid., 80; *TP, Florida*, 25: 207.

22. Hernandez to Secretary of War, Adjutant General's Office, Letters Received (AGOLR), M567, Roll 124, H–15.

23. The description of military preparations of the Seminoles is based on Hartley, 19; on Sprague's interrogation of warriors after they were captured, 105; and on letters and diaries of American soldiers quoted in *Army & Navy Chronicle*.


*Part Three:* The Second Florida War, 1835–1842

7. *Osceola's Campaign*

1. *Territorial Papers, Florida*, 26: 216–217.

2. Judge Augustus Steele to the secretary of war, enclosing depositions by Ransome Clark, SWLR, M221, Roll 16; *A&NC*, 4, no. 24, (1837): 369–370; Crofutt, *Hitchcock Diary*, 87–88. See Frank Laumer's *Massacre* for a carefully documented, detailed account of the Dade incident. He states that the names of the other two survivors reported by Clark to have died of their wounds actually appear on active duty in later army records.

3. K. W. Porter, "Three Fighters for Freedom," *JNH*, 28, no. 4, (1943): 65–72.

4. *ASPMA*, 6: 561; *TP, Florida*, 25: 218.

5. W. and E. Hartley, *Osceola*, 137–140, 150–151.

6. Hernandez to SW Lewis Cass, AGOLR, M567, Roll 124, H–15.

7. K. W. Porter, "Florida Slaves and Free Negroes in the Seminole War, 1835–1842," *JNH*, 28, no. 4, (1943): 390–421; *ASPMA*, 6: 21–23.

8. *A&NC*, 3, no. 21, (1836): 320–321.

9. J. L. Williams, *The Territory of Florida*, 223.

10. J. T. Sprague, *The Florida War*, 95. Information about activities in the Indian camps comes from interviews with Seminole prisoners of war, in Sprague and from Hartley.

## 8. The United States Army Strikes Back

1. Hernandez to SW, AGOLR, M567, Roll 124, H-15; James Gadsden to the President, 14 January 1836, *TP, Florida*, 25: 224–226.

2. *ASPMA*, 6: 63; John Bemrose, *Reminiscences of the Second Seminole War* (*Reminiscences*), 78.

3. AGOLR, M567, Roll 123, G-63; *A&NC*, 2, no. 10, (1836): 168.

4. AGOLR, M567, Roll 123, G-65; *United States House Document 78*, 25th Cong., 2d Sess., (1838); *A&NC*, 2, no. 15, (1836): 225–226.

5. Abraham Eustis to Winfield Scott, 26 March 1836, SWLR, M222, Roll 32, T-32.

6. M. M. Cohen, *Notices*, 162.

7. John Bemrose, *Reminiscences*, 78; *A&NC*, 4, no. 12, (1837): 177–179.

8. J. L. Williams, *The Territory of Florida*, 234–235.

9. *A&NC*, 4, no. 11, *United States Senate Document 227*, 25th Cong., 2d Sess., (1838).

10. After being thoroughly snubbed in Washington and Tallahassee, Mrs. Eaton finally spent the happiest years of her life in Europe.

11. AGOLR, M537, Roll 40, C-18.

12. J. L. Williams, *The Territory of Florida*, 247.

13. Ibid.

14. The Green Corn Festival celebrated the ripening of the corn crop and symbolized the beginning of a new year.

15. J. L. Williams, *The Territory of Florida*, 249.

16. *Dictionary of American Biography* (*DAB*), 2: 422.

17. J. L. Williams, *The Territory of Florida*, 257.

18. *TP, Florida*, 25: 344–359; *ASPMA*, 6: 992; Ibid. 7: 986–989; *United States House Document 78*, 25th Cong., 2d Sess., (1838); *United States Senate Document 278*, 26th Cong., 1st Sess., (1840); J. L. Williams, *The Territory of Florida*, 263–264.

19. J. T. Sprague, *The Florida War*, 97.

20. *A&NC*, 2, no. 7, (1836): 99. The letter is quoted in many sources, yet there are documents showing Abraham signed with an *X*. It seems quite possible that he could not read or write and may have delivered an oral message to General Clinch.

21. *A&NC*, 7, no. 14, (1838): 220.


## 9. Emigration, the Alternative to Resistance

1. H. Carlton, District Attorney at New Orleans, to SW Lewis Cass, OIALR, M234, Roll 288.

2. Wiley Thompson to Elbert Herring, 10 June 1834, Ibid.

3. *ASPMA*, 6: 485.

4. Ibid., 534.

5. Joseph Harris to Wiley Thompson, 23 August 1835, enclosed in report to Commissioner of General Subsistence, Letters Received, OIA (CGSLR, OIA) Entry 198; Harris to General George Gibson, 29 April 1835, *ASPMA*, 6: 534–536.

6. Harris to Gibson, 13 November 1835, *ASPMA*, 6: 556; Harris to Gibson, 23 October 1835, CGSLR, OIA, Entry 198.

7. *ASPMA*, 6: 561; Ibid., 7: 562.

8. *ASPMA*, 6: 476.

9. Ibid., 569–570.

10. Harris to Lewis Cass, 4 June 1836, CGSLR, OIA, Entry 198.

11. Jefferson Van Horne to Gibson, OIA, "Florida Emigration," Preliminary Inventory 163, Entry 198, File 67. All references to the overland route are taken from this document.

12. C. J. Kappler, *Treaties*, 2: 344–345.

13. Grant Foreman, *Indian Removal: The Emigration of the Five Civilized Tribes of Indians*, 340; Harris to Cass, 25 July 1836, OIA, "Florida Emigration."

14. Joseph Harris to C. A. Harris, 1 April and 3 May 1837; Joseph Harris to Gibson, 4 June 1836; Joseph Harris to Lewis Cass, 25 July 1836, CGSLR, OIA, PI 63, Entry 198.

15. Foreman, *Indian Removal*, 340–341.

16. *A&NC*, 8, no. 14, (1839): 220.


## 10. General Thomas S. Jesup's Campaign, 1836–1837

1. *ASPMA*, 7: 821–822, 825–826; AGOLR, M567, Roll 144, J-9 through J-15.

2. *A&NC*, 4, no. 4, (1837): 53; AGOLR, M567, Roll J-19.

3. *ASPMA*, 7: 827–831; AGOLR, M567, Roll 144, J-27.

4. *A&NC*, 5, no. 13, (1837): 41.

5. Ibid., 4, no. 9, (1837): 129–130; AGOLR, M567, Roll 144, J-19.

6. *A&NC*, 4, no. 9, (1837): 131–132.

7. Ibid.

8. *ASPMA*, 7: 829–830.

9. *A&NC*, 4, no. 24, (1837): 378.

10. *United States House Document 225 (USHD 225)*. 25th Cong., 3d Sess., 21–22.

11. AGOLR, M567, Roll 144, J-60, J-63.

12. Ibid., J-65; *ASPMA*, 7: 825–828; *A&NC*, 4, no. 17, (1837): 265.

13. *A&NC*, 4, no. 36, (1837): 348; *ASPMA*, 7: 871.

14. *A&NC*, 4, no. 25, (1837): 393.

15. Ibid., 4, no. 15, (1837): 234; T. S. Jesup to Adjutant General Jones, *ASPMA*, 7: 848.

16. *A&NC*, 4, no. 15, (1837): 234.

17. *USHD 225*, 22; *ASPMA*, 7: 832.

18. *USHD 225*, 9.

19. Ibid., 11.

20. Ibid., 20.

21. *ASPMA*, 7: 882. Creeks had fought in every battle against the Seminole allies and hoped to clear their debt against the United States government for lost slaves by claiming those captured as part of their salary.

22. Foreman, *Indian Removal*, 349.

23. J. R. Motte, *Journey*, 143; *A&NC*, 5, no. 24, (1837): 382.

24. W. and E. Hartley, *Osceola*, 221.

25. *ASPMA*, 7: 825–826; K. W. Porter, "Florida Slaves and Free Negroes in the Seminole War, 1835–1842," *JNH*, 28, no. 4, (1943): 408.

26. Porter, "Florida Slaves and Free Negroes," 405–408.

27. *USHD 225*, 22; Motte, 119–123 (An assistant surgeon, he gives a colorful eye-witness account of the expedition).

28. Motte, 131–137; Hartley, 225.

29. J. T. Sprague, *History of Florida*, 216–218.

30. Ibid., 190.

31. Here is another Negro who must have known both Cherokee and Seminole as well as English, yet he is not even dignified with a name.

32. K. W. Porter, "Seminole Flight from Fort Marion," *FHQ*, 22, (January 1944): 113–133.

33. *ASPMA*, 7: 890; *USHD 78*, 25th Cong., 2d Sess., (1838), 196. Jesup resented the interference of the Cherokees, fearing they were too sympathetic to the Seminoles.

34. *USHD 225*, 11–12.

35. Hartley, 237.

36. *ASPMA*, 7: 986–989; *USSD 227*, 25th Cong., 2d Sess., (1838): 1–13.

37. Sprague, 212.

38. Ibid., 214.

39. Charles H. Coe, *Red Patriots: The Story of the Seminoles*, 21.

40. Motte, 207–210.

41. *ASPMA*, 7: 811.

### 11. General Jesup's Second Campaign

1. W. and E. Hartley, *Osceola*, 243–244.

2. George Catlin, *Letters and Notes on . . . North American Indians*, 2: 219.

3. Ibid., 219–220.

4. Ibid.

5. Weeden to Catlin, in footnote, Ibid., 219–220.

6. C. H. Coe, *Red Patriots*, 103, 117–118.

7. *Niles National Register*, 53, (3 February): 353; whole number 1375; Washington City.

8. As if there were not enough other horrors in the Florida war, there is a particularly grisly ending to the death of Osceola. Dr. Weedon cut off his head and kept it. Weedon's son-in-law inherited the gruesome relic and gave it to Dr. Valentine Mott of the New York Medical School where it was lost in a fire in 1866; Mark F. Boyd, "Asi-Yaholo or Osceola," *FHQ*, 33 (January and April 1955): 303–305; May McNeer Ward, "The Disappearance of the Head of Osceola," *FHQ*, 33, (January-April 1955): 193–201; Hartley, 247–249.

9. *United States House Document 219 (USHD 219)*, 25th Cong., 2d Sess., 1–5.

10. *ASPMA*, 7: 290.

11. *A&NC*, 4, no. 19, (1837): 299.

12. Ibid., 298–299.

13. Ibid., 6, no. 7, (1838): 105.

14. Powell to Dallas, 17 January 1838, *Niles Register* 53: 388; Powell to Secretary of the Navy, 27 January and 6 February 1838, Officers' Letter; George E. Buker, *Swamp Sailors*, 56–63.

15. *USHD 219*, 6–8; Coe, 180–181.

16. Coe, 134.

17. *TP, Florida*, 25: 494.

18. Coe, 135.

19. *TP, Florida*, 25: 495.

20. Coe, 135.

21. Ibid., 136.

22. *TP, Florida*, 25: 495.

23. Coe, 127.

### 12. The Second Emigration

1. *A&NC*, 6, no. 3, (1838): 42.

2. Ibid., no. 19; 297.

3. John Reynolds to C. A. Harris, *United States House Document 225 (USHD 225)*, 25th Cong., 3d Sess., (1839), 97.

4. OIALR, M234, Roll 289, D-438; T. S. Jesup to John Reynolds, *USHD* *225*, 26; Special Order No. 4, *USHD 225*, 81.

5. *USHD* 225, 91.

6. Reynolds to Harris, 2 June 1838; Reynolds to General Matthew Arbuckle, 12 June 1838; Arbuckle to Reynolds, Ibid., 102–104.

7. Reynolds to J. Morrison, 14 June 1838, Ibid., 101.

8. *A&NC*, 7, no. 3, (1838): 45.

9. Grant Foreman, *Indian Removal*, 367–369.

10. *A&NC*, 7, no. 3, (1838): 44.

11. C. J. Kappler, *Treaties*, 395.

12. E. C. McReynolds, *The Seminoles*, 230–231.

13. *A&NC*, 8, no. 13, (1839); 205. Abraham was still acting as an interpreter in the third Florida war.

14. W. K. Porter, "Seminole Flight from Fort Marion," *FHQ*, 22 (January 1944): 129. Porter says John Cavallo (Horse John in Spanish) became Gopher John, government interpreter, after he surrendered with Alligator.

15. Joseph Harris to George Gibson 13 September 1836, CGSLR, OIA, PI 163, Entry 120.

16. Ibid.

17. John Page to Commissioner of Indian Affairs, 18 June, 1841, OIALR, M234, Roll 289.


*13. General Zachary Taylor's Campaign, 1838–1839*


1. Zachary Taylor to Adjutant General R. Jones, 5 January 1839, AGOLR, M567, Roll 196, T-13; *A&NC*, 9, no. 6, (1839): 89; J. T. Sprague, *The Florida War*, 225.

2. *A&NC*, 8, no. 24, (1839): 379.

3. From a glossary of terms compiled by John Lee Williams, *The Territory of Florida*, 276.

4. Sprague, 252.

5. Since the officers said the same of Osceola and Coacoochee, perhaps the Seminoles behaved this way in general.

6. Sprague, 503.

7. *A&NC*, 8, no. 24, (1839): 380.

8. Ibid.

9. C. H. Coe, *Red Patriots*, 143–144.

10. Ibid.

11. *A&NC*, 8, no. 24, (1839): 380.

12. Coe, 147.

13. *A&NC*, 8, no. 23, (1839): 364.

14. Coe, 150.

15. *A&NC*, 8, no. 24, (1839): 381. If army reports of crop destruction have any validity, the women and children could grow crops on the top of the smallest hammock.

16. Sprague, 232–233.

17. *A&NC*, 10, no. 4, (1840): 50.

18. Ibid., 76–77.

19. Ibid., 6, no. 22, (1838): 346.

20. J. R. Giddings, *The Exiles of Florida*, 272.

21. Ibid., 274.

22. OIALR, "Florida Superintendency," M234, Roll 288, 29 March 1837, item 685.

23. McReynolds, 243–246.


## 14. General W. K. Armistead's Campaign, 1840–1841

1. *A&NC*, 7, no. 24, (1838): 386–387.

2. Ibid.

3. *TP, Florida*, 25: 411.

4. *A&NC*, 8, no. 3, (1839): 39.

5. Ibid., 10, no. 3, (1840): 34.

6. J. T. Sprague, *The Florida War*, 248.

7. AGOLR, M567, Roll 202, A-261, A-268, A-274.

8. Ibid., A-295.

9. *TP, Florida*, 26: 224–225.

10. W. A. Crofutt, *Hitchcock Diary*, 123.

11. John Page to C. A. Harris, 9 December 1840, OIALR, M234, Roll 289.

12. *A&NC*, 11, no. 25, (1840): 395.

13. Crofutt, 124.

14. Ibid., 125.

15. AGOLR, M567, Roll 202, A-312, A-331, A-349, A-354.

16. *A&NC*, 4, no. 19, (1837): 298–299.

17. G. E. Buker, *Swamp Sailors*, 100–101.

18. Ibid., 107–109.

19. Sprague, 254.

20. Buker, 114.

21. AGOLR, M567, Roll 222, A-34; Sprague, 248–254.

22. John Page to Commissioner of Indian Affairs, 24 January 1841, OIALR, M234, Roll 289.

23. Sprague, 257.

24. Crofutt, 125.

25. Sprague, 260.

26. Crofutt, 125–127.

27. AGOLR, M567, Roll 222, A-140.

28. Grant Foreman, *Indian Removal*, 378.

29. Sprague, 262–263.

30. AGOLR, M567, Roll 241, W-228. Major Thomas Childs assisted in the capture; Colonel William Gates, ignoring Worth's wishes, shipped the chief to New Orleans.

31. Sprague, 264–265.

### 15. Colonel W. J. Worth's First Campaign, 1841

1. *Appleton's Encyclopaedia of American Biography*, 6: 615–616.

2. J. T. Sprague, *The Florida War*, 270–273.

3. AGOLR, M567, Roll 241, W-215.

4. Sprague, 270–273.

5. Ibid., 275.

6. AGOLR, M567, Roll 241, W-220.

7. Ibid., W-259.

8. Enclosure in W-259, Ibid.

9. J. K. Mahon, *History of the Seminole War*, 13.

10. Sprague, 279–281.

11. Ibid., 270; *United States House Executive Document 262*, 27th Cong., 2d Sess., (1847): 47.

12. AGOLR, M567, Roll 241, W-288.

13. Sprague, 288.

14. Ibid., 289.

15. Ibid., 290–293.

16. *A&NC*, 12, no. 37, (1841): 293; Sprague, 301–302.

17. AGOLR, M567, Roll 243, W-386, W-402; Ibid., Roll 244, W-483.

18. The description of this camp came from Sampson, a Negro who had once been a slave of Gad Humphreys. Sampson had been captured by the Indians and spent two years with Osceola. Now he was acting as a messenger and interpreter for the army, Sprague, 318–319.

19. AGOLR, M567, Roll 244, W-543; *A&NC*, 12, no. 44, (1841): 349.

20. Sprague, 323–324.

21. AGOLR, M567, Roll 244, W-543.

22. Grant Foreman, *Indian Removal*, 379.

## 16. Colonel Worth's Navy Campaign

1. AGOLR, M657, Roll 243, W-421.

2. G. E. Buker, *Swamp Sailors*, 118.

3. AGOLR, M567, Roll 260, W-26; McLaughlin to Worth, 25 October 1841, Ibid., Roll 244, W-474.

4. Report of Major Thomas Child's expedition into the Everglades, AGOLR, M567, Roll 244, W-438; *A&NC*, 12, no. 41, (1841): 322.

5. J. T. Sprague, *The Florida War*, 352.

6. Buker, 124.

7. Ibid., 127.

8. AGOLR, M567, Roll 260, W-30; Sprague, 359–367 (Sprague takes his material from a journal kept by C. R. Gates of the Eighth Regiment.)

9. AGOLR, M567, Roll 244, W-516; *A&NC*, 12, no. 47, (1841): 372.

10. Buker, 124–125, 126.

11. Sprague, 305.

12. John Bemrose, *Reminiscences*, 99.

13. Ibid., 94–98.

14. *A&NC*, 13, no. 10, (1841): 156; Buker, 128–129, 131; Sprague, 384–386.

15. *A&NC*, 13, no. 7, (1841): 110; George Henry Preble, "The Diary of a Canoe Expedition . . . ," *A Monthly Review of Military and Naval Affairs, The United Service*, Series 1, 8: 366.

16. Preble, 367; AGOLR, M567, Roll 261, W-48. Fort Center had been activated by Colonel Worth who ordered Captain George A. McCall to be there with six to nine thousand rations to support McLaughlin's men. Obviously there was no shortage of food with nature providing so bountifully as Preble reveals.

17. John Rodgers to McLaughlin, 12 April 1842, in Preble, 359–360.

18. Worth to McLaughlin, 20 June 1842, Ibid., 374.

19. Preble, 358–376, gives a detailed account of Rodgers' expedition.

20. Buker, 136.

21. Ibid., 139.

22. AGOLR, M567, Roll 260, W-26.

23. Sprague, 429–435.

24. M. M. Cohen, *Notices*, 222.

25. *A&NC*, 13, no. 10, (1841): 155.

## 17. Colonel Worth's Final Thrust

1. J. T. Sprague, *The Florida War*, 396.

2. Ibid., 397.

3. Ibid., 400.

4. AGOLR, M567, Roll 261, W-52; *A&NC*, 12, no. 52, (1841): 411.

5. Sprague, 428–429.

6. AGOLR, M567, Roll 261, W-54.

7. Sprague, 430.

8. AGOLR, M567, Roll 261, W-47, W-48; A&NC, 13, no. 4, (1842): 59–60.

9. *United States House Executive Document 262*, (*USHED 262*), 27th Cong. 2d Sess., 9; AGOLR, M567, Roll 261, W-48; Sprague, 438.

10. AGOLR, M567, Roll 261, W-105.

11. Sprague, 441.

12. AGOLR, M567, Roll 261, W-105.

13. Sprague, 441.

14. AGOLR, M567, Roll 261, W-54, W-58, W-68.

15. *TP, Florida*, 26: 436–439; AGOLR, M567, Roll 261, W-74.

16. Sprague, 440–445.

17. Ibid., 450.

18. *USHED 262*, 19.

19. Sprague, 454, 443–444.

20. AGOLR, M567, Roll 261, W-148.

21. Ibid., W-177.

22. Sprague, 454–460; *USHED 262*, 22–23; J. K. Mahon, *History of the Second Seminole War*, 307–308; AGOLR, M567, Roll 261, W-177.

23. Sprague, 468.

24. *A&NC*, 13, no. 18, (1842): 281; *USHED 262*, 30.

25. Sprague, 468. Chiefs had walked into army camps before to "negotiate" while stock-piling food and ammunition. Often the plan worked. No one could predict when American patience would end and the gamble fail.

26. Ibid., 469.

27. *A&NC*, 13, no. 18, (1842): 281.

28. Sprague, 482–483.

29. Ibid.

30. AGOLR, M567, Roll 262, W-230.

31. *A&NC*, 2, no. 7, (1836): 99.

32. E. C. McReynolds, *The Seminoles*, 157.

## 18. Colonel Josiah H. Vose's Non-Campaign, 1842

1. The boundary ran roughly from the mouth of Pease Creek to the head of Lake Istokpoga, down the Kissimmee to Lake Okeechobee, through the lake and the Everglades to the Shark River, along it to the Gulf and back to the starting point.

2. AGOLR, M567, Roll 262, W-352, W-264.

3. Ibid., Roll 260, V-64, item 15.

4. AGOLR, M567, Roll 262, W-264, W-269; *United States House Executive Document 262 (USHED 262)*, 27th Cong., 2d Sess., 45.

5. AGOLR, M567, Roll 262, W-270, W-352.

6. *USHED 262*, 8–9; AGOLR, M567, Roll 261, W-47.

7. *TP, Florida*, 26: 524–525, 551.

8. AGOLR, M567, Roll 262, W-352; Sprague, 487.

9. J. T. Sprague, *The Florida War*, 494–495.

10. AGOLR, M567, Roll 260, V-57, V-66.

11. William H. Powell, ed., *List of Officers of the Army of the United States from 1799 to 1900*, 648.

12. *TP, Florida*, 572, 552–553.

13. AGOLR, M567, Roll 260, V-65, V-58.

14. For details of the Armed Occupation Act, see pp. 189, 252.

15. AGOLR, M567, Roll 262, W-328; *TP, Florida*, 26: 950.

16. *TP, Florida*, 26: 552–553.

17. Ibid., 548–549.

18. AGOLR, M567, Roll 260, V-73, item 24.

19. *TP, Florida*, 26: footnote, 557.

20. AGOLR, M567, Roll 260, V-45.

21. Mahon states another officer claimed the chief was seriously ill. J. K. Mahon, *History of the Second Seminole War*, 317.

22. Sprague, 499–500.

23. J. K. Mahon, *History of the Second Seminole War*, 317.

24. Sprague, 502.

25. Ibid.

26. Ibid., 505–507.

27. AGOLR, M567, Roll 260, V-66, item 17.

## 19. The Final "End" of the Second Florida War, 1842

1. AGOLR, M567, Roll 263, W-603.

2. Fort Stansbury was located on the Wakulla River, nine miles above St. Marks, footnote in *TP, Florida*, 26: 549.

3. W. A. Crofutt, *Hitchcock's Diary*, 167–168.

4. "In 1830 and 1831, Edgar Allen Poe was a cadet at West Point under the instruction of Captain Hitchcock, and for the first six months stood near the head of his class, but becoming restless and indifferent, he was cashiered and dismissed from the service," in Crofutt, footnote, 63.

5. Crofutt, 52–94.

6. Ibid., 122–129.

7. Ibid., 165–166. Ten million is way below the cost of the second Seminole war. J. K. Mahon, *History of the Second Seminole War*, 326, estimates the cost at

between thirty and forty million. No analysis of costs has been made—probably because appropriations bills often contained a lump sum for the suppression of Indian hostilities, making it nearly impossible to separate the cost of the Creek uprising from that of the Seminole war; *United States Senate Document 278*, 26th Cong., 2d Sess., 1840, and *United States House Report 582*, 28th Cong., 1st Sess., 1844, deal with expenditures of the war; *USHR 582* inquired into the high cost of the naval operations but absolved Lieutenant John T. McLaughlin of collusion with his suppliers or of wasteful practices; Mahon, 323.

8. AGOLR, M567, Roll 259, H-28.

9. Ibid., Roll 263, W-603.

10. Fort Preston cannot be related to a modern place name.

11. AGOLR, M567, Roll 259, H-280.

12. Crofutt, 168–169.

13. AGOLR, M567, Roll 263, W-652.

14. Crofutt, 170.

15. Ibid., 170–171.

16. J. T. Sprague, *The Florida War*, 501; Crofutt, 167–173.

17. Crofutt, 173.

18. Ibid.

19. J. K. Mahon, *The History of the Second Seminole War*, 326.

*Part Four:* THE THIRD FLORIDA WAR, 1848–1858

### 20. The Final Indignity

1. J. T. Sprague, *The Florida War*, 513. Sprague leaves twelve warriors unidentified as to race or tribe.

2. OIALR, M234, Roll 289, A-290.

3. AGOLR, M567, Roll 403, C-377.

4. Ibid., C-388.

5. Ibid., C-372.

6. OIALR, M234, Roll 289, I-291, K-36.

7. AGOLR, M567, Roll 403, C-449.

8. Ibid., C-493.

9. Ibid., C-515.

10. *United States Senate Executive Document 1 (USSED 1)*, 31st Cong., 1st Sess., 134 and 120.

11. Ibid., 122.

12. Ibid., 136.

13. Ibid., 128–132.

14. Ibid., 128.

15. Ibid., 120.

16. OIALR, M234, Roll 289, D-227, D-234, D-247.

17. Ibid., D-251.

18. Ibid., D-256.

19. Ibid., D-262.

20. Ibid., D-278.

21. Ibid., G-152, D-154.

22. Ibid., H-1120, H-1123, I-291.

23. E. C. McReynolds, *The Seminoles*, 250–255, 269.

24. Ibid., 266–267.

25. AGOLR, M567, Roll 425, C-297.

26. Records of the United States Continental Commands, 1820–1920, RG 393, Part 1, Entry 1615, item 76, p. 46.

27. AGOLR, M567, Roll 426, C-563.

28. *United States Senate Executive Document 71 (USSED 71)*, 33rd Cong., 1st Sess., 27; C. H. Coe, *Red Patriots*, 201.

29. AGOLR, M567, Roll 426, C-493.

30. Coe, 203–204.

31. USACC, 1820–1920, RG 393, Part 1, Entry 1615, 2.

32. *USSED 71*, 26.

33. Coe, 206.

34. OIALR, M234, Roll 291, I-130.

35. RUSCC, 1820–1920, RG 393, Part 1, Entry 1615, 1: item 15, p. 73; *USSED 71*, 9.

36. Ibid., 85–86.

37. *USSED 71*, 12–15.

38. Ibid., 16–20.

39. RUSCC, 1820–1920, RG 393, Part 1, Entry 1615, 2: 48–50.

40. Ibid., 3: 18.

41. *USSED 71*, 20–21, 27–18.

42. Ibid., 24–65.

43. USACC, 1820–1920, RG 393, Part 1, Entry 1615, 3: 45.

44. C. M. Brevard, *A History of Florida*, 2: 13.

45. USACC, 1820–1920, RG 393 (v. 74, Old Book 242) Entry 1616, item 78.

46. McReynolds, 275.

47. Coe, 219.

48. *United States Senate Executive Document 1, (USSED 1)*, 35th Cong., 2d Sess., 81.

49. Coe, 219.

50. McReynolds, 287.

51. *USSED 1*, 35th Cong., 2d Sess., 81.

52. The number of years the war dragged on differs according to when one starts counting. Twenty-three years includes the second Florida war from 1835 to 1842 and the third Florida war from 1849 to 1858 but if one counts the attempts to annex Florida and the attacks on the Indians and maroons from 1810 to 1818, the conflict spans thirty years—including two "cold" wars during 1818–1835 and 1842–1849. 53. Coe, 221.

# Bibliography

THE FLORIDA WARS are a fascinating subject because they were documented by a number of highly articulate participants who published their experiences. Meyer M. Cohen, *Notices*, with a group of young aristocrats from South Carolina, rushed to join the militia in order to gain glory while he saved the citizens of Florida from onslaughts of the cruel savages. He lost most of his illusions but never his sense of humor as he coped with the realities of war. John Bemrose and Jacob Rhette Motte, brought to Florida to tend the ill and wounded, recounted vividly all facets of life in the Florida army. George Catlin, timely as always, arrived at Fort Moultrie just in time to paint Osceola and other prominent chiefs imprisoned there. He listened to the story of each man as he painted. His impressions are part of a two-volume record of his trek around the continent to record the native leaders before they disappeared. John Lee Williams, *The Territory of Florida*, one of its earliest residents, loved the land, was fascinated by the natives and participated in the war. All these experiences are reflected in his work. John T. Sprague's *The Florida War* gives not only a soldierly account of the actions but a very human picture of the enemy—both the people and the land—his army was fighting. Major Ethan Allen Hitchcock's diary is full of word pictures of the baffling Florida war and of caustic comments on its cost and futility. Years later, Rear Admiral George Henry Preble would pull from his files and publish a diary he had kept as a passed midshipman while on one of the major navy campaigns. He would argue that historians were neglecting the role of his branch of the service when they dealt with the Florida wars. To read his day-by-day account of life in a swamp boat is to feel one is there.

Equally absorbing are some of the fine secondary sources which have probed deeply into one particular aspect of the wars. Rembert Patrick, *Florida Fiasco*, explores both the actual invasion during the plot to annex East Florida in 1812 and the evidence of secret support of the administration for the abortive and illegal attempt. Herman J. Viola's chapter on Andrew Jackson's 1818 invasion of Florida assembles and interprets the primary sources used in congressional investigations of that incident in the series, *Congress Investigates*. Frank Laumer, *Massacre*, has dug up, piece-by-piece, the evidence necessary to flesh out the hundred or so men who moved out with Major Francis L. Dade when they marched from Fort Brooke to relieve the undermanned garrison at Fort King. Laumer follows every step of the way—in archival material and on the site—their march to death, in a beautifully detailed account of the first battle of the second war and what led up to it. While Sprague is the basic on-site source for the second war, John K. Mahon's annotated bibliography in his *History of the Second Seminole War* provides a comprehensive accumulation of other primary sources. George E. Buker concentrates on the largely neglected naval contribution to the second war in his well-documented *Swamp Sailors*. Incorporating legend with verified facts (and clearly labeling each category), William and Ellen Hartley, in *Osceola*, focus on the brief but brilliant era of the chief's vital leadership in the early days of the second war, giving both the man and the times a reality and immediacy rare in history books. Charles H. Coe, *Red Patriots*, brings to life the third Seminole war—that epilogue to the first two wars—scarcely touched on by most authors.

Underlying, connecting, and verifying the primary and secondary accounts of what took place in the Florida wars is the mass of government documents in the National Archives. Because of the efficiency and willingness of that institution's personnel in all departments as well as in the main library, it is possible to track down any source, however tenuous or remote it may be.

*The Army & Navy Chronicle*, thirteen volumes of a professional journal for military men (1835–1842), is full of newspaper articles, letters to editors, and official military documents quoted verbatim. It is a treasury of opinions, vignettes, arguments, and humor which help the researcher feel he is part of that time. Equally valuable are the seventy-six volumes of the *Niles Register* (1811–1849) found in the history library at the Navy Yard, Washington, D.C.

Working over a period of more than three decades, Dr. Kenneth Wiggins Porter brought to light long-ignored information on the role of blacks in the Florida wars. Published mostly in the *Journal of Negro History* and the *Florida Historical Quarterly*, his work is a rich lode of primary sources and of acute and sensitive insights into people, events and the motivations of interaction among blacks, Indians, and whites. Like Sprague, his work must be the basis for all students of the Florida wars.

Crucial to a real understanding of what went on between the three races in those wars is an unpublished master's thesis by Michael Paul Duffner. In "The Seminole-Black Alliance in Florida: an Example of Minority Cooperation," he has brought together and interpreted well, a mass of anthropological and historical data to explain the unique example of two minorities uniting to protect themselves from a superior force. His work is sociologically, as well as historically, significant for it points the way for similar coalitions today and in the future.

There is no question but that the primary and secondary sources recounting this little-known war on the outskirts, as it were, of our society, provide a moving account of the gallantry and folly displayed when three races of people met and mingled in a battle over possession of a beautiful, yet treacherous, land and over the right to stand tall on it.

### PRIMARY SOURCES: MANUSCRIPT MATERIALS

ADJUTANT GENERAL'S OFFICE, Record Group 94 (RG 94), National Archives (NA).

Letters Sent, Main Series (1800–1890), on Microfilm 565 (M565) 63 Rolls.

Letters Received, Main Series, (1822–1860) on M567, 636 Rolls.

DEPARTMENT OF INTERIOR, RG 48, NA.

Documents Relating to the Negotiation of Ratified and Unratified Treaties with Various Indian Tribes (1801–1869) on Microfilm T494, 10 Rolls.

JESUP, MAJOR GENERAL THOMAS S., Papers, RG 94, NA.

MAPS, CARTOGRAPHIC SECTION, NA.

*No. 1141*, RG 75: "Map of the Seat of War in Florida," compiled by order of General Zachary Taylor, Tampa Bay, Florida, 1839, (from surveys of Captain John Mackay and Lieutenant J. E. Blake, Hq. of the Army of the South.

*No. 4343*, RG 75: "Map of the Seat of War in Florida, 1836."

*No. 40, Pre-Federal Maps* (Special List 26), United States 45: "A New Map of Georgia, with part of North Carolina, Florida, and Louisiana Drawn from Original Draughts assisted by the most approved maps and charts, collected by Eman[uel] Bowen, Geographer to his Majesty," Published in 1764 by T. Osborne, London, 1 inch approximately 40 miles, 17 × 23 inches: Shows roads, trails, towns and Indian villages.

*No. 167, Florida* in *Selected Maps of States and Territories* (Special List 29), "Map of Florida, . . ." by John Lee Williams, 1837. Shows natural features, Indian towns, white plantations and tillable land, etc.

*No. L66*, RG 77: "Map of the Seat of War in East Florida," 1837, compiled from various data in the U.S. Topographical Bureau under the direction of Colonel John J. Abert, U.S. Topographical Engineer.

*No. L75*, RG 77: "Sketch of Major Dade's Battle Ground taken from the Report of Edwin Rose, Lieutenant, U.S. Artillery.

*No. L247*, Item 2, RG 77: "Theater of Military Operations in Florida During 1835, 1836, 1837."

*No. L247*, Item 30, RG 77: Showing a triangle of the Southern Tip of Florida from Charlotte Harbor across to Locha Hatchee down to Cape Sable and Key Largo, indicating camps of resisting Indian Chiefs, 1840–1841.

*No. L247*, Item 48½, RG 77: "Map of the Route Passed Over By Bvt. Col. William Davenport's Command between 15th Dec., 1838, and 9th Jan., 1839, from a Reconnaissance by J. Edmund Blake, 1st Lieut. Top. Eng's."

OFFICE OF INDIAN AFFAIRS, RG 75, NA.

Commissioner of General Subsistence, Letters Received, Preliminary Inventory 163, Entry 198, File 67.

Florida Superintendency, Letters Received (1824–1850), on M234, Rolls 288–291.

Office of Indian Affairs, Letters Sent, 1824–1881, Rolls 1–60.

Seminole Agency, Letters Received, (1824–1876), on M234, Rolls 800, 801, 802, 806.

RECORDS OF THE UNITED STATES SENATE, RG 46, NA.

SECRETARY OF THE NAVY, RG 45, NA.

Letters Sent to Officers (1798–1865) on M149, 86 Rolls.

Letters Received from Commanders, (1804–1886), on M147, 124 Rolls.

Letters Received from Officers below the Rank of Commander, (1802–1884), on M148, 518 Rolls.

SECRETARY OF WAR, RG 107, NA.

Letters Received, Registered Series, (1801–1870), on M221, 317 Rolls.

Letters Received, Unregistered Series, (1789–1861) on M222, 34 Rolls.

Register of Letters Received, Main Series, (1800–1879), 134 Rolls.

UNITED STATES ARMY CONTINENTAL COMMANDS, (1820–1920), RG 393, NA.


PRIMARY SOURCES: PRINTED GOVERNMENT DOCUMENTS

*American State Papers*, NA:

Foreign Relations, 6 volumes, 1789–1828.

*Indian Affairs*, 2 volumes, 1832–1834.

*Military Affairs*, 7 volumes, 1832–1860.

KAPPLER, CHARLES J., *Indian Affairs: Laws and Treaties*, 3 volumes, 57th Cong., Document 452, Washington, D.C.: Government Printing Office (GPO), 1904.

*State Papers & Publick Documents of the United States, 1789–1818*, Series 1, volume 9, (1812–1815). Edited by Thomas B. Wait, Library of Congress.

*Territorial Papers of the United States, Florida Territory (TP, Florida)*, volumes 22–26. Compiled and edited by Clarence E. Carter, Washington, D.C.: GPO, 1957–1962, NA.

UNITED STATES CONGRESSIONAL SET, NA.

*USED 1*, 35th Cong., 2d Sess., (1858–1859)

*United States House Document 119 (USHD 119)*, 15th Cong., 2d Sess., (1818–1819), "Inquiry into Jackson's Reasons for Attacking the Negro Fort."

*USHD 122*, 15th Cong., 2d Sess., (1818–1819), "Inquiry into Attack on Negro Fort."

*USHD 267*, 24th Cong., 1st Sess., (1836), "Report on Causes of Hostilities."

*USHD 271*, 24th Cong., 1st Sess., (1836), "Supplemental Report on Causes of Hostilities."

*USHD 78*, 25th Cong., 2d Sess., (1838) "Inquiry into Campaigns of Generals Scott and Gaines; Documents Pertaining to Jesup's Campaign."

*USHD 219*, 25th Cong., 2d Sess., (1838), "Jesup's Conduct of the War."

*USHD 285*, 25th Cong., 2d Sess., (1838), "Memorial of the Cherokee Mediators."

*USHD 225*, 25th Cong., 2d Sess., (1839), "Captured Negroes."

*USHD 8*, 26th Cong., 2d Sess., (1840), "Expenditures in the War."

*USHD 247*, 27th Cong., 2d Sess., (1842), "Expenditures in the War."

*USHD 582*, 29th Cong., 1st Sess., (1844), "Expenditures in the Florida Squadron."

*USHD 82*, 28th Cong., 1st Sess., (1844), "Indians Remaining in Florida."

*USHD 253*, 28th Cong., 1st Sess., (1844), "Indians Remaining in Florida."

*United States House Executive Document 14* (*USHED*), 15th Cong., 2d Sess., (1818) "The Seminole War."

*USHED* 17, 19th Cong., 2d Sess., (1826), "Florida Indians."

*USHED 262*, 27th Cong., 2d Sess., (1842), "Secretary of War to Commander in Florida."

*United States Miscellaneous Document 55*, 36th Cong., 1st Sess., (1860), "Ferreira vs. the United States."

*United States Senate Document 512*, (*USSD*), 23rd Cong., 1st Sess., 5 volumes, (1831–1833), "Indian Emigration."

*USSD 152*, 24th Cong., 1st Sess., (1836), "Hostilities in Florida."

*USSD 227*, 25th Cong., 2d Sess., (1838), "General Taylor's Report on Okeechobee."

*USSD 224*, 24th Cong. 2d Sess., (1837), "Inquiry into Campaigns of Scott and Gaines."

*USSD 507*, 25th Cong., 2d Sess., (1838), "General Jesup's Report of his Command."

UNITED STATES CONGRESSIONAL SET, NA

*USSD 278*, 26th Cong., 1st Sess., (1840), "Correspondence Between General Call and the War Department."

*USSD 42*, 25th Cong., 3d Sess., (1839), "Armed Occupation of Florida."

*USSD* 88, 25th Cong., 3d Sess., (1839), "Armed Occupation of Florida."

*USSD 93*, 25th Cong., 3d Sess., (1839), "Armed Occupation of Florida."

*USSD 163*, 25th Cong., 3d Sess., (1839), "Armed Occupation of Florida."

*USSD 39*, 30th Cong., 1st Sess., (1848), "Report on Armed Occupation Act."

*United States Senate Executive Document 1*, (*USSED*) 31st Cong., 1st Sess., (1849–1850). "Annual Reports to the President."

*USSED 71*, 33rd Cong., 1st Sess., (1853–1854). "Annual Reports to the President."

*United States Statutes at Large*, volume 3, Little, Brown & Co., 1854. NA.

## PRIMARY SOURCES: BOOKS

BASSETT, JOHN S., ed., *Correspondence of Andrew Jackson*. 2 vols. Washington, D.C.: Carnegie Institution of Washington, 1926–1935.

BEMROSE, JOHN. *Reminiscences of the Second Seminole War*. Edited by John K. Mahon. Gainesville: University of Florida Press, 1966.

CATLIN, GEORGE. *Letters and Notes on the Manners, Customs, and Conditions of the North American Indians*. 2 vols. London, 1844. New York: Dover Publications, Inc., 1973.

CHATEAUBRIAND, FRANCOIS A. *Travels in America*. 1791. Lexington: University of Kentucky Press, 1969.

COHEN, MYER M. *Notices of Florida and the Campaigns*. 1836. Gainesville: University of Florida Press (Facsimile Reproduction), 1974.

COMMAGER, HENRY STEELE. *Documents of American History*. 7th ed. New York City: Appleton-Century-Crofts, 1963.

CROFUTT, W. A., ed. *Fifty Years in Camp and Field: Diary of Major Ethan Allen Hitchcock, U.S.A.* New York, London: G.P. Putnam Sons, The Knickerbocker Press, 1909.

DOWLING, DAN J. *Sketch of the Seminole War by a Lieutenant*. Charleston: 1836.

HENING, WILLIAM WALLER, *The Statutes at Large Being a Collection of all the Laws of Virginia, from the First Session of the Legislature, in the year 1619*. 1823. Charlottesville: University Press of Virginia (Facsimile Reprint), 1969.

McCALL, GEORGE. *Letters from the Frontier*. Philadelphia: 1868.

McKENNEY, THOMAS L. and Hall, James, *History of the Indian Tribes of North America with Biographical Sketches and Anecdotes of the Principal Chiefs*. 2 vols. Philadelphia: Daniel Rice and James G. Clark, 1842 (folio).

MORSE, JEDIDIAH. *Report to the Secretary of War on Indian Affairs*. New Haven, 1822.

MOTTE, JACOB RHETT. *Journey into Wilderness: An Army Surgeon's Account of Life in Camp and Field During the Creek and Seminole Wars, 1836–1838*. Edited by James F. Sunderman. Gainesville: University of Florida Press, 1963.

RAWICK, GEORGE P., ed., *The American Slave: A Composite Autobiography*. Volumes 1–25, Florida Narratives. Westport, Connecticut: Greenwood Publishing Company, 1972.

ROMANS, BERNARD. *A Concise Natural History of East and West Florida*. 1775. Gainesville: University of Florida Press (Facsimile and Reprint Series), 1962.

SPRAGUE, JOHN T. *The Origin, Progress, and Conclusion of the Florida War*. New York / Philadelphia: Doubleton, Appleton & Co., 1848.

VIOLA, HERMAN J. "Andrew Jackson's Invasion of Florida, 1818," *Congress Investigates: A Documented History*. 5 vols. Edited by Arthur M. Schlessinger, Jr. & Roger Bruns. New York and London: Chelsea House Publishers with R. R. Bowker Co., 1975.

WILLIAMS, JOHN LEE. *The Territory of Florida or Sketches of the Topography, Civil and Natural History of the Country, the Climate, and the Indian Tribes from the First Discovery to the Present Time with a Map, Views, etc.* New York: A. T. Goodrich, 1837.

## PRIMARY SOURCES: PERIODICALS

*Army & Navy Chronicle*. 13 vols. Edited and published by B. Homans, Washington, D.C., 1835–1842. References to this journal are not, as a rule, listed by author.

*Niles National Register (Niles Register)* 76 vols. 1811–1849. Baltimore, Washington & Philadelphia. Edited and published by H. Niles and others. References not listed by author.

PREBLE, REAR ADMIRAL GEORGE HENRY. "The Diary of a Canoe Expedition into the Everglades and Interior of Southern Florida in 1842." *A Monthly Review of Military and Naval Affairs, The United Service,*

Series 1, 14 vols. 1879–1886, 8: 358–376. Philadelphia: L. R. Hammersly & Co., 1883.

WRIGHT, I. A., ed. "Dispatches of Spanish Officials Bearing on the Free Negro Settlement of Gracia Real De Santa Teresa De Mosè." *Journal of Negro History*, 9, (April 1924): 144–195.


## SECONDARY SOURCES: BOOKS

ABEL, ANNIE HELOISE. *The American Indian as Slaveholder and Secessionist.* Cleveland: Arthur H. Clark Co., 1915.

*Appleton's Cyclopaedia of Biography.* 6 vols. Edited by James Grant Wilson and John Firke. New York: Appleton Co., 1887.

BENNETT, LERONE, JR. *Before the Mayflower: A History of the Negro in America, 1619–1964.* Baltimore: Penguin Books, 1970.

BENTON, THOMAS H. *Thirty Years View: A History of the Working of the American Government for Thirty Years 1820–1850.* 2 vols. New York: D. Appleton and Company, 1875.

BILLINGTON, RAY A. *American History before 1877.* Paterson, New Jersey: Littlefield, Adams & Co., Inc., 1965.

——*American History after 1865.* Paterson: Littlefield, Adams & Co., Inc., 1965.

BRAWLEY, BENJAMIN. *A Social History of the American Negro.* 1921. New York: The Macmillan Co., 1970.

BREVARD, CAROLINE MAYS. *A History of Florida: From the Treaty of 1763 to Our Own Times.* 2 vols. Deland, Florida: Florida Historical Society, 1924.

BUKER, GEORGE E. *Swamp Sailors.* Gainesville: The University of Florida Press, 1975.

COE, CHARLES H. *Red Patriots: The Story of the Seminoles.* 1898. Gainesville: The University of Florida Press, (Facsimile Reproduction), 1974.

COTTERHILL, ROBERT S. *The Southern Indians: The Story of the Civilized Tribes Before Removal.* Norman: University of Oklahoma Press, 1966.

CRANE, VERNER C. *Tne Southern Frontier, 1670–1737.* Ann Arbor: University of Michigan Press, 1964.

DEGLAR, CARL. *Neither Black nor White.* New York: The Macmillan Co., 1971.

*Dictionary of American Biography.* 20 vols. New York: Charles Scribners Sons, 1928–1937.

DOHERTY, HERBERT J., JR. *Richard Keith Call*. Gainesville: University of
    Florida Press, 1961.
DOUGLAS, MARJORY STONEMAN. *The Everglades: River of Grass*. New York:
    Rhinehart and Co., 1947.
DOWNEY, FAIRFAX. *Indian Wars of the United States Army, 1776–1865*. New
    York: Doubleday and Co., Inc., 1963.
DYER, BRAINERD. *Zachary Taylor*. Baton Rouge: Louisiana State University
    Press, 1946.
ELLIOTT, CHARLES W. *Winfield Scott: The Soldier and the Man*. New York:
    The Macmillan Co., 1937.
FORBES, JACK D. *The Indian in America's Past*. Englewood Cliffs, New
    Jersey: Prentice-Hall, Inc., 1964.
FOREMAN, GRANT. *The Five Civilized Tribes*. Norman: The University of
    Oklahoma Press, 1966.
———— *Indian Removal: The Emigration of the Five Civilized Tribes of Indians*.
    1932. Norman: University of Oklahoma, 1972.
FOSTER, LAURENCE. *Negro-Indian Relationships in the Southeast*. Philadelphia:
    University of Pennsylvania Press, 1935.
FRANKLIN, JOHN HOPE. *From Slavery to Freedom: A History of American
    Negroes*. New York: Alfred A. Knopf, 1967.
FRECH, MARY L. AND SWINDLER, WILLIAM F., eds. *Chronology and Documen-
    tary Handbook of the State of Florida*. Dobbs Ferry, New York:
    Oceana Publications, Inc., 1973.
GIDDINGS, JOSHUA R. *The Exiles of Florida: The Crimes Committed Against
    the Maroons Who Fled from South Carolina and Other Slave States
    Seeking Protection under Spanish Laws*. 1858. Gainesville: The
    University of Florida Press, (Facsimile Reproduction), 1964.
GILBERT, MARTIN. *American History Atlas. 112 maps from earliest times to the
    present*. New York: Macmillan Publishing Co., Inc., 1968.
GINZBERG, ELI AND EICHNER, ALFRED S. *The Troublesome Presence: Ameri-
    can Democracy and the Negro*. New York: Mentor Books, 1966.
HARPER, FRANCIS., ed. *The Travels of William Bartram*. New Haven: Yale
    University Press, 1958.
HARTLEY, WILLIAM AND ELLEN. *Osceola: The Unconquered Indian*. New
    York: Hawthorn Books, Inc., 1973.
HENNOKOGAN, HILDE., ed. in chief. *The American Pictorial Atlas of United
    States History*. New York: American Heritage Publishing Co.,
    1966.
HODGE, FREDERICK WEBB. *Handbook of American Indians North of Mexico*.
    2 vols. Washington, D.C.; GPO, 1910.

HORAN, JAMES D. *The McKenney-Hall Portrait Gallery of American Indians.* New York: Crown Publishers, Inc., 1972.

HORTON, JAMES AFRICANUS. *West African Countries and Peoples.* Edinburgh: Edinburgh University Press, 1969.

JOSEPHY, ALVIN M. *The Patriot Chiefs.* New York: Viking Press, 1961.

KATZ, WILLIAM LOREN. *Eyewitness: The Negro in American History.* New York: Pitman Publishing Co., 1969.

KRAUS, MICHAEL. *The United States to 1865.* Ann Arbor: University of Michigan Press, 1959.

LAUBER, A. W. *Indian Slavery in Colonial Times within the Present Limits of the United States.* New York: Longmans, Green and Co., 1913.

LAUMER, FRANK. *Massacre.* Gainesville: University of Florida Press, 1968.

LURIE, NANCY OESTRICH. "Indian Cultural Adjustment to European Civilization." *Seventeenth Century America: Essays in Colonial History.* Edited by Morton James Smith. New York: W.W. Norton & Co., 1959.

MacCAULEY, CLAY. *The Seminole Indians of Florida.* Smithsonian Institution, Bureau of American Ethnology, Fifth Annual Report, 1883–1884. Washington, D.C.: GPO, 1887.

McMASTER, JOHN B. *A History of the People of the United States from the Revolution to the Civil War.* 8 vols. New York: Doubleday, Appleton & Co., 1883–1913.

McREYNOLDS, EDWIN C. *The Seminoles.* Norman: University of Oklahoma Press. 1957.

MAHON, JOHN K. *History of the Second Seminole War, 1835–1842.* Gainesville: University of Florida Press, 1967.

MELTZER, MILTON. *Hunted Like a Wolf.* Farrar, Straus and Giroux, 1972.

MONETTE, JOHN W., MD. *History of the Discovery and Settlement of the Valley of the Mississippi by the Three Great Powers: Spain, France and Great Britain. The Subsequent Occupation, Settlement and Extension of the Civil Government by the United States until the Year 1846.* 2 vols. New York: Harper and Brothers, 1846.

MORRIS, ALLEN. *Florida Place Names.* Coral Gables: University of Miami Press, 1971.

MORRIS, RICHARD B., ed. *Encyclopedia of American History.* New York: Harper & Rowe, 1965.

NASH, ROY. *A Survey of the Seminole Indians of Florida.* Senate Document 314, 71st Cong., 3d Sess., 1931, Washington, D.C.

PATRICK, REMBERT. *Florida Fiasco.* Athens: University of Georgia Press, 1954.

POWELL, WILLIAM H., ed. *List of Officers of the Army of the United States from 1779 to 1900.* Detroit: Gale Research Co., 1967.

PRUCHA, FRANCIS PAUL. *A Guide to the Military Posts of the United States, 1789–1895.* Madison: State Historical Society of Wisconsin, 1964.

———, ed. "The Indian in American History." *American Problem Studies.* Hinsdale, Illinois: The Dryden Press, Inc., 1971.

PUCKETT, NEWHELL MILES. *The Magic and Folk Beliefs of the Southern Negro.* 1926. New York: Dover Publications, 1969.

QUARLES, BENJAMIN. *The Negro in the American Revolution.* New York: W. W. Norton & Co., 1961.

SWANTON, JOHN R. *The Indians of Southeastern United States*: Smithsonian Institution, Bureau of American Ethnology Bulletin 137. 1946. Grosse Point, Michigan: Scholarly Press, 1969.

——— *Religious Beliefs and Medical Practices of the Creek Indians.* Smithsonian Institution, Bureau of American Ethnology, 42nd Annual Report, 1924–1925, Washington, D.C., 1928.

——— *Social Organization and Social Usages of the Indians of the Creek Confederacy.* Smithsonian Institution, Bureau of American Ethnology, 42nd Annual Report, 1924–1925, Washington, D.C., 1928.

TEBBEL, JOHN. *The Compact History of the Indians Wars.* New York: Hawthorn Books, Inc., 1966.

TEBEAU, CHARLTON. *A History of Florida.* Coral Gables: University of Miami Press, 1971.

VAN EVERY, DALE. *Disinherited: The Lost Birthright of the American Indian.* New York: William Morrow and Co., 1966.

WISSLER, CLARK. *The American Indian.* Gloucester: Peter Smith, 1957.

## SECONDARY SOURCES: PERIODICALS

APTHEKER, HERBERT. "Maroons within the Present Limits of the United States." *Journal of Negro History,* 24, (April 1939): 167–184.

BOYD, MARK F. "Asi-Yaholo, or Osceola." *Florida Historical Quarterly (FHQ)* 33, (January and April 1955):249–305.

——— "Florida Aflame: Background and Onset of the Seminole War, 1835." *FHQ,* 30, (July 1951): 1–115.

COVINGTON, JAMES W. "The Armed Occupation Act of 1842." *FHQ,* 40, (July 1961): 41–52.

——— "Cuban Bloodhounds and the Seminoles." *FHQ,* 33, (October 1954): 111–119.

DODD, DOROTHY. "R. K. Call versus the Federal Government on the Seminole War." *FHQ*, 31, (January 1953): 163–180.

GOGGIN, JOHN M. "The Seminole Negroes of Andros Island, Bahamas." *FHQ*, 3 (January 1946): 201–210.

GREENLEE, ROBERT F. "Folktales of the Florida Seminole." *Journal of American Folklore*, 58, no. 228, (1945): 38–43.

HOLMES, JACK D. L. "The Southern Boundary Commission, the Chatahoochee River, and the Florida Seminole, 1799." *FHQ*, 46, (April 1966): 321–322.

HOYT, WILLIAM D., ed. "A Soldier's View of the Seminole War: Three Letters of James B. Dallam." *FHQ*, 25, (April 1947): 359–362.

IRVING, WASHINGTON. No Title, *A&NC*, 11, (1840): 294–295.

JOHNSTON, JAMES HUGO. "Documentary Evidence of the Relations of Negroes and Indians." *JNH*, 14, (January 1920): 26–42.

KROGMAN, WILTON M. "The Racial Composition of the Seminole Indians of Florida and Oklahoma." *JNH*, 19, (October 1934): 404–428.

MAHON, JOHN K. "British Strategy and Southern Indians." *FHQ*, 44, (April 1966): 290–315.

MILLIGAN, JOHN D. "Slave Rebelliousness and the Florida Maroon." *Prologue*, 6, (Spring 1974): 4–18.

MOORE, JOHN HAMMOND. "A South Carolina Lawyer Visits St. Augustine, 1837." *FHQ*, 43, (April 1965): 368–375.

PORTER, KENNETH WIGGINS. "Abraham." *Phylon*, 2, no. 2, (1941): 105–116.

———— "Billy Bowlegs in the Seminole Wars." *FHQ*, 15, (January 1967): 227–239.

———— "The Cowkeeper Dynasty of the Seminole Nation." *FHQ*, 30, (April 1952): 341–349.

———— "The Episode of Osceola's Wife: Fact or Fiction?" *FHQ*, 25, (July 1947): 92–98.

———— "Florida Slaves and Free Negroes in the Seminole War, 1835–1842." *JNH*, 28, (1943): 390–421.

———— "John Caesar: Seminole Negro Partisan." *JNH*, 31, (1946): 190–207.

———— "The Founder of the Seminole Nation." *FHQ*, 28, (April 1949): 360–372.

———— "The Negro Abraham." *FHQ*, 25, (July 1946): 1–43.

———— "Negroes and the East Florida Annexation Plot, 1811–1813." *JNH*, 30, (1945): 9–29.

———— "Negroes and the Seminole Indian War, 1817–1818." *JNH*, 36, (July 1951): 249–280.

—————— "Negro Guides and Interpreters in the Early Stages of the Seminole War, December 28, 1835—March 6, 1837." *JNH*, 35, (April 1950): 174–182.

—————— "Negroes on the Southern Frontier, 1670–1763." *JNH*, 33, (January 1948): 33–74.

—————— "Notes on Seminole Negroes in the Bahamas." *FHQ*, 24, (July 1945): 56–58.

—————— "Notes Supplementary to 'Relations Between Negroes and Indians.'" *JNH*, 28, (July 1933): 282–321.

—————— "Osceola and the Negroes." *FHQ*, 33, (January and April 1955): 235–244.

—————— "Relations Between Negroes and Indians within the Present Limits of the United States." *JNH*, 27, (July 1932): 287–367.

—————— "Seminole Flight from Fort Marion." *FHQ*, 22, (January 1944): 113–133.

—————— "Three Fighters for Freedom." *JNH*, 28, (1943): 51–72.

—————— "Tiger Tail." *FHQ*, 24, (January 1946): 216–217.

Siebert, Wilbar H. "Slavery and White Servitude in East Florida, 1726–1776." *FHQ*, 10, (July 1931): 3–25.

Smith, Joseph R. "Letters from the Second Seminole War." Edited by John K. Mahon. *FHQ*, 36, (April 1958): 331–352.

Smith, Julia F. "Slave Trading in Antebellum Florida." *FHQ*, 50, (January 1972): 251–262.

Smith, Rhea M. "Racial Strains in Florida." *FHQ*, 11, (July 1932): 118–130.

Southall, Eugene P. "Negroes in Florida Prior to the Civil War." *JNH*, 19, (January 1944): 78–86.

Stafford, Robert Charles. "The Bemrose Manuscript on the Seminole War." *FHQ*, 28, (April 1940): 286–296.

Sturtevant, William C. "The Medicine Bundles and Busks of the Florida Seminoles." *Florida Anthropologist*, 7, (May 1954): 31–70.

—————— "Seminole Myths of the Origins of Races." *Ethnohistory*, 10 (1963): 80–85.

Ward, May McNeer. "The Disappearance of the Head of Osceola." *FHQ*, 33, (January–April 1955): 193–201.

Wik, Reynold M. "Capt. Nathaniel Wyche Hunter and the Florida Indian Campaigns." *FHQ*, 39, (July 1960): 66–80.

Williams, Edwin L., Jr. "Negro Slavery in Florida." *FHQ*, 28, (July 1949): 95–102.

WYLLYS, RUFUS KAY. "The East Florida Revolution of 1812–1814." *The Hispanic American Historical Review*, 9, (November 1929): 415–445.


SECONDARY SOURCES: UNPUBLISHED WORKS

DUFFNER, MICHAEL PAUL. "The Seminole-Black Alliance in Florida: An Example of Minority Cooperation." Masters Thesis, George Mason University, Fairfax, Virginia, 1973.

GALLAGHER, ARTHUR, JR. "A Survey of the Seminole Freedmen." Master's Thesis, University of Oklahoma, 1951.

SAMETH, SIGMUND. "A Study of Creek-Negro Relations." Master's Thesis, University of Oklahoma, 1940.

# Index